Roger C. Parker's

Guide to Web Content and Design

Eight Steps to Web Site Success

MIS:
PRESS

A Division of Henry
Holt and Company, Inc.
New York

MIS:Press
A Division of Henry Holt and Company, Inc.
115 West 18th Street
New York, New York 10011
http://www.mispress.com

First Edition—1997

Library of Congress Cataloging-in-Publication Data

Parker, Roger C.
      Roger C. Parker's Guide to Web content and design / Roger C. Parker.
        p.   cm.
      ISBN 1-55828-553-9
      1. Web sites—Design. 2. Content analysis (Communication) I. Title.
    TK5105.888.P369   1997   97-42048
    025.04—dc21   CIP

Associate Publisher: *Paul Farrell*

Managing Editor: *Shari Chappell*   **Editor:** *Rebekah Young*
Copy Edit Manager: *Karen Tongish*   **Copy Editor:** *Winifred Davis*
Production Editor: *Kitty May*   **Indexer:** *Richard Genova*

Acknowledgments

BOOKS ARE TEAM PROJECTS!

Although my name appears as author, *Web Content and Design* wouldn't exist without the mentoring of Paul Farrell, the publisher at MIS:Press and Rebekah Young, my editor at MIS:Press. Their patience, encouragement, and perspective helped me refine my focus and create a much different and better book than I had originally proposed. I especially appreciate Paul's encouragement to "Write the book you want to read!" What wonderful words for a writer to hear!

I also appreciate the encouragement of Margot Maley at Waterside Productions, who kept in daily contact, following the progress of this book.

As usual, my family's contribution is important. This includes my wife, Betsy, as well as my sons, Christopher, Zachary, and Ryan, who were forced to live with the "absentee father" syndrome. Special thanks go to Christopher, many of whose illustrations make their print debut in this book.

Numerous software vendors also contributed to the success of this book, including Sonya Schaefer, Peter Card, and Loni Singer from Adobe, Bill Davis from Monotype, Louise Domenitz from ITC, and numerous members of the Front Page and Publisher team from Microsoft, including Larry Engel, Linda Mitchell, Tammy Shiley, and Brent Johnson. Special thanks go to Tom D'Andre from Lexmark for helping me create lasting memories of many of the Web sites I've visited.

Special thanks also go to those who so graciously allowed samples of their Web sites to be included in this book.

Foreword

Imagine a world filled with automobiles, none of which have steering wheels. Imagine those automobiles zooming down the highways, driven by motorists who have never earned a driver's license.

Now, you can stop imagining and switch your attention to the reality of the World Wide Web, where most Web sites are like high-powered cars minus steering wheels and most Webmasters are well-meaning technicians who haven't a clue as to what it takes to earn a license to drive.

A depressingly large number of companies have launched Web sites and found themselves on the trail to oblivion, with stopovers in desperation, frustration, and poverty. This has happened because most businesses in cyberspace do not understand two basic facts:

1. How similar Web marketing is to other marketing
2. How different Web marketing is from other marketing

In *Web Content and Design*, Roger C. Parker enlightens Web-minded businesses about these facts. If he were to stop there and leave readers in an enlightened state, that would certainly be enough to make this an incredibly valuable book. But he does not stop there. He continues on, leading readers by the hand from understanding the Web to taking solid action about marketing on the Web. Guerrillas know that profits are to be found in taking action.

And Roger C. Parker proves beyond doubt that he is a cyber-guerrilla of the highest order. His ammunition is truth and he wields it like the mightiest of swords.

He pulls no punches in examining all the facets of a profit-producing Web site—preventing readers from overlooking key ideas that spell the difference between success and failure. His concept of a balanced approach might also be termed a sane approach or a complete approach because if you dare to launch or continue maintaining your own Web site without Roger C. Parker's insights, you are either insane or your site will be incomplete. Or both.

Unlike a TV spot, a brochure, or a direct mail letter that is eventually finished, a Web site is never finished but is always a work in progress, a living, evolving thing. Or else.

In this book, you'll learn the details most Web site creators overlook, the areas that are neglected, the keys to succeeding online, the reasons many people fail, the truths you just have to know in order to succeed.

Some books cover some of these factors. I've never seen any book that covers all of them—that is, until I read *Web Content and Design*. Now, I more clearly understand why most Web sites are dismal failures for the businesses they are supposed to help. Better yet, I know how to transform them from failures into successes—and now, you do, too.

In *Web Content and Design*, you'll learn the realities of the cybermarketplace. What I personally like best about the book is that it asks you questions and when you have answered them, you have a roadmap to your own personal success.

Do you have an inkling as to what would be the most winning and meaningful content to put on your Web site? You'll be asked questions and when you have answered them, you'll know exactly what content to provide.

Do you know all the tasks that a Web site involves? You'll have them in clear focus after you complete this book and you'll be able to attend to them—much to the delight of your customers and your bottom line. Your automobile will have a steering wheel. You'll have a driver's license. And you'll be able to zoom about in cyberspace with confidence and aplomb.

One billion? Two billion? Five billion? I'm trying to figure how many dollars have been wasted by Web site owners who lacked the information in this book. I can use those same figures, and even more optimistic ones, when I consider how many dollars will be earned by those who learn to master their Web content and design.

I know one thing for sure: Many of them will be readers of Roger C. Parker's masterful book on the topics that any far-sighted business owner must embrace in order to wise up to the Web.

Jay Conrad Levinson
Author, *Guerrilla Marketing* series of books

Contents in Brief

Contents

Chapter 10: Producing Your Web Site 171

Section 4: Harvest, Promotion, and Maintenance . . 191

Chapter 11: Follow-Up and Closure 193

Chapter 12: Promoting Your Web Site 201

Chapter 13: Maintaining Your Web Site 215

Introduction

What the Web Is,
and What the Web Isn't

The Web is not about design: The Web is about marketing! Or, rather, the Web is about the intersection between your the goals of your firm and the needs of your customer, client, employee, or supporter.

The Web is about *information*, not entertainment! It's about results, not awards. The Web is not about creativity as much as it's about communicating with those whose needs you must satisfy in order to succeed.

For too long, the Web has been viewed as a designer's playground, with each designer trying to "out-create" the other. The introduction of a new generation of Web authoring software, however, has changed all this. Now you can create powerful Web sites even if you don't know, or don't want to know, HTML and other programming languages.

This is not to suggest that the Web lacks excitement or doesn't present creative challenges. What it does imply is that creativity must be used with discipline and restraint, in a goal-directed manner, never losing focus on the intersection between your goals and your customer's needs.

HOW THIS BOOK DIFFERS FROM OTHER BOOKS ABOUT THE WEB

Numerous books have been written on designing for the Web. All too often, however, these books have approached the Web from a design, or creative, point of view, rather than from a marketing point of view. As with any fast-advancing technology, the focus of these books was often on technology and technique, at the expense of relevance to the day-to-day marketing challenges facing the typical business owner.

Many of the books that did stress marketing aspects of the Web were either too theoretical or too oriented to the needs of large, multinational corporations competing in the much-touted global business environment.

My goal was different. I wanted to create a book that the typical entrepreneur or manager could use as a step-by-step guide to creating a Web site that would reflect their firm's goals as well as their customers and client's needs. In other words, I wanted to break down the walls between marketing and design. I wanted to stress content—information—in a way that no other book has done. I wanted to show how the Web fits into an overall marketing program including prospect, follow-up, and closure, Web site promotion, and constant improvement.

I also wanted to avoid the technobabble which, unfortunately, scares many business owners away from the Web—or encourages them to hire expensive outsiders who often don't know the firm's business and the firm's customers as well as the business owner does.

This may not be the only Web book you purchase. As you become comfortable with the Web and begin working with any of the excellent software programs available, I encourage you to consider specialized books that will complement the eight-step marketing approach outlined in this book.

THE WEB AS CATALYST

One of the most exciting aspects of the Web is the way it often serves as a catalyst for a firm's taking an entirely new look at their marketing and communications programs.

The creation of a Web site often provides firms that have muddled along to victory for several years with the motivation to re-examine their fundamental core values and the benefits they offer their customers. Thus, the creation of a Web site provides you with an opportunity to review your firm's marketing activities in the context of a new and exciting environment. Instead of reviewing business goals and customer needs in the single dimension offered by print communications, the Web provides an opportunity to review your firm's goals and customers' needs in the context of color, sound, and movement.

This provides you an opportunity to review and fine-tune all of your firm's internal and external print and point-of-purchase communications, as well as to become involved in the most exciting business communications tool since the telephone.

WHERE THIS BOOK CAME FROM

Perhaps like you, I was a relative late-comer to the Web. I was initially skeptical about all of the hype about cyberspace and global markets. After all, I sit here in Dover, New Hampshire, overlooking Tuttles Red Barn, the oldest continuously operating family farm in America. What possible use could I have for the Web? I enjoy retail experiences; I enjoy going to car dealerships, bookstores, and reading newspapers. What could the Web offer me as a consumer and as a writer, consultant, and seminar provider?

The turning point came when Buddy Guy, one of the nation's finest blues performers, came to Boston to perform at Harbor Lights, a relatively new venue. We called about tickets and were told that only BB106 and BB107 were available. "BB106 and BB107 What kind of tickets are these?" I asked.

"Check the seating location on our Web site, and see for yourself," the ticket seller told us.

"I can do that?" I replied.

Within seconds, we had accessed the Harbor Lights Web site and ascertained that BB106 and BB107 were, indeed, good tickets and, from that moment on, I was hooked on the Web.

HOW THE WEB WORKS FOR ME (AND HOW IT CAN WORK FOR YOU)

Since then, the Web has enriched my life as both a consumer and as a writer and consultant. As a consumer, I have attended more concerts and purchased more books than ever before, and have bought more products more intelligently than ever before. By allowing me to check for last-minute airline and concert ticket availability, the Web has made it possible for me to visit friends whom I previously wouldn't have been able to visit and to attend concerts that I otherwise wouldn't have attended. I've been able to access articles in long out-of-print magazines. And, to my wife's chagrin, I must admit, the Web has helped me locate rare railroad models which I'd never have been able to find in local stores.

More important, my business has greatly expanded and has become more fun because of the Web—just as yours will, too, when you follow the eight-step program described in this book for establishing your own Web presence. For example:

◆ When prospective clients call and want to know what I've done, instead of stopping work and preparing a presentation kit for them and sending it to them via overnight express service, I simply refer them to my Web site, *http://www.rcparker.com*, and tell them to check me out. This alone has saved me thousands of dollars in brochure printing and shipping costs.

◆ Readers who encounter and enjoy one of my articles or books can easily locate *other* books and articles that I've written. And I can easily inform them of new books and upcoming seminars.

Most important, and most often overlooked, the Web is a highly personal medium. I receive e-mail from Web site visitors throughout the world and have greatly expanded my circle of friends and—in the process—expanded my reach of potential book buyers, seminar attendees, or consulting/copywriting clients. The next time I'm in London, San Francisco, or India, I have standing invitations for supper from visitors to my Web site who have contacted me and begun to exchange communications.

A REVOLUTION IN PROGRESS

The Web is not going to go away. It is only going to grow in importance in the months and years that follow.

If you have a business and want it to grow to its fullest and most profitable potential, the Web is the way to go. Not the Web at the expense of other advertising and marketing media, but the Web in partnership with other advertising and marketing media. And not the Web as a single event, but the Web as an ongoing process integrated into all of your firm's ongoing marketing and management activities.

Start by following the eight steps outlined in this book and let me know how things work out for you! Contact me through my Web site located at *http://www.rcparker.com*.

Roger C. Parker
Dover, NH

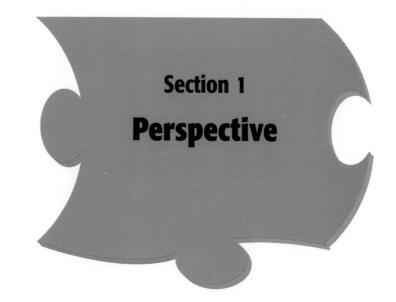

Section 1

Perspective

Chapter 1

Why the Web?

Deciding How to Put the Web to Work For You

The Web is the most important business and sales tool of the 1990's—and beyond. Although traditional media—radio and television broadcasts, printed books, magazines, and newspapers—will continue to be important to our lives, more and more of our friends and associates will receive information from the World Wide Web. Your firm's customers and prospects will increasingly depend on the Web for information and commerce. Indeed, your competition may already be taking advantage of the Web, decreasing your pool of potential buyers.

Never underestimate the power of the Web. The Web is here to stay, and whether your primary market is across town or across the country—or even overseas, you can and should be using the Web.

WHAT IS THE WEB AND WHAT MAKES IT SPECIAL?

The Web is important because it permits you to *immediately* communicate *great amounts* of *selective* and *updated information* in *color* at remarkably *low cost*. Let's look at each of these advantages the Web, alone, can help your firm compete more efficiently and effectively.

Immediacy

The Web makes it easy for you to get your message out as quickly as possible. Changes to your Web site can be posted the day you make them. After you have added, deleted, or updated the information at your Web site, it takes just seconds to post your Web site—making the new, updated information available to visitors to your Web site.

Compare this to the weeks, often months, it usually takes to produce, print, and mail a newsletter or catalog. Often, by the time the newsletter or direct mailer arrives in the prospect's mailbox, the information is out of date.

Because you can easily update your Web site, you can easily keep it up to date. Consider the difference between a printed college student directory and the same information posted on the Web. *Immediately* upon publication, the printed directory is probably out of date because some students have dropped out and others have enrolled while the directory was printed and distributed. The same student directory on the Web, however, can be updated *daily* without incurring printing or distribution costs other than the labor involved in updating the Web site.

Great Amounts of Information

The Web permits you to communicate as much information as you need to achieve your goals. On the Web, costs do not increase as the amount of information you communicate increases. Unless your Web site grows so large it exceeds the base amount your Internet Service Provider charges, it doesn't matter whether your Web site consists of eight pages, eighteen pages, or eighty pages.

This is in direct contrast to print publishing where printing costs increase proportionate to the amount of information. Postage costs also increase as you increase the size, number of pages, and weight (which increases as you add pages) of your publication. Indeed, printing and postage costs are relatively inflexible in that they jump rather than smoothly increase. This is because publications are typically printed in *signatures* consisting of multiples of four pages. (That's why you often encounter four- and eight-page newsletters, but rarely six-page newsletters.)

Personalized Information

The Web is an *interactive* medium, which means that visitors to your Web site can concentrate on just those topics of interest to them. Few Web visitors will read every page. But they don't have to, because the Web permits you to offer something for everyone without concern for the high costs of wasted circulation that occur when you advertise a specialty product in a mass medium, like in a newspaper or on a Top 40 or Oldies radio station.

This element of selectivity, of course, puts an added burden on you to promote your Web site and design a navigation system that will make it easy for visitors with defined interests to locate your Web site and quickly access the information they desire. Web sites of Realtors permit you to search for homes in any area of the country by specifying just the price range and desired number of bedrooms. Likewise, you can search for bargains in pre-owned luxury automobiles. A further example is shown in Figures 1.1 and 1.2.

Color and Photography

Print color is notoriously expensive—especially in the relatively small quantities needed by most businesses. For this reason, color in print is usually restricted to high-budget and high-volume applications, that is, those occasions when you can afford to print enough pieces to justify the high costs of color publishing. Although the print costs of color publishing continue to drop, it is still far more expensive, in terms of both preparation and printing, than black-and-white printing.

Photography, too, inevitably increases print costs. Not only do color photographs cost more than black-and-white photographs, but also the larger the photograph, the higher the production and printing costs.

The Web, however, doesn't care about color. It costs no more to publish a color photograph on the Web than a black-and-white one (although the burden is on you to prepare the color photograph in such a way that extended downloading times are avoided).

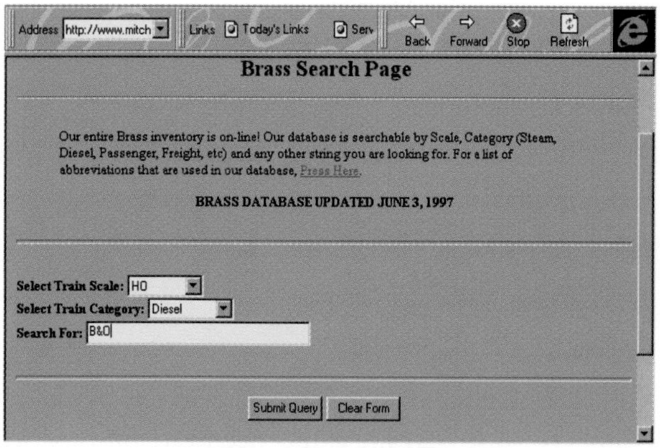

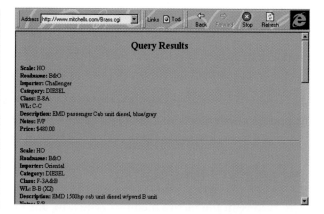

Figure 1.1 Model railroaders visiting the Web site of Mitchell's Hobby Shop can view just those models which fit their desired category, scale, and prototype railroad.

Figure 1.2 The Web allows a hobby shop in Delaware to promote inexpensively its inventory to modelers located throughout the nation—indeed, throughout the world.

Low Cost

Web publishing is inexpensive. Indeed, because of its freedom from expenses related to quantity, quality, or color, the Web is often called a *leveling field* in that it allows even small businesses to compete with large businesses and produce Web sites that are as attractive and meaningful as firms with huge advertising budgets.

Chances are, your firm can't afford to advertise in the *New Yorker* or on *Late Night with David Letterman*. But, you *can* produce a Web site that is as impressive and effective as any from firms with huge advertising budgets. The burden is on you, however, to determine your message, provide the information your market desires, and present it as attractively as possible.

It's within your power to produce a Web site that is as impressive and effective as any from firms with huge advertising budgets. The burden is on you, however, to determine your message, provide the information your market desires, and present it as attractively as possible.

MARKETING ON THE WEB

The success of your Web site will be based not so much on the colors, layout, and typefaces you employ as on your ability to provide the right content (i.e., information) at the right time. This identifying the stages of the buying cycle and appropriately tailoring your Web site's content to the various market segments involved in buying from you (Figure 1.3).

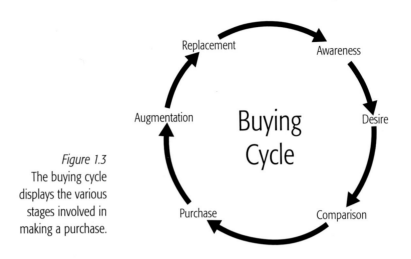

Figure 1.3
The buying cycle displays the various stages involved in making a purchase.

Stages of the Buying Cycle

Start by analyzing the six stages involved in buying most products and services. These include:

1. *Awareness* is a precondition of any purchase. Your market has to be aware that your product or service exists and understand the benefits that it offers. Your market also has to be aware that your firm is capable of providing the product or service. Market expansion follows education. The more you educate your market to the advantages offered by your product or service, the larger your market will be.

2. *Desire* follows awareness. At this stage, your prospect becomes increasingly convinced of the desirability of purchasing your product or service. The better job you do of convincing them of both the desirability of the product and the desirability of buying from you, the more your market will need to buy from you. The more information you provide at this point, the faster desire turns into *need*.

3. *Comparison* follows. At this stage, your market is likely to compare your offering—your product or service's price-performance ratio, if you will—with your competition's. Success occurs to the extent the content of your Web site provides your prospects with reasons to buy from your product, right now. After desire has been aroused, if you don't make the sale, there's a good chance one of your competitors will—or the prospect will lose enthusiasm for your product or service.

4. *Purchase* is just one of the steps, not the goal, of a strong Web marketing program. Intelligent marketers realize that the purchase is just the start of a relationship that should continue result in follow-up sales and word-of-mouth recommendations.

5. *Enhancement* occurs when the original purchase results in additional purchases. Often, one purchase leads to another, for example, a television buyer realizes that their new television reveals the inadequacies of their current videocassette recorder or decides to add an audio/video receiver and additional speakers so they can convert their living room into a home theater with sound as advanced as the video. Likewise, the purchase of an author's best-selling book often results in readers purchasing earlier books by the same author—or similar books by other authors. Augmentation also occurs when a purchase requires the purchase of supplies or accessories: videocassette tape, razor blades, and so forth.

6. *Replacement*, or repurchase, occurs when the original purchase wears out or no longer provides satisfaction. Replacement, of course, begins the cycle all over again—and is contingent upon *awareness*—the original first step. Replacement often results not from dissatisfaction with the original purchase, but—paradoxically—from satisfaction with the original purchase. The happier you are with a car that can go 0 to 60 miles per hour in 8 seconds, the happier your are likely to be (or think you will be) with a car that can go from 0 to 60 miles per hour in 6 seconds. Likewise, a 17-inch computer monitor shows you how much you've been missing with a 15-inch computer—and makes you want to purchase a 20-inch monitor!

Because it makes it practical for you to communicate inexpensively, efficiently, and continuously with your market, your Web site can make it easy not only to take advantage of the buying cycle but to spin the wheel at increasing rates of speed—constantly generating new desires, new needs, and new word-of-mouth recommendations.

Analyzing Your Market and Its Information Needs

The content of your Web site should be tailored to the needs of the various markets that you firm must satisfy. Creating a Web site that pleases you in terms of design is unlikely to lead to early retirement in Florida. Rather, you must identify the market—or markets—you want to attract and tailor the content of your Web site to them at the various stages of the buying cycle (see Figure 1.4). Your goal is to tailor the contents of your Web site to the point in the buying cycle where you can most efficiently communicate with your market. Alternatively, you can custom-tailor Web content for prospects at various points in the buying cycle.

Your firm's primary market contains two categories of prospects:

◆ *Buyers about to make a decision.* These are prospects you are currently negotiating with at your place of business, their place of business, or on the telephone (or the Web itself).

◆ *Prospects who have expressed an interest* in buying by either visiting your store or contacting you for information. Think of these as the *uncommitted* who are in the market, but are not convinced that your firm offers the best choice.

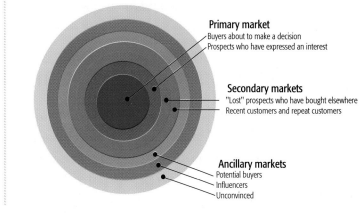

IDENTIFYING YOUR MOST EFFICIENT WEB MARKET

Figure 1.4
Success comes from identifying the most efficient target markets for your Web site, so that you know what types of information to provide.

Primary market
Buyers about to make a decision
Prospects who have expressed an interest

Secondary markets
"Lost" prospects who have bought elsewhere
Recent customers and repeat customers

Ancillary markets
Potential buyers
Influencers
Unconvinced

Your firm's secondary market also contains two categories of prospective buyers:

◆ *Lost prospects* you spent time with but who either purchased from one of your competitors or who didn't buy from anyone. Even though you lost them this time, chances are—compared to the population as a whole—that they will purchase the same or similar product or service in the future. Since these individuals have already spent time with you and are familiar with you and your products, you have already established a comfort zone with them that predisposes them to buying from you at that time.

◆ *Recent customers and repeat customers.* Recent customers are ideal prospects for either upgrading their purchase or purchasing necessary supplies and recommended accessories. Recent customers are valuable because, due to the newness of their purchase, they are the ones their friends and co-workers turn to for information and recommendations. Recent customers are, thus, excellent candidates for generating positive word-of-mouth recommendations.

There are many ancillary—or tertiary—markets. To consider just a few example of these important but lower priority buyers:

◆ *Potential buyers* are those who should purchase your product or service, but haven't done so in the past—probably because they are not aware of the advantages you and your product and services offer. If you have developed an accounting software program for mortuaries, for example, your potential market consists of mortuaries that have not yet bought from you (or a competitor). Potential buyers haven't even approached the awareness stage yet.

◆ *Influencers* include the press and other high-profile individuals whose opinions and recommendations are respected by those buying your firm's products and services. Make the influencers—book and movie reviewers, for example—happy and they'll sell your product and services for you! Influencers are important because they can build awareness for potential buyers as well as reinforcement for your primary and secondary market.

◆ The *unconvinced segment* of your market is aware of your existence, and the benefits of your product or service, but is not yet ready to buy.

CHOOSING THE RIGHT TYPE OF WEB CONTENT

In today's enthusiasm for the Web, it's easy to overlook the fact that visitors to your Web site aren't looking for entertainment or a display of your graphic prowess. Web site visitors are searching for information. Your challenge is to determine the desired information and make it as accessible as possible. As we'll see in later chapters, design is important because it can either hide or reveal information…but design, for its own sake, is relatively unimportant.

Design is important because it can either hide or reveal content, but design—for its own sake—is relatively unimportant.

Types of Information

Your key to making the most of the Web is directly proportional to your ability to determine the information your market needs in order to make a favorable decision—one that will support your firm's or organization's goals.

Information takes numerous forms. Information isn't just specifications. To succeed, your Web site has to translate specifications and features into easily understood benefits.

The information your market requires can take many forms. In the following pages, let's review a few of the many forms that information can take and the issues your information can resolve.

Making the Right Buying Decision

Clients and customers want to know what to look for when making buying decisions.

Buyers live in a world of information overload. There are too many products and services competing for the buyer's attention. There are too many similar, or near-similar, products and services. Buyers need information that will build their confidence in their ability to make the right choice. Insecure customers would rather postpone a purchase than make a mistake. Wouldn't you rather eat at a steak house than a fancy French restaurant where the waiters and waitresses might make fun of your mispronunciation of the main course?

CONTENT AND MARKET SEGMENTS

Analyzing your various market segments and their position in the buying cycle is central to the success of your Web efforts.

The likelihood of immediate purchase decreases as you move away from your primary market. This isn't to say you should ignore your secondary and ancillary markets, but you should be aware that ignoring your core market and concentrating exclusively on secondary and ancillary markets is unlikely to produce the results you're looking for on the Web.

This fact may explain why so many Web sites are destined to fail: They concentrate on marginal prospects–the gray areas at the fringes of the market–rather than concentrating on their firm's core markets where immediate results are more likely to be generated (see Figure 1.6).The more meaningful the content–or information–contained on your Web site, the more likely it is that you can cause migration towards your core market. Working from the outside in, let's analyze the role that meaningful content can provide to each of your market segments.

ANCILLARY MARKETS

- ◆ Content can create a market where none exists by explaining the benefits of your product or service.
- ◆ Content can encourage influencers to recommend your product to their constituencies and provide them with the information they need to communicate effectively.
- ◆ Content can build awareness among potential buyers, adding them to the buying cycle.

SECONDARY MARKETS

- ◆ Content can give you a second chance at prospects who originally bought elsewhere (or who didn't buy).
- ◆ Content can reinforce prospects who are at the comparison stage of the buying cycle.

PRIMARY MARKET

- ◆ Content can support augmentation sales to recent customers, showing them how to gain even more satisfaction from their recent purchase.
- ◆ Content can provide the information and motivation that active customers need to cross the line and buy from you.

Content–appropriate and meaningful information–is the single most important characteristic of all market segments. Each segment has its own information requirements. In to each market segment, Web site appearance is less important than content.

MOVING AWAY FROM YOUR PRIMARY MARKET

MOVEMENT TOWARDS YOUR PRIMARY MARKET

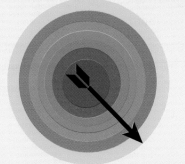

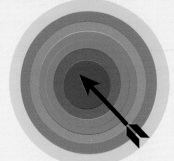

Figure 1.5 The likelihood of immediate purchase decreases as you move away from your primary market.

Figure 1.6 Content–information–can cause movement towards your core market.

The more expensive the product, the more prospective buyers need to know the lay of the land. They need to know the questions to ask and the vocabulary to use asking the questions. They need to know how to recognize quality and how to avoid mistakes. Your Web site will contribute to your firm's success to the extent you provide this information.

Buyers need information that will build their confidence in their ability to make the right choice. Insecure customers would rather postpone a purchase than make a mistake.

Saving Money

One of the most important driving forces is the urge to save money. Everyone wants to save money. There are two ways to save money. One way is to purchase something for less than others are selling it for. Another option is to buy a less expensive, but equally satisfying, alternative.

In either case, the Web can help you market your firm more efficiently. If you want to offer your customers lower prices, the Web can help by reducing your advertising and promotion costs as well as the costs of fulfillment (i.e., getting the product into your customer's hands electronically, or by eliminating printing and mailing tickets—like airlines are doing). The Web also allows you to build immediacy into your offers by making it possible to promote limited-quantity specials that could not be efficiently advertised in traditional media because of higher cost.

The Web's ability to provide you with the space you need to tell a convincing story helps you if you want to explain to customers why your lesser-known product may be a better deal than the more expensive, more heavily advertised product.

Providing Detailed *Why Buy* Information

One of the oldest sayings in advertising is "the more you tell, the more you sell." Direct-marketers have known this for years…which is why your mailbox is filled with eight-page letters from association presidents describing how your donation will help save the world or why you can't live without the latest *Home Sites of the Nashville Great's* photo album.

In the past, expensively produced brochures, newsletters, and direct-mail pieces were usually the most tangible form of reinforcement. Now, however, the Web makes it easier to build confidence in prospective buyers as well as help previous buyers avoid post-sale remorse (and product returns).

Finding Out Where to Buy

Looking for the nearest Mercedes-Benz dealer in your area? The Web offers both you and the Mercedes-Benz dealer a decidedly better alternative than the local telephone book. For one thing, being computer-based, in many cases it will be faster and easier to locate the dealer through the Mercedes-Benz dealer listing on the Web than it would be to locate the phone book and pore through listings of the clutter of multiple dealer listings.

More important, the Web offers the Mercedes-Benz dealer a much better opportunity to explain not only where they are located, but why they can do a better job of selling you a Mercedes-Benz than any other dealer in the area. Their Web site can contain far more information than even the largest newspaper ad; it can not only include a map showing their location, list their hours of operation, and describe their service facilities but can also contain a list of their current new inventory as well as pre-owned specials.

Upcoming Events

Web-based calendars listing upcoming events are becoming increasingly important. Brochures and direct-mail pieces get lost…or, at the very least, are rarely around when needed. If your firm or organization sells tickets to special events, the Web makes it easy for your to encourage your market to spend their money on you on the day they decide to go out.

The Web sites of most performing arts organizations, for example, include a calendar highlighting important dates. Click on a desired date, and you're taken to a page describing what's going on that day in great detail. Again, the Web makes a great deal of information accessible when it's wanted. (And, if the concert is canceled or sold out, the information on the Web can quickly be updated at far less cost than sending members and ticket holders a postcard.) Figures 1.7 and 1.8 demonstrate similarly convenient information access.

By permitting you to efficiently offer your market specialized, timely information about upcoming events—sales, clinics, seminars, or special promotions—the Web avoids the costs and hassles required if you were to attempt to keep your market informed by printing and mailing the same information…information that would, in many cases, be lost by the time the prospects in your various market segments were ready to buy.

Customer Support and Reinforcement

By providing the luxury of low-cost space, the Web lets you to do a better job of explaining the ins and outs of a product before and after the sale. The Web makes it easy to show buyers how to make the most of their purchase, and, at the same time, the Web makes it easy to solve post-sales

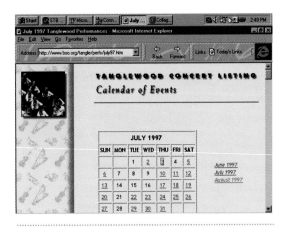

Figure 1.7 Click on a July date when you want to attend a Boston Symphony Orchestra concert at their summer home in Tanglewood.

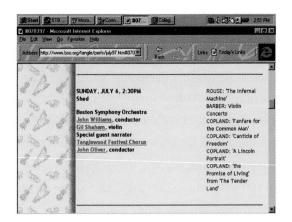

Figure 1.8 You'll be taken to a page describing the concert that's taking place that day. At that point, you can go even further and locate more detailed information by clicking on the text links (indicated in red).

problems. This post-sale reassurance pays great dividends not only in reducing the cost of customer service, but by creating satisfied customers who will grow your business as they recommend your firm to their friends.

Weber, for examples, sells outdoor barbecues. Their Web site (*http://www.weberbbq.com*) features barbecue recipes. By offering recipes, the Weber company makes it easier for its buyers to enjoy their purchase—as well as positions itself as an authority in the barbecue field.

In a similar manner, the Web excels at customer support. Customer support is one of the least understood and most often neglected aspects of the Web, even though satisfied buyers are likely to become repeat buyers and influence friends and associates. The Web makes it easy to generate such satisfied customers by providing them with the information they need to get the most out of their purchase (see Figure 1.9).

Content is central to all of the above categories. Whether helping buyers make the right choice, save money, attend upcoming events, or providing after-sale pleasure or problem-solving information, content is the one thing all the above categories have in common. Unless your business is entertainment or graphic design, success will come to the extent that you view the Web not as an entertainment medium but as a content medium.

Unless your business is entertainment or graphic design, success will come to the extent that you view the Web not as an entertainment medium but as a content medium.

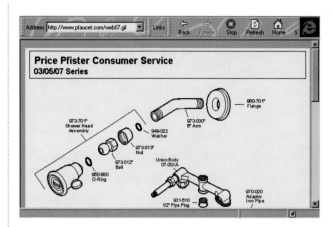

Figure 1.9
The Price-Pfeister company's Web site contains detailed drawings of all its faucets, making it easy for home owners to repair a leaking faucet themselves, instead of calling a plumber.

PUTTING THE WEB TO WORK

One of the best ways to appreciate the breadth of opportunities the Web offers you is to compare it to existing types of marketing communications and see how the Web can communicate information faster and at lower cost.

Advertisements

Print advertisements can build awareness or show buyers how to save money. Advertising costs can quickly mount, however, and there are relatively few media that allow you to efficiently target your primary and secondary markets. Color always costs extra. Most advertisements also suffer from a great deal of waste circulation…you're paying to advertise to people who are unlikely to buy from you. In addition, unless your pockets are deep, advertisements offer only a limited amount of space to tell a complete story.

In addition, the lead times for placing many advertisements in magazines reduces the immediacy they offer. Broadcast advertisements make it equally difficult to target desired audiences. Broadcasts further reduce the amount of information you can communicate.

By promoting your Web-site address in your advertisements, however, you can complement your advertising and increase its efficiency by telling more of a story. Use your media advertisements, in other words, to attract prospects to your Web site where you can tell a more complete and up-to-date story.

Brochures

Brochures are silent salesmen that continue selling long after a face-to-face encounter. Because brochures can provide a lot of selling space—much more than most advertisements—they're great reinforcers at the point of sale to your primary market. Brochures permit you to describe how your firm differs from the competition and what this means to buyers.

Brochures are inflexible, however. Once they're printed, it's impossible to modify their content. On the other hand, brochures provide more space to provide convincing arguments than advertisements do. Printing and distribution costs further limit the effectiveness of most brochures…especially if you want to include color and photographs, or print brochures on a quality paper. Because of the nature of printing, you generally have to print large quantities of brochures in order to bring per-copy costs down to reasonable levels.

Always include your Web site address on your brochures and consider your Web site another opportunity to reinforce your brochure by repeating information that describes how your firm differs from the competition.

Newsletters

Newsletters make it easy to maintain awareness among your secondary market segments. Newsletters can be more credible than advertisements or brochures because they present your selling arguments in an editorial, as opposed to a brag-and-boast format. Newsletters are more likely to be saved than advertisements and can be cost-efficient to produce and print in relatively low quantities.

Newsletters are ideal to describe your firm's competence by including case studies and by answering frequently asked questions. Newsletters generally provide even more storytelling space than brochures, and, since they are less expensive to produce, their information can be frequently updated. Newsletters are an ideal vehicle for keeping your previous customers informed about new products—and new ways to enjoy existing products. Newsletters thus can help maintain the enthusiasm of your secondary markets and encourage augmentation and replacement sales.

Time and money are the biggest drawbacks associated with newsletters. Months can go by between the time you agree on the content of a newsletter and the time it finally arrives in your customer or prospect's mailbox. Newsletters also require you to maintain an up-to-date mailing list. If you don't mail frequently and keep your list up to date, you're apt to be discouraged by the amount of undeliverables the Post Office returns to you.

The Web permits you to communicate the same credibility-building information in the same educational format as newsletters without incurring printing and postage costs. Your Web site can be consider a free "update-able" newsletter that you make available to all of your markets.

Most important, as described in Chapter Eleven, at no cost you can send e-mail to your customers and prospects informing them when your Web site newsletter has been updated with new information.

At no cost, you can send e-mail to your customers and prospects informing them when your Web site newsletter has been updated with new information.

Postcards

Postcards are quick and easy to prepare and cost less to mail than newsletters. Postcards are great for generating immediate response by describing special events and stressing money-saving opportunities. The amount of information postcards can communicate is relatively limited, however.

Postcards are ideal for communicating with your secondary market and following up with prospects who don't buy on their first sales encounter with you.

You can communicate the same late-breaking-news/special-event information free via e-mail to your customers and prospects if your Web site provides compelling reasons visitors should register their e-mail with you. The more information you provide in your Web site, the more likely visitors are to provide you with their e-mail addresses.

Telephone Calls

A telephone call can be considered the ultimate inexpensive advertisement (assuming it's a local call, of course!). The only expense is your time or your staff's time. E-mail, however, to a mailing list of enthusiastic Web site visitors permits you to communicate equally effectively with prospects and customers by freeing you from telephone tag.

Flyers

Flyers, inexpensively produced and printed single-sheet publications describing an upcoming event or promotion, can be used to build enthusiasm among your primary and secondary markets. Distribution is always a problem, however. What can you do to get your message into the right market segments at the right time—and how much information can you provide on a single sheet of paper?

Your Web site can be considered a point-of-sale flyer targeted directly to your target market, because only those persons interested in buying are likely to be visiting your Web site. The advantages of flyers can also be equaled by e-mail sent to the appropriate market segments.

Billboards

Billboards are great at building awareness, but it's hard to translate awareness into immediate sales. Billboards are noticed by a lot of people, but only a relatively small number are likely to represent prospects for your firm's product and services.

The Web equivalent to the awareness-building power of billboards is to promote your Web site to as many search engines as possible, as described in Chapter Twelve. In addition, if you have a well-chosen Web site address, as described in Chapter Four, you may be able to effectively promote your Web site address by including it on your billboards.

Instructions

Businesses often spend a great deal of staff time answering the same questions over and over from both prospects and previous buyers. Many firms are frustrated by the necessity to print detailed documentation and instructions that are likely to quickly go out of date. The Web makes it easy to help customers and prospects informed keep themselves about solutions to problems.

Internal Directories and Procedures Manuals

As firms grow, internal communication becomes more and more difficult. It becomes harder and harder to keep staff address and phone-extension information up to date. More and more money ends up being spent on nonrevenue-producing projects like directories and procedures manuals that are likely to quickly go out of date.

An *intranet*—internal Web site—makes it easy for employees to share information with each other without incurring printing, distribution, or environmental costs.

Sales Encounters

More and more sales are being done over the Web. It's becoming easier to order a book from an on-line bookstore than to put up with mall traffic or visit a computer store—and find that you know more about computers than their staff does. More and more Web sites are making it easier and easier to customize your purchase (see Figure 1.10) and also find out how much it will cost to finance or lease it.

The above analogies represent just a few of the ways the Web can reduce your costs of doing business by helping you communicate more effectively with your primary, secondary and ancillary markets.

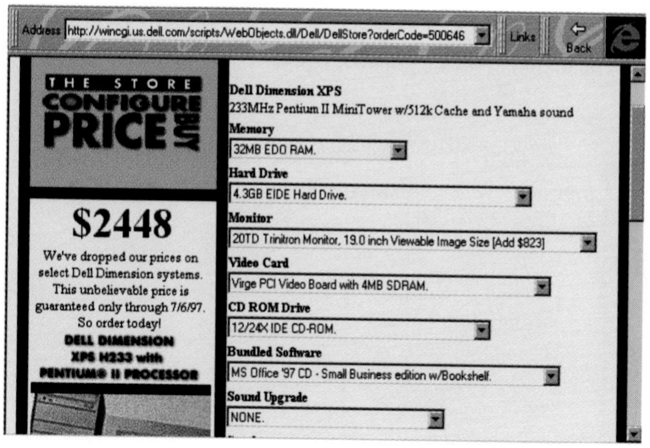

Figure 1.10
Dell's online computer store makes it easy to sell yourself a computer custom-configured to your specific needs—and find out how much it will cost to lease. The price shown at left will change to reflect your specific choices.

CONCLUSION

The Web offers you a new and powerful way to communicate with the various market segments your business must satisfy in order to survive and grow.

Content—good, solid information—is the key to success. But filling your Web site with facts isn't enough. The facts have to be presented and interpreted in a manner appropriate to the needs of Web visitors at various stages of the buying cycle. This requires you to balance long-term and short-term goals…which, in turn, forces you to consider how to integrate the Web into both your firm's daily operations as well as its long-term goals.

Ultimately, the Web is about decisions. These decisions include:

◆ To which market segment should you tailor your messages?

◆ What information do members of the various market segments require?

◆ How can you make this information as attractive and easy to access as possible?

◆ How much information do you need in order to put the Web to work?

◆ Who is going to do the work?

These are just a few of the questions we'll be discussing in the following chapters.

How Do You Want to Use the Web?

Use the Web Strategy Worksheet below to review the advantages and disadvantages of the various ways you presently communicate with your primary, secondary, and ancillary markets. As you review your current marketing activities, search for ways you can adapt to the Web the advantages and strategies you're presently employing, and search for ways you can use the Web to increase your firm's ability to communicate with current and prospective buyers.

WEB STRATEGY WORKSHEET

Traditional media analogy	Advantages to your firm	Disadvantages to your firm	Target Market segment	Present level of utilization	Can Web site accomplish the same function?
Advertisements					
Brochures					
Newsletters					
Postcards					
Telephone call					
Billboards					
Instructions					
Internal directories and procedures manuals					
Sales encounters					

Chapter 2

Eight Keys to Success

Establishing a Successful Web Site Development Cycle

Balance and *program* are the keys to establishing a successful Web site marketing program. One without the other simply isn't enough.

◆ *Balance* comes from placing equal emphasis upon each of the eight elements that make up a successful Web site. Your site is likely to fail if you fall into the trap of stressing one or two elements at the expense of the others.

◆ *Program* involves making an ongoing commitment to promoting your Web site and keeping it up to date with new material. It's not enough to spend a week creating a Web site and then leave it alone for six months. Success requires consistent follow-through on the leads your Web site creates and constantly updating and improving your Web site. It's essential that your Web site be integrated into your firm's ongoing marketing program.

Many Web sites fail to achieve their full potential because too much emphasis is placed on the Web site's appearance or the technology used to create it. Appearance, of course, is important, but it's not the whole story. A good-looking Web site without meaningful content is as unlikely to succeed as a well-designed Web site with good content that nobody visits because the site is not promoted or a site that generates responses which are not acted upon.

> *Many Web sites fail to achieve their full potential because too much emphasis is placed on the Web site's appearance. A good-looking Web site without meaningful content is as unlikely to succeed as a well-designed Web site with good content that nobody visits, or a site that generates responses which are not acted upon.*

EIGHT KEYS TO SUCCESS

There are eight steps involved in creating an effective Web site based on balance and program. Before proceeding further, let's take a brief look at each of these steps (see Figure 2.1). Then, in the following chapters, we'll take a more detailed look at each element and relate it to your goals, your market, your available time, and budget and hardware/software resources.

Planning involves creating a community of information with your Web site visitors, based on examining your marketing goals and reconciling them with your customer and prospect's needs. Planning involves asking questions like: "What do I want my Web site to do for me—what do I expect to accomplish?" This often requires taking a new look at your present business and your business plan and identifying areas where the Web can augment your present business as well as lay the groundwork for a future business.

WEB SITE SUCCESS: Equal Emphasis on Eight Key Elements

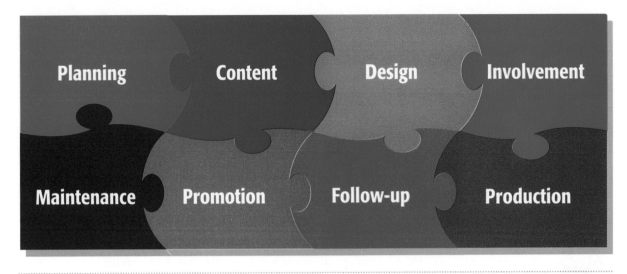

Figure 2.1 Successful Web sites include eight key elements, each of which deserves equal attention.

Planning also involves establishing realistic expectations for your Web site. Unless your business represents the exception rather than the rule, your Web site will probably start out playing a supporting role in your firm's marketing—although there is every indication that Web site marketing will only grow in importance in the coming years.

Planning involves research—spending time on the Web checking out what others are doing on the Web and becoming familiar with the terminology and technology of the Web.

Most important, planning involves asking the right questions, questions like:

◆ Whom do you want to attract to your Web site?

◆ What types of information are these visitors likely to want?

◆ What action do you want your Web site visitors to take?

◆ What information do they need to make a decision that benefits your firm? This often requires *listening* to your clients and customers and noting concerns and questions that come up over and over again.

Planning also involves determining an appropriate URL—or Web site address—for your firm. As will be described in Chapter 4, there's often more to determining an effective URL than simply placing *http://www* in front of your firm's name and adding *.com* after it.

There's more to determining an effective URL than simply placing http://www *in front of your firm's name and adding* .com *after it.*

Content involves determining the categories of information you want to include on your Web site, and how best to communicate this information—i.e., in text or in graphics. Your goal is to identify areas where your goals and the goals of your Web site visitors intersect. The key to developing meaningful content is to put yourself in your customer or client's shoes and asking yourself: "If I were a prospect for my firm's products or services, what questions would I want answered?"

Developing meaningful content is based on answering two fundamental and closely-related questions:

◆   What information *do your prospects need* to know in order to buy from you?
◆   What information *do you know* that will convince prospects to buy from you?

As we'll discuss in Chapter 5, you probably already know more about your subject than you think you do. You know more about the trends going on in your field than your prospects do; success comes from establishing your credibility by providing your prospects with information and guidance. Success comes from overcoming the myopia of everyday knowledge and building your credibility by using your Web site to answer the questions you answer over and over again in your everyday sales encounters.

Design involves choosing a *look* for your Web site—a unique combination of colors, layout, and typography that will simultaneously make your message inviting and easy to read as well as project a memorable image that will set your firm apart from the competition.

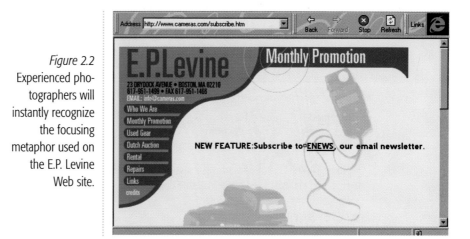

Figure 2.2
Experienced photographers will instantly recognize the focusing metaphor used on the E.P. Levine Web site.

In today's media-filled world, it's not enough that you provide meaningful content on your Web site; it's equally important that the content be presented as attractively as possible. Given the choice between an easy-to-read Web site and a cluttered, slow-loading Web site, which do you think your visitors will spend more time visiting? Carefully consider and answer the following questions:

◆ How can I deliver the desired information in as accessible and convincing a form as possible?

◆ How can I structure the information so that it is as easy to locate as possible?

◆ How can I make my Web site respond as quickly as possible to my visitor's queries?

Successful design is often based on creating a *theme*—an emotional organizing concept that will strike a responsive chord in the Web site visitor's mind. For example, the E. P. Levine company in Boston specializes in photographic equipment. Accordingly, the central metaphor of their Web site is the split-image focusing prism that comes into focus on each page (see Figure 2.2). This is a metaphor every experienced photographer will instantly relate to. Sheer genius! The focusing metaphor is strengthened by the pale background images of light meters and other tools that trade photographers are likely to recognize.

Design involves making color and typeface choices that appropriately reflect your business and set it apart from the competition. Design involves choosing a layout flexible enough to accommodate the particular blend of text and graphics you want to include on your site, yet consistent enough to project a unified image in your customer's mind.

Design also involves dividing the information found on your Web site into meaningful categories. Your goal is to make it as easy as possible for Web site visitors to immediately access desired information (see Figure 2.3). Often the easiest way to do this is to use software programs

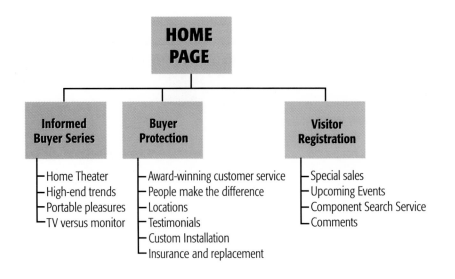

Figure 2.3 Software programs that can create organization charts make it easy to display visually the location of information in your Web site's hierarchy.

like Software Publishing Corporation's ActiveOffice or presentation programs like Microsoft PowerPoint to create an organization chart that displays the structure of your, or your client's, Web site. Working visually will greatly speed up your work.

There are three aspects of involvement. The first is navigation. Navigation involves developing ways for Web site visitors to move from topic to topic. Your goal is to make it as easy as possible for visitors to your Web site to quickly locate desired information. The Internet is a nonlinear form of communication. Few visitors to your Web site will start on page one and read every page of your Web site. Rather, visitors will want to prioritize their visit and go directly to the pages containing the information they desire.

The second aspect of involvement is based on beginning a process that culminates in a relationship between you and your Web site visitor—a relationship that, ideally, itself culminates in making a sale. Involvement can be as simple as asking Web site visitors to register, in order to

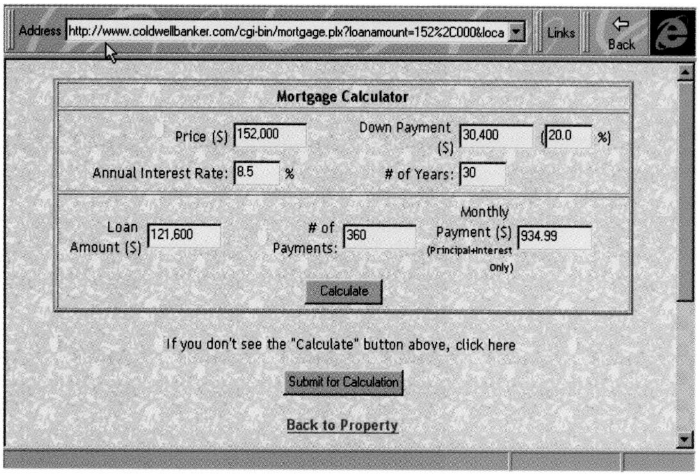

Figure 2.4
The mortgage calcula-
tors found on most real-
tor's Web sites, like the
Coldwell-Banker site
above, allow you to
determine whether or
not you can afford the
home of your dreams as
well as try out different
down payments and
interest rates.

capture their names and addresses for later follow-up. Or, you can go as far along the sales process as you desire, often helping your Web site visitors prequalify and presell themselves before you even speak to them.

Automotive dealers and realtors are perhaps in the vanguard of Web involvement. Coldwell-Banker's Web site not only allows you to "shop" a given city or neighborhood for homes that meet your specific price, number of bedroom, and number of bathroom criteria. After selecting and viewing a picture of a home of possible interest, you can actually use the built-in mortgage calculator to see if you can afford the house! (See Figure 2.4.)

Registration and feedback are yet other ways of encouraging visitor involvement.

◆ Feedback permits you to find out what visitors think about your Web site and identify other topics they would like you to include.

◆ Registration allows you to capture your visitor's e-mail address so that you can build a relationship with them, keeping them informed about special promotions and upcoming events.

E-mail should be considered an essential part of your Internet experience. It is vital that you adopt e-mail as a primary communications tool. Web sites should contain e-mail links to you.

Production

Production involves technology: choosing the best way to create your Web site and post it on the Internet. Production involves making appropriate hardware and software choices. Production also involves mastering as much technology as you need to achieve your content and design goals—or knowing when to delegate production to others and locating appropriate assistance. Production issues include:

◆ What's the easiest and most efficient way for me to get online?

◆ Which software should I choose?

◆ How do I choose the right Internet Service Provider?

◆ Who should do the work of creating my Web site?

◆ How do I overcome the technological limitations of the Web as discussed in Chapter 8, "The Web Is Not a Page"?

Production also involves testing all links of your Web site, to make sure that all pages are properly connected and keeping all links to external Web sites up to date.

Follow-up

Follow-up involves harvesting the fruits of your labor. It also involves integrating your Web site into your firm's day-to-day operations. It's not enough to generate leads from the Web; you have to do something with them! Follow-up involves management issues of delegation and responsibility as well as—possibly—adopting new technology (i.e., e-mail). For example:

◆ Who is going to read and respond to e-mail?

◆ Who will create and maintain a database of Web site prospects?

◆ Who is going to fulfill requests for information?

◆ Who is going to answer questions and respond to comments from Web visitors?

Time has to be appropriated for these functions, which will inevitably increase in volume as your Web site becomes increasingly successful. Although, in the beginning, the same individual (possibly you!) will both create and maintain your Web site and follow up on the leads it generates, later on you probably will want to separate Web maintenance (described below) from prospect follow-up.

Web sites that no one visits are failures, no matter how meaningful their content or how well designed they are. It's vitally important that you do everything possible to make your Web site as visible as possible through both conventional and electronic means. It's important that you establish a promotional plan involving three distinct phases:

◆ First, you have to make sure your Web site address is as visible as possible. Every advertisement, brochure, business card, instruction book, letterhead, proposal, and newsletter should contain your Web site address.

◆ Second, first-time visitors should find your Web site as easily as possible by making it possible for search engines to list your Web site address in the appropriate categories. This involves both notifying search engines of your Web site's existence as well as including in your Web pages the key words that independent search engines rely on to locate Web sites.

◆ Third, you'll want to investigate co-marketing relationships with other Web sites so that you can link your Web site to theirs.

One aspect of co-marketing involves identifying complementary, but not competitive, Web sites and cross-linking your Web site to theirs, that is, they list your Web site as a recommended link and you recommend their Web site as a valuable resource. The more meaningful the content you provide on your site, the easier you will probably find it to cross-link your site with others.

The more meaningful the content you provide on your site, the easier you will probably find it to cross-link your site with others.

Maintenance

No Web site should ever be considered completed. Keep your Web site fresh. It should be in a state of constant improvement. On the most practical level, you'll want to constantly review and refine your Web site from the spelling and links point of view. Inevitably, typographical errors appear on even the best Web sites and these should be fixed as soon as possible. Links to other sites, too, must be constantly checked because others are constantly refining their Web sites.

There are other aspects of maintenance; for example:

◆ Adding new information: In order to attract repeat visitors, you should add new information at regular intervals.

◆ Deleting (or archiving) out-of-date information. (*Archiving* involves reducing the visibility of older information so that new information will be more prominent.)

◆ Improving navigation on the basis of comments from Web site visitors so that your most popular features are as easy to locate as possible.

Maintenance also involves speeding up your Web site by improving your mastery of your software so that graphics, for example, will download faster.

CYCLE VERSUS STEPS

Although the eight elements of a successful Web site were depicted as pieces of a puzzle in this chapter, perhaps a better way to view them is as a continuous cycle. A successful Web site is never finished. Most important, a successful Web site is not the result of a linear series of steps. Rather, a successful Web site is the result of an ongoing process—or cycle. Your Web site has to become an integral part of your firm's ongoing marketing program, not an event that, once completed, is neglected in the press of day-to-day business.

A successful Web site is never finished and is not the result of a linear series of steps. Rather, it's the result of an ongoing cycle.

Why a Cycle?

Each element of a successful Web site is constantly affecting the other elements. For example:

◆ Your Web site's content and design should influence the URL, or Web site address, that you choose.

◆ Content and design should be reviewed and updated on the basis of involvement, that is, feedback from Web site visitors.

◆ Production influences design: As your mastery of your software improves, you'll be able to add new impact to your Web site's design.

◆ Follow-up will become more important as you improve your Web site's content and design and become more successful promoting your Web site.

◆ Planning and involvement will influence content as you get a better picture of what's working and what's not working on your Web site.

Basically, each element of your Web site influences every other element…and all should be in a constant state of review and improvement.

Implications

A Web site, thus, requires more than just creation and posting. It requires close integration with your firm's overall marketing and selling strategies. It involves monitoring technology and the trends affecting businesses large and small so that you can keep your Web site and your business as efficient and productive as possible.

A successful Web site is not a one time event like a brochure or a newsletter. Rather, a Web site is more like an ongoing philosophy that can infuse new life into even tired businesses, or businesses that have grown in spite of themselves and previously limited marketing and promotion efforts.

Because it involves so many time-consuming activities and human resources, as described above, a Web site is also as much a management concern as a creative concern. Successful Web sites bring up questions like "Who is going to do the work?" both before and after the Web site is posted.

The Web as Catalyst

Because it impacts so many areas of a firm's operation, many firms have found that a successful Web site can result in a dramatic improvement in the firm's marketing by forcing owners and managers to take a fresh, close look at the basic questions underlying their firm's marketing:

- Who are our customers?
- What are they buying?
- What are our clients and customers really buying?
- What are the key concerns of our customers and clients?
- Why are they buying from us instead of our competitors?
- Are we projecting an image appropriate to our view of ourselves and our customers?

CONGRATULATIONS

As you read the chapters that follow, you're taking the first step toward revitalizing your business by integrating and taking competitive advantage of what will probably turn out to be the century's most powerful technology into your firm's everyday activities.

Chapter 3

The Web Is Not a Page

An Introduction to Web Page Design

Web pages are more than printed pages transmitted electronically. Web pages are fundamentally different from print media. They offer both more opportunities and more challenges. For this reason, you can't simply take print documents—like ads, brochures, and newsletters—and convert them into Web pages.

The opportunities offered by Web design include the ability to include more information—and more types of information—without incurring major printing and distribution costs. The Web offers space to communicate as much information as you want without increasing distribution (i.e., printing and postage) costs—once created, a Web site with seventy-five pages doesn't cost more than a Web site with ten pages. Color and photographs are "free," so you can communicate more effectively, again, without incurring increased production and printing costs. If appropriate, you can even easily enhance your message with sound and movement.

OVERVIEW OF WEB PAGE DESIGN CHALLENGES

The challenges of Web design begin with the nature of on-screen reading—many people find reading from a computer screen harder than reading from a printed page. In addition, a number of popular design techniques, such as multicolumn snaking layouts, don't translate to the Web. Web site visitors don't want to have to continuously scroll from the bottom of one column to the top of the next.

Navigation—or the steps needed to locate desired information—is also more complex on the Web than on a printed page. Web navigation implies more than simply flipping through the pages of a magazine (typically from back to front) and stopping at interesting pages or looking up a page number in the index or table of contents of a book and turning to the page.

Finally, there's the element of lack of control. After a printing press is turned on, every copy of the book, brochure, or newsletter that emerges looks the same, regardless of the conditions where it is read (i.e., the type of reading chair present in the room where the document is read doesn't change its appearance). Presently, however, you lose this predictability on the Web because of differing computer hardware and software used by different Web site visitors. Here are some of the ways you lose control:

◆ *Typography*: You lose control over the appearance of type on the Web. You lose control over the typeface and the type size your Web site visitor will use to read your message. With the exception of type saved as a graphic (discussed later in this chapter), your message will be delivered using the typeface and type size selected as defaults in the Web site visitor's browser software, not yours. You lose control over letter and line spacing, control essential to preparing good-looking print communications. You lose the ability to control hyphenation and the use of "true" punctuation—opening and closing quotation marks (" ") and em (—) and en (–) dashes. You also lose the ability to use typographic subtleties like TRUE SMALL CAPS and old style figures (numbers with descenders like 3, 4, 5, 7, and 9).

◆ *Color*: You also lose absolute control over colors and flexibility. Every computer monitor is slightly different. In addition, to accommodate the greatest number of Web site visitors, you'll probably want to limit the number of colors used on your Web site. Also, to ensure quality results on the widest possible range of computers, you are limited in your color choices. Choose the wrong colors, and you might be dismayed by the way the colors turn on when viewed on a different computer platform or on a monitor driven by a computer with less sophisticated graphics capability than yours.

♦ *Size and proportion*: There is also no uniformity in the size of the screen used to display your Web site. Image size and the specific browser software used to display your Web site will differ from visitor to visitor. The size and location of text and graphics may shift depending on the specific Web site browser used. Most important, although vertical pages are the norm in print communications, that is, the height of the pages is typically greater than their width—and you see an entire page at a glance—Web pages are almost always viewed as horizontal slices of partial pages.

Implications

The Web represents a technological revolution in progress. Like most revolutions, it has its advantages and disadvantages. But for individuals and businesses interested in survival, growth, and profitability, the advantages far outnumber the disadvantages. It's just that you have to be aware of the challenges and work around them as necessary until advancing technology reduces the numbers of disadvantages.

It's important to note that there are already ways to get around most of the problems out-lined above, but they usually involve additional complexity on either your part—that is, your need to invest time mastering the latest technology (such as Cascading Style Sheets)—or the will-ingness of visitors to your Web site to acquire additional fonts and software (such as Adobe Acrobat Reader). The issue is not the money involved—it's the time. Software like Adobe Acrobat Reader can be downloaded for free from the publisher's Web site, and there are many sources of free fonts that you can use to design your Web site and that your visitors can download for free. But how many of your potential Web site visitors are going to want to add additional software and fonts to their computer just to view your Web site, the way you intended? In addition, as an inevitable consequence of your Web site becoming more sophisticated, Web site visitors will have to wait longer for files containing graphics to be downloaded.

How many of your potential Web site visitors are going to want to download additional software and fonts to their computer just to view your Web site?

WEB PAGE ARCHITECTURE

Before going further, let's review the basics of the Web. A Web site consists of an opening, or home, page connected or linked to several other pages. In most cases, depending on the software used to create them, these pages can be as long as necessary (unlike pages in a book or newsletter, which are always of uniform size, i.e., page 9 is unlikely to be physically longer than page 1).

Home Page

Your home page represents the location where Web site visitors enter your *URL*—Web site address—into their browser. The top half of your home page is called the *opening page*. The opening page represents your Web site visitor's first encounter with your Web site. And its size is limited: Although you have been used to thinking in terms of vertical eight-and-one-half by eleven-inch pages coming out of your ink-jet or laser printer, visitors to your Web site will only encounter a horizontal view roughly equal to one-half of that space.

The importance of the opening page area of your home page is similar to the expression on your face as you meet someone for the first time or the image visitors to your home get as they approach your home and park in the driveway. First impressions last and you only get one chance to make a first impression! If visitors like what they see on the top half of your home page, they'll likely scroll down for clues as to the *content*—or type of information—you're offering at your Web site. On the other hand, if Web site visitors don't like what they see, or if you make them wait, or if you don't offer them a reason for either scrolling further down your home page or clicking on a link to another page, they are likely to click on the Back button of their browser and leave your Web site forever.

The importance of the top part of your home page is similar to the expression on your face as you meet someone for the first time....

CHARACTERISTICS OF A GOOD HOME PAGE

A successful home page satisfies eight characteristics. A home page should:

1. *Identify* the firm (or organization) responsible for the Web site.
2. *Describe* the type of products or services the firm sells and the benefits that buyers enjoy (or the benefits that members of an organization enjoy).
3. *Identify the content* (i.e., information) provided at the Web site and the benefits that visitors will gain by visiting the various pages linked to the home page.

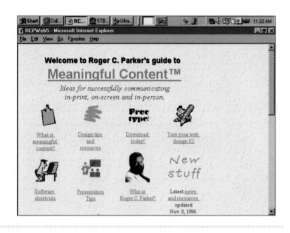 

Figure 3.1 A Web site that only offers options lacks the focus that a particular product or service would provide.

Figure 3.2 Web sites that immediately focus on a particular product or theme are more involving and can create urgency.

4. *Display and explain links* to the other pages located at the Web site.

5. Differentiate the firm *by emphasizing its philosophy or the unique customer benefits that set it apart from its competition.*

6. *Project an appropriate emotional image* through the words, colors, typeface, and layout used.

7. *Provide a hook* that will immediately involve visitors and encourage them to spend time at the site. This can be a teaser describing a special event or product, or the beginning of your feature article. Web pages that begin the sale are always more interesting than unfocused sites that just present a number of options.

8. *Load as quickly as possible* since visitors are quick to leave slow-loading Web sites.

We'll return again and again to these eight essential characteristics. Few home pages succeed in accomplishing all eight goals, but it's important to state them as ideals toward which your designs will gravitate.

WHAT MAGAZINES CAN TEACH WEB SITE DESIGNERS

The top half of your home page should resemble the front cover of a magazine.

The next time you're at a new stand or bookstore, study the front covers of the magazines on display. Notice that the front covers of most magazines contain more than just the publication's name. The front covers of most magazines sell the contents of each issue. There's usually a dominant photograph plus a headline and brief paragraph promoting a feature article. The titles of several other articles inside usually also appear on the cover.

Typically, there will also be a tagline that identifies the magazine's target market or explains what makes the magazine unique, that is, *Seattle Gardening* magazine's tagline might be "For those who want to make the most of rain instead of sun."

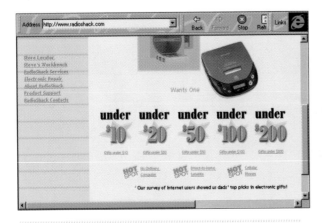

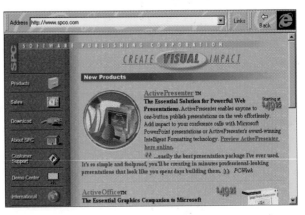

Figure 3.3 Within seconds of reaching this site, you're likely to be involved in choosing which product to buy.

Figure 3.4 This home page illustrates how to simultaneously project an image, offer numerous options (i.e., links), and involve the visitor by focusing on a specific product.

AN ALTERNATIVE APPROACH

An alternative approach is to provide a sequence of carefully chosen experiences that lead up to the home page and its eight characteristics. Instead of a single home page, this scenario offers a progression of screens that immediately involves the Web site visitor. Each screen communicates a single thought and contains a large link for Web site visitors to click on before they can proceed further.

This type of progression drives home the message contained on each screen and, because it requires the Web site visitor to click on the key word to continue, it involves them from the start.

The appearance and content of each screen, of course, has to be carefully considered in order to pique the Web site visitor's curiosity and encourage them to continue as the sequence builds up to a climax that satisfies the eight characteristics of a successful home page (see Figures 3.5 through 3.8).

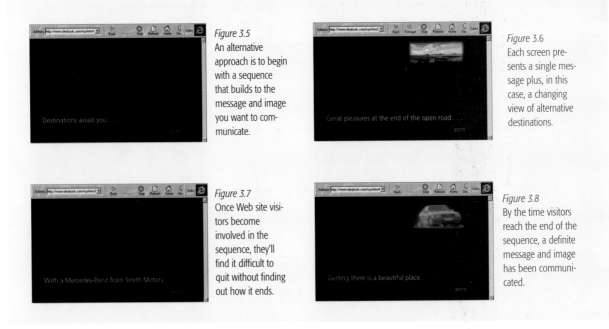

Figure 3.5 An alternative approach is to begin with a sequence that builds to the message and image you want to communicate.

Figure 3.6 Each screen presents a single message plus, in this case, a changing view of alternative destinations.

Figure 3.7 Once Web site visitors become involved in the sequence, they'll find it difficult to quit without finding out how it ends.

Figure 3.8 By the time visitors reach the end of the sequence, a definite message and image has been communicated.

Links

Links form the framework that connects the various pages of your Web site. There are several types of links. Links can consist of:

◆ *Highlighted words*: Links can be words that appear in a different color in the text of your document. Click on a highlighted word, and you will be taken to a different location on the same page in the Web site, a different page in the Web site, or even to an entirely different Web site. Text links can also be grouped together along the top, bottom, or one of the sides of a Web page.

◆ *Buttons or icons* grouped together at the top, bottom, or one of the sides of a page. A *button* is generally a circle or a rectangle, often with a three-dimensional appearance, containing a word that describes the contents of the page it links to. An *icon* is a stylized graphic image—like the knives-and-forks symbols indicating restaurants located on Interstate Highways or the internally recognized symbols for male and female rest rooms that visually communicate their meaning.

◆ A *navigation bar* containing several text links, buttons, or icons grouped together against a different-colored background along one edge of the screen.

◆ An *image map* consisting of an illustration containing *hot spots* which, when clicked on, take the Web site visitor to different pages. (You'll know when the pointer of your Web site browser is located over a hot spot because it turns into a hand.) A medical Web site might open with an image map of the human body. Clicking on the elbow would take you to a page discussing elbow injuries, clicking on the forehead might take you to a page discussing headaches. Or, by clicking on a particular state in the United States, you can locate information, resources, or businesses located within the state. (See Figures 3.9 and 3.10.)

◆ *Bookmarks* are specialized types of links. Bookmarks are destinations within articles (typically subheads) that text links placed at the start of the article take the Web site visitor to.

Text links change color after they have been clicked on, and a third color is used to indicate currently selected links. This allows Web site visitors to see at a glance whether they have already visited a page as well as their current location.

Clip-art—or generic illustrations—can also be used to indicate links. When using clip art as links, your software can add borders to identify the clip-art as a link and indicate when the link has been visited (or is currently being visited). (See Figures 3.11 and 3.12.)

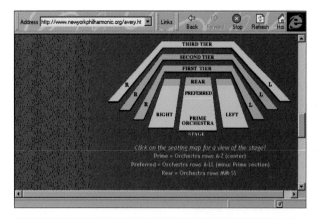

Figure 3.9 Image maps present many interesting creative options. You can preview the view of the stage from your proposed seat at Lincoln Center by clicking on the seat's location.

Figure 3.10 Each audience location is linked to a photograph showing you the view you'll get when seated in that particular location.

Characteristics of Effective Links

Links should be as obvious as possible. To avoid ambiguity, icons should be accompanied by text that explains the function of the icon. Text descriptions of icons and graphic links are also important since many Web site visitors use text-only browsers. Others temporarily turn graphics off in order to speed up their Web browsing.

Buttons and icons should be as small as possible so that their files will small, making it possible for them to load as quickly as possible. Their appearance should be consistent with the overall image of the Web site.

Insert Alt tags whenever possible. Most Web authoring programs make it easy to add them. Alt tags provide a text description of icons and graphic links as they are being downloaded. Alt tags allow Web site visitors to get an idea of the structure of your Web site as buttons and icons are downloading. Another advantage of Alt tags is that sometimes, when the Internet is busy, one or more buttons and icons may fail to load. If you have provided an Alt tag, however, visitors will still be able to determine where the incomplete link image leads.

WHERE DO BUTTONS, ICONS, AND CLIP-ART COME FROM?

There are numerous ready-to-use sources of buttons and icons. Most Web site authoring software contains dozens—or hundreds—of ready-to-use icons and buttons. Additional icons and buttons can be downloaded on the Web from the Web sites of various software publishers and other Web sites that seek to increase traffic—like book publishers or authors promoting their books. You can also easily create your own icons and buttons using the drawing tools that come with your word processing or Web site authoring program.

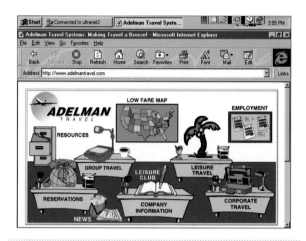

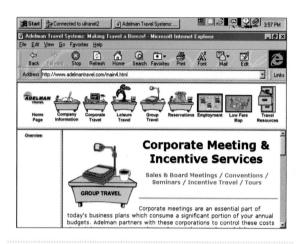

Figure 3.11 Illustrations accompanied by explanatory text quickly direct you to the appropriate pages of this travel agency's Web site.

Figure 3.12 Once you reach a desired page, the other links remain visible on the screen, so you can easily visit another agency resource.

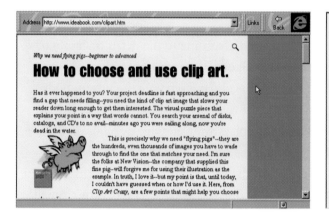

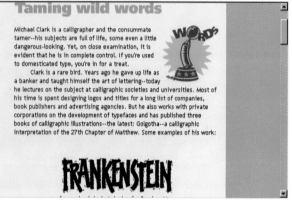

Figure 3.13 Note the different typefaces and colors used on each of the home page links.

Figure 3.14 Note how the headline typeface and the color of the right-hand border match the link that brought you to this point.

Figure 3.15
Similarly, the headline typeface and border color on this page match the originating link.

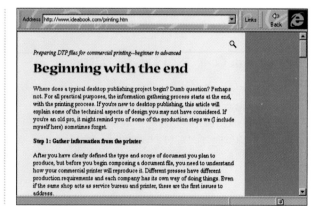

Links offer tremendous creative opportunities. For example, you can color code your site by relating the colors used for links to the headlines or graphic accents on the pages they link to. You can also use appearance to relate link to page by using the same typeface for headlines on linked pages as were used on the home page links. (See Figures 3.13 through 3.15.)

A *site map* is a page of your Web site that shows the hierarchy of your Web site's contents. Site maps make it easy for Web site visitors to directly access the information they're interested in. Site maps become increasingly important as your Web site grows and becomes more complex when you add additional layers of information.

Words, Words, and More Words

The bulk of your site's content is likely to be words—that is, text. Although technology for downloading fonts—typeface designs—along with Web sites is advancing, at present there are primarily two types of text. The success of your Web design efforts depends on your ability to make the right choice of these types at any given time.

◆ *Tagged text* immediately downloads and is formatted according to the defaults chosen by your Web site browser. You have only relative control over the appearance of tagged text. You can establish a hierarchy for headlines and subheads, and separate them from body copy, but you cannot control the specific typeface or type size used to display the text on your visitor's browser. The specific typeface that displays your message depends on the typefaces available on your visitor's computer and the typefaces they have chosen as defaults in their Web browser. The specific sizes of the various headlines, subheads, and the body copy is determined by your visitor's choice among the Normal, Large, Larger, Small, or Smaller options in their Web browser.

◆ *Formatted text* consists of text has been saved as a graphic file and downloads as a graphic. Formatted text offers you absolute control over the appearance of the type. You can use any desired typeface and it will display at exactly the size you want on your visitor's computer—

LINKS AND CONDENSED TYPEFACE DESIGNS

The condensed typeface designs discussed in the next section, such as Arial Narrow, are ideal for use in links, as they occupy significantly less space. By using these typefaces, you can reduce the size of your buttons by almost 30 percent without a loss of legibility! (See Figure 3.16.)

Figure 3.16
You can reduce the size of your buttons and links by over 20 percent by using condensed typefaces.

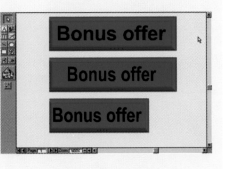

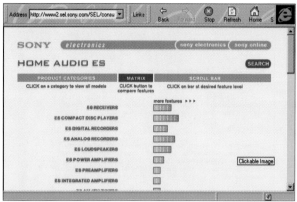

Figure 3.17 In addition to helping visitors access information, the colors used for links can play a major role in creating the image the Web site projects.

Figure 3.18 Links can be visual metaphors that describe the quality level of the products on the linked pages.

regardless of whether or not the typeface is available on your visitor's computer. You can also stretch or compress the type, modify letter, word, and line spacing, or set the type against a photograph or colored background. Formatted text permits you to use typeface variations like condensed and/or extra heavy fonts or refinements like correct punctuation, true small caps, and old style figures. The only disadvantage to formatted text is that the files take time to download. The larger the text, and the more colors used, the longer it will take the type to download.

Characteristics of Effective Web Text

Fast-loading tagged text is always preferable to formatted graphic text that inevitably downloads more slowly. Although you sacrifice control over appearance, visitors to your Web site will have more time to concentrate on your site's content (see Figure 3.19).

Font versus Typeface

Typeface refers to a specific typeface design, i.e., Times New Roman, Arial, or Frutiger–designed by Adrian Frutiger. Font refers to a variation of the typeface. Most typefaces contain several variations. Bold, italics, and bold italics are the most common variations.

Many typeface designs contain several weight and width variations. These offer additional capabilities for you to style your documents. Condensed fonts maintain the look of the typeface but permit you to include more words in a given space. Light versions of a typeface are characterized by thinner strokes–the lines making up each character. Heavy or black fonts use thicker strokes.

Think of it this way: Frutiger is a typeface design–a particular arrangement of shapes that communicate the letters of the alphabet. Frutiger Italic, Frutiger Light, Frutiger Condensed, and Frutiger Condensed Extra Black are font variations that maintain the same basic look but communicate as though using different volume levels or tones of voice. Each font variation consists of a separate file.

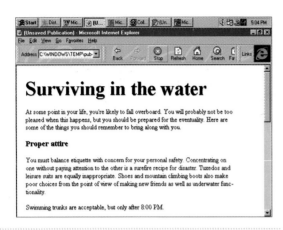

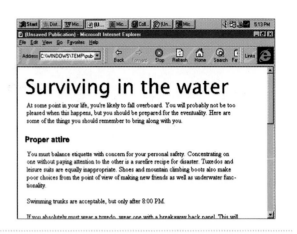

Figure 3.19 Tagged text defaults to the Web site viewer's default typeface, typically Times New Roman. As a result, only heading levels will be shown.

Figure 3.20 Replacing the headline and subhead with graphic files containing formatted text set in an informal contemporary typeface projects a different image even though the words are the same.

SIMILARITIES BETWEEN THE USE OF TEXT ON THE WEB AND IN PRINT

There are six ways that the successful use of text on the Web resembles the successful use of text in print. These six methods are:

1. Limit line length. Whether encountered in a newsletter printed or read on the Web, long lines of text are boring because the pages lack visual contrast—empty space before and/or after each line. Long lines of text are hard to read because your Web site visitor's eyes have to make numerous left-to-right movements as they scan each line. In addition, the longer the line, the more chance there is that Web site visitors will get lost at the end of a line—and either start to reread the line they have finished reading or inadvertently skip down two lines.

2. Avoid setting words and sentences exclusively in upper case. Words set in upper-case characters (capital letters) occupy more space and are significantly harder to read than the same words set in lower-case letters. Readers in print and on the screen depend on word-shapes to identify, or decode, each word. Words set in upper-case type form rectangles, whereas words set in lower-case type create unique shapes because of the way some letters are tall (b, l, t, etc.) and other characters contain elements that drop down (g, y, p).

3. Center with care. Centered text is harder to read because readers have to search for the beginnings of each line. Centered text also creates more boring pages because the empty space surrounding each line is equally divided between the left- and right-hand margins of each line, instead of being concentrated to either the left or the right of the line, where it is more noticeable. Long text passages set entirely in centered text are especially annoying. Another problem with centered text is that, if your visitor is viewing text at a large size, the first line of a two-line centered headline may extend completely across the page, leaving a single word isolated on the second line.

4. Strive for legibility, that is, maximum foreground/background contrast. Black text against a white or off-white (i.e., cream or ivory) background is easiest to read. Black text against a gray background is significantly harder to read, as is dark blue text against a light blue background. Be especially careful when placing text on top of photographs or against textured backgrounds or gradient fills (where the background makes a transition from light to dark or from one color to another).

5. Edit to the bone. Shorter is always better. In print or on the Web, short words, short sentences, and short paragraphs are always preferable to long words, long sentences, and long paragraphs. Whether in print or on the Web, your readers are in a hurry. The faster they can assimilate your message, the better.

6. Always chunk your content, that is, break up your message into numerous short elements, each introduced with a subhead. The more subheads you include, the easier it will to maintain reader momentum and keep them involved. Each subhead permits you to advertise the contents that follow. On the Web and in print, each subhead present readers with an additional entry point into your message.

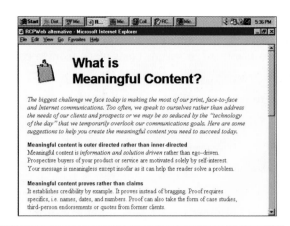

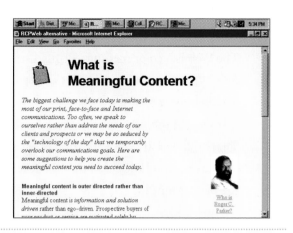

Figure 3.21 Long lines of text create visually boring, hard-to-read Web pages.

Figure 3.22 Reducing line length creates more open, attractive, and easy-to-read Web pages plus creates space for secondary features.

Figure 3.23
Short line lengths
make text easy to
read and provide
space for illustra-
tions. (Note the
way the currently
active link is high-
lighted in a
second color.)

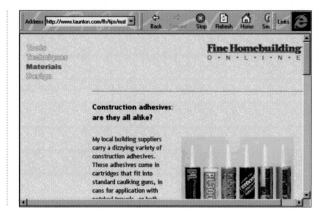

Limited amounts of graphic text, however, can be used to project a unique image—an image that can make your Web site memorable and set it apart from the competition's. Graphic text is ideal for use in titles, headlines, subheads, or tags (see Figure 3.20).

Alt tags are useful when using formatted text, so that Web site visitors can preview a brief description of the text while the file is downloading.

Always limit line length. Lines should contain fewer than sixty characters. Long lines of text create boring, hard-to-read Web pages (see Figure 3.21). A great deal of your Web design success depends on your ability to create Web pages that contain lines of the appropriate length. Web site visitors will willingly read extended text topics if the lines are short and the page contains empty space that provides visual contrast (see Figures 3.22 and 3.23).

Foreground and Background Colors

The Web is a color medium. Printed color always costs extra—in supply costs when using a color ink-jet printer in your office, or in preparation and printing costs at a commercial printer. Color is free, however, on the Web. It's to your advantage to take maximum advantage of it.

The default colors for the Web consist of black text against a rather dismal gray background. Thankfully, most Web authoring programs make it relatively easy to simultaneously change text and background colors, so that the text will always form a strong and easy-to-read contrast with the background.

Black text against a white background is a popular combination. However, many visitors may object to spending a lot of time at Web sites containing white backgrounds. Extended staring at a white screen can be very tiring. Remember that color on the Web is *projected* color. Web site visitors are, in effect, staring into the lens of a slide projector. For this reason, subdued colors or lightly patterned backgrounds offer a pleasing alternative.

Characteristics of the Effective Use of Color on the Web

Like all design choices, color should augment, rather than dominate, your Web site. Although "free," color should be used consistently and with restraint. With the exception of using color to visually connect home page links with the pages they are linked to, if you use black text on your home page, use black text throughout your Web site. Don't change from black text on your home page to blue text on another page, for example, without a good reason.

Avoid bright, solid-colored backgrounds, like reds, yellows, oranges, or greens. These can quickly become very tiring in large doses. It is also harder to choose text colors that can be easily read against bright colors for extended amounts of time.

Beware of overusing *reversed* text, that is, white or yellow type placed against a black or dark blue background. This is especially true if there is any chance that visitors to your Web site are going to print out your pages (as many will) on a color printer. Remember that backgrounds don't show up when you print from a Web browser! Thus, unless your Web site visitor remembers to switch the settings on their printer (which few will), they will be unable to read the white or yellow text after it is printed on white paper.

Limit your color choices to the 216 "platform-safe" colors. These ensure that the vast majority of visitors will be able to view your Web site, regardless whether their computer is using the Apple Macintosh, Microsoft Windows, or Unix operating system. These colors can be found—identified by number—on many Web sites and in many books. In addition, these 216 colors will reproduce cleanly on monitors driven by the most popular type of graphics cards. Your computer may possess more sophisticated graphics capabilities than the computers of many of your Web site visitors. Platform-safe colors become increasingly important as the size of the area covered by the color increases. Colors beyond the 216 platform-safe colors don't cause problems in photographs, for example, but they do when used for text or Web site backgrounds.

When you use colors outside, or beyond, the 216 safe colors, the colors will *dither*, or look granular on your visitor's monitor. This is because your visitor's computer will attempt to emulate the colors you have specified by mixing them on screen (i.e., your Web visitor's computer attempts to create a specific shade of orange by displaying a combination of red and yellow pixels—or dots—next to each other and relies on your visitor's eyes to group them together.)

Be especially careful when using gradient fills—text, backgrounds, or illustrations containing smooth transitions between full saturation to a light tint, or transitions from one color to another. In addition to dithering caused by attempts to create intermediate colors, gradients inevitably create *banding*—where adjacent colors group together and create unsightly shapes.

Visuals

Web pages without visuals can be very boring—no matter how exciting the content. Therefore, most Web sites employ a variety of visuals. Visuals can take many forms:

◆ *Photographs* come in several varieties. Scanned images are photographs unique to your Web site that have been converted into digital files using an image scanner. Today, you can scan either photographic enlargements or the original slide or film negative. You can also take your own digital photographs with the new breed of digital—or filmless—cameras now appearing. Prices for these cameras keep going down while their image quality is increasing. You can also purchase stock photographs from numerous sources. Although not unique to your Web site, these can effectively communicate mood and atmosphere for a fraction of the cost of hiring professional models and photographers or traveling to remote locales.

◆ *Illustrations* excel at communicating atmosphere and emotion. Illustrations often load significantly faster than photographs, especially if attention has been paid to their size and the number of colors they contain. You can either create your own illustrations, commission custom illustrations, or purchase off-the-shelf illustrations done in a variety of styles. You can even employ picture-fonts, which are typefaces containing illustrations instead of alphabet characters.

Web TV has an even more limited color bandwidth—it can recreate fewer colors—than the 216 platform-safe colors. If your Web site promotes a consumer product likely to attract Web TV viewers, you'll want to limit your color choices even more.

◆ *Business graphics* translate words and numbers into relationships and trends. A pie chart makes part whole relationships instantly visible. An organization chart does a better job of displaying hierarchy than would numerous paragraphs of text. You can use flowcharts and timelines to display sequence or cause-and-effect relationships. Various types of charts can be created by even the most basic spreadsheet programs and many hardware or software vendors include business graphics programs with their offerings. Stand-alone programs like *Visio* or utilities like Software Publishing Corporation's *Active Office* provide additional sources of business graphics.

Characteristics of Effective Visuals

Speed is the most important issue you should be concerned with when employing visuals. The larger the visual, and the more colors it contains, the longer it will take to download. Although the cost of personal computing continues to decline and Web performance is making rapid gains, graphics still take time to download. The faster your graphics load, the happier your visitors will be.

A great deal of your Web site success will be determined by the skills you develop handling graphics. One major aspect of this involves choosing how much information you need to include in the files of illustrations and scanned images. Remember that most computer monitors can only display 72 dots per inch. Thus, it doesn't make sense to scan photographs at the higher resolutions characteristic of images scanned for printing on your office printer or to take them to a commercial printer for quantity duplication. Also, you can often reduce file size by eliminating unnecessary colors.

Alt tags should always be used when placing graphics. Alt tags can provide a short description of each graphic as it is being downloaded. Interlaced visuals maintain your Web site viewer's interest as the graphics file downloads by providing a rough outline of the image that gets progressively clearer as the file downloads.

Employ *thumbnails* whenever possible. Instead of including large graphics that every Web site visitor has to download, include a small version of it which, when clicked, links to a larger version of the graphic. This way, only those who want to see the graphic, and are (presumably) willing to wait for it to download, will have to wait.

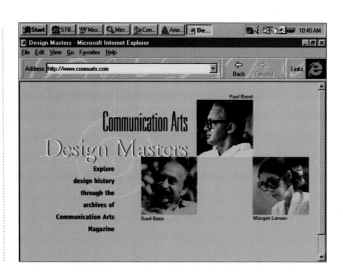

Figure 3.24
Careful sizing and table-based alignment of visuals are keys to creating Web sites that project a professional image.

TOOLS OF WEB PAGE DESIGN

Having taken a look at the various elements of Web site and Web page architecture, let's investigate the tools you use when assembling a Web site. Your major tools are:

◆ Tables

◆ HTML tags

◆ Frames

◆ Graphics files

Let's take a look at each of these important tools.

Tables

Tables are one of the fundamental tools of Web design. It's hard to overestimate the importance of tables. They permit you to define the horizontal and vertical placement of the various text and graphic elements included on your Web page. Tables are the Web equivalent of the column grids that print designers use to lay out books and newsletters. This may come as a surprise to you because, on the Web, most tables are hidden, that is, you do not see the horizontal and vertical gridlines that create the cells that organize the various text and graphic elements. Cells are created where rows and columns intersect each other.

Whenever you run across a good-looking Web page a page that contains short lines of text surrounded by plenty of attractive empty space—or breathing room—open your Web browser's View menu and select Source. Chances are, you'll see various references to TB. Such TB references are a clue that tables were used to create the Web site. In addition to framing your text with breathing room (I'm resisting a strong temptation to use the term "white space" at this point. Since you may not be using white for your Web site background, I won't use the term), you can also use tables to place subheads next to the text they introduce (instead of above the text they introduce). You can also use tables to create the Web equivalent of parallel columns of text.

Whenever you run across a good-looking Web page... open your Web browser's View menu and select Source. Chances are, you'll see various references to tables.

Tables are used even when you are not aware of their existence. Many Web authoring programs allow you to continue to use the column and grid layouts characteristic of print communications. Other programs allow you to drag-and-drop text and graphic elements into any desired location on the Web page. In both cases, however, these programs automatically create tables in the background when they prepare your Web site files for posting on the Web. It's just that you're not aware of it!

You can also use tables to organize links. Tables maintain consistent spacing between the links. One of the major advantages of text links placed in tables is that the links can load very quickly, without the delays characteristic of graphic links. You can also use tables to link captions to photographs so that they don't inadvertently become separated.

Characteristics of the Effective Use Of Tables

Tables are used well when they are used consistently throughout your Web site. This means that text and graphic placement remains consistent from page to page, so that the same amount of space separates text columns from the left and right edges of the screen.

The use of tables does not have to result in boredom, however. Most Web authoring software makes it easy to combine table cells, so that, for example, you can hang headlines and subheads to the left of the text they introduce.

Consistent alignment is a characteristic of the effective use of tables. Tables can ensure that text and graphics are accurately and consistently aligned with each other, rather than floating around on the page. Tables can help ensure that pages will appear the same, and elements will remain properly aligned, regardless of the typeface or type-size choices specified in the visitor's browser.

HTML Tags and Styles

HTML stands for *HyperText Markup Language*, a universally agreed-upon list of tags that Web browsers depend on to determine the size and alignment of text as well as to decide between displaying serif or sans serif text. HTML tags are typically placed before and after the various text elements that comprise your page, page titles, headlines, subheads, normal text, and numbered lists.

In the past, you had to manually add these tags before and after the various text elements on your page. Now, however, many word processing, page layout, and Web authoring programs permit you simply to highlight the various categories of text and apply HTML tags by choosing the desired heading level, body, or numbered list formatting options by selecting them from the style menu.

USING TABLES AS A DESIGN TOOL

Tables are remarkably easy to use as a design tool. They can be easily created with most word processing and Web authoring software programs. Here's a simple three-step guide to using tables to reduce line length, build visual contrast into every page, and emphasize the hierarchy of your Web page's content.

1. Start by creating a seven-column table that extends the width of your page (see Figure 3.25).

2. Combine cells, using your software's Merge Cells command, to create larger cells or containers for subheads and text. Insert placeholder text to indicate where subheads and text will appear (see Figure 3.26).

3. Replace the subhead and placeholder text with your Web page's desired content and format the subhead by applying the appropriate styles or tags (depending on the software you are using) (see Figure 3.27).

When you view the completed table in your browser, you'll be impressed at how good your page looks!

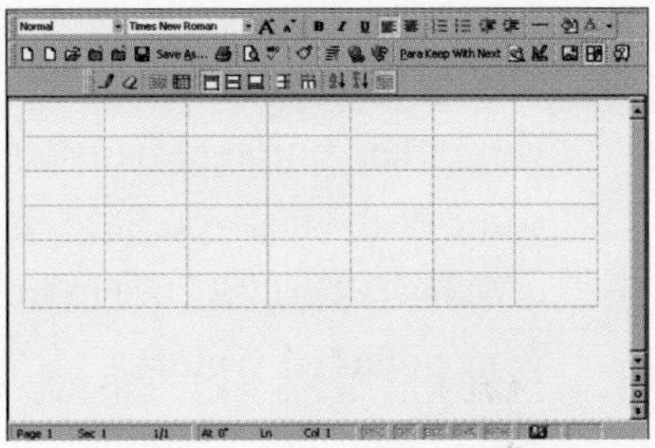

Figure 3.25
The starting point for a good-looking page is to create a seven-column table.

Figure 3.26
Combine cells to indicate the placement of subheads and text and insert placeholder text.

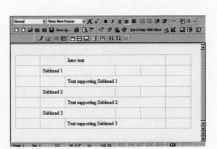

Figure 3.27
Replace placeholder text with the desired text and format the subheads.

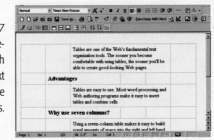

Although familiarity with HTML tags is not necessary in order to create effective Web pages, familiarity with HTML can greatly expand your creative options. One of the most useful HTML codes, for example, is the Block Quote tag, which indents the left- and right-hand margins of text, reducing line length and adding air to your Web pages without requiring you to add tables.

Characteristics of the Effective Use of HTML

Universality is one characteristic of the effective use of HTML. *Universality* means that Web pages will appear the same—or nearly the same—regardless of the browser used to view the Web site. Although most HTML features have been agreed upon by the major browser publishers, features are by no means identical through all browsers in use. By sticking to mainstream HTML tags, you'll avoid disappointing your visitors who are using a different Web browser. For this reason, you should install the latest as well as (when possible) earlier versions of both Microsoft Explorer and Netscape Navigator on your computer, and you should test your Web site with both current and earlier versions of both browsers.

You should also test your Web site with the Web browsers offered by online services like America Online and CompuServe. In addition, you should test your Web site on different computing platforms, that is, test your Web site on your friend's Macintosh if you created it on a computer running Microsoft Windows, and vice versa. You may be disappointed to find that some of the tags you have employed may not be universally supported. (And, remember, you, as a Web site designer, are more likely to have the latest Web site browser installed than many of your potential visitors.)

Practicality is another characteristic of the appropriate use of HTML codes. There's never enough time. New information is likely to turn up just as you think you have completed your Web site. If your Web site is overly complicated, chances are you won't have time to update it. If you have used HTML appropriately, however, updating your Web site won't be as much of a problem.

Although you can go a long way without learning HTML, you'll probably end up wanting to familiarize yourself with it, if only to discover how especially good-looking pages were created.

Frames

Frames are another major design tool. Frames permit you to display more than one file on the screen of your Web site visitor's monitor at a time. Typically, these frames will be of vastly different size. The bulk of your Web site's content will appear in the largest frame that contains a vertical scroll bar, so visitors can read down the page. One, or more, smaller frames, usually without scroll bars, will appear along the top or side edges of the screen.

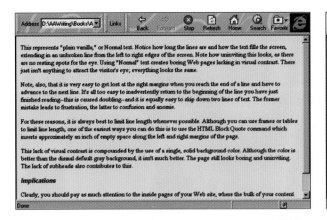

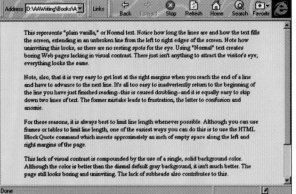

Figure 3.28 Pages containing long lines of Normal text are visually boring and hard to read.

Figure 3.29 Reformatting Normal text using the Block Quote tag indents the text, reducing line length and adding visual contrast to the page.

Frames offer several major advantages. Frames can:

♦ Assist navigation by allowing you to always display your Web site's navigation links. By always keeping links visible, you make it easy to keep your Web site visitors informed of where they are and of other interesting content at your site.

♦ Add a noticeable message to each page. This can be a *banner*, or rectangle of advertising, that will remain on the screen regardless of how far down the Web site visitor scrolls in the article they are reading. Banners can remain static or change at predetermined intervals. Banners can also contain your firm's logo and motto, reminding your Web site visitor that they are visiting your site.

♦ Add interest to your Web site by providing visual contrast. You can use one background color for the frames containing your Web site's navigation links and another for the frame containing your message. These colors can be optimized for the contents of each frame, that is, you can use light text against a dark background for the frame containing navigation links and dark text against a light (or white) background for the frame containing extended text.

Characteristics of the Effective Use of Frames

Paradoxically, the ability to view a Web site without frames is a very desirable characteristic. Because many Web browsers do not support frames, you may want to create two versions of your site: one using frames; one without frames.

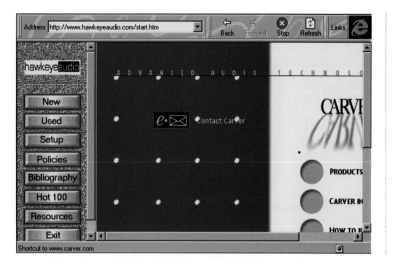

Figure 3.30
The frame, at left, containing the firm's name and internal Web links, retains control of visitors to your site while they temporarily visit another site. (Note the blue borders which indicate previously visited links.)

The background colors of the frames must complement each other. Instead of fighting each other, the colors should not only maintain text legibility but should project an image appropriate for your message and one you want your Web site to project.

Frames offer yet another advantage: They permit you to link your Web site to other sites without losing your visitor. By continuing to display a banner identifying your Web site in a frame along the top of the page, frames keep your Web link visible, thereby reminding visitors that they are really at your site (see Figure 3.30). This can save you a lot of time, because your visitors can access boilerplate information at other sites without your having to recreate it yourself for their use.

Graphics Files

Graphics files consist of visuals, like a scanned—or digitized—version of your logo as well as files containing visuals and formatted text. Successful Web site design and production involve:

◆   Keeping these files as small as possible when creating them so they will download as quickly as possible.

◆   Choosing the right type of file to further increase downloading speeds. Some software programs do this automatically, but others leave you to choose between the two primary types of files (discussed in Chapter 10).

◆   Organizing the files so you can locate them as quickly as possible when producing your Web site and placing them on the desired pages.

One essential difference between printed pages and Web pages is that printed pages are *static* in that the "files" that comprise them remain in place when read. Each page generally consists of a single file which may contain files—the illustrations. Web pages, however, are assembled on the fly as they are displayed on the monitor of your visitor's computer. Each screen, or view, of your Web page typically contains several files that have to be downloaded and organized by your visitor's browser as they are accessed by your Web site's links.

As your Web site becomes more complex, it's inevitable that downloading time will increase and there will be more opportunities for problems.

Characteristics of the Effective Use of Graphics

Effective graphics share these characteristics:

◆ They download as quickly as possible.

◆ They are as universal as possible, allowing the content at your Web site to benefit as many potential visitors as possible.

◆ There are as few opportunities for things to go wrong as possible.

These issues will be treated in greater detail in Chapter 10, "Producing Your Web Site."

HOW WEB PAGE DESIGN DIFFERS FROM PRINT DESIGN

Because print and Web technology differs so much, you can't just take print documents like brochures and newsletters and make Web pages out of them. There are a lot of changes you have to make. These changes are discussed in the following sections.

Reformatting Columns

Multicolumn formats, where the text snakes from the bottom of one column to the top of the next, don't work on the Web. Visitors don't want to—or simply won't—continually scroll from the top to bottom of one column and then return to the top of the next and, again, scroll down. A three-column format would be especially bothersome on the Web and would probably not be read at all. Each Web screen should contain all of the information the Web site visitor needs at that point.

The only time two-column formats may work on the Web is if the contents of the columns consist of disconnected information, such as a list of resources of approximately equal weight that can be read across as well as down.

Smaller Photographs and Illustrations

Web sites require smaller photographs. Although photographs don't increase content distribution costs the way photographs increase production and printing costs at a commercial printer, large photographs increase downloading time, often to the point where your visitor may leave your site in favor of a faster-loading one.

Options include reducing the size of the photographs and manipulating them so the files contain the minimum amount of information necessary to communicate effectively.

Modifying Color Choices

Bright background colors can be very distracting on the Web. Bright colors are more annoying on the Web than in print because of the difference between the relatively pure (i.e., bright) color projected on the screen of a computer compared to color reflected off the surface of a printed sheet of paper. Bright colors that can be tolerated on a sheet of paper often become annoying when viewed in large quantities on a computer screen.

In addition, it's very possible that there are no direct platform-safe Web colors equivalent to the colors used in your print communications. You may have to choose similar, but not exactly the same, colors for backgrounds and text because the specific colors and shades used in print (where there are virtually no limitations to your color choices) do not correspond to a platform-safe Web color.

Navigation

Navigation is far more difficult on the Web than in print. Although readers can scan an entire printed page at a glance, they can rarely see an entire Web page in its entirety. This makes it harder for them to scan a Web site or an article and make read or not-read decisions based on the relevance of the content to their needs and interests.

For this reason, Web sites require careful link architecture. At every point, Web site visitors have to know what their options are. At the beginning of an article, for example, Web site visitors should be able to view links that describe the structure of the article by showing the subheads—or topics—discussed in the article. Inside an article, it should be easy for Web site visitors to discontinue reading and immediately return to the home page or locate a different topic and quickly ascertain if it offers desired or interesting content.

Chunking

Conciseness is even more important on the Web than in print. Words, sentences, and paragraphs have to be as short as possible. It's important that as much content as possible be visible at a time, reducing the need for the Web site visitor to scroll. When sentences and paragraphs are too long, it's likely that important information may disappear off the top of the screen when visitors scroll down.

SIX KEYS TO SUCCESSFUL WEB DESIGN

There are many implications of the shift from print to the Web. The following are the six key elements of successful Web design. If you consistently follow these guidelines, you can't help but design and create a good-looking, easy-to-read Web site.

1. Smaller Is Always Better

The text and graphics contained on many Web pages are simply too large.

Large is bad because large objects reduce the number of items that can fit on your home page. Large graphic elements, like your firm's logo, prevent your home page from containing additional reasons to explore your Web site further. Often, links to information elsewhere on the site are visible only if the visitor scrolls further down the page… which few visitors will bother to do unless the top half of the page provides compelling reasons to scroll down.

There are other advantages to small:

◆ Small means faster loading, whether the file contains formatted text, your firm's logo, or other types of visuals.

◆ Small means space for more teasers. Each screen can contain links to more content options located elsewhere on your Web site.

◆ Small means more room to begin the relationship by offering more content and more ways for Web site visitors to respond to your offer and begin a relationship with you.

◆ Small provides space for you to build immediacy as soon as possible into your Web site.

It's important to remember that there is a fundamental difference between a Web page and a magazine or newspaper advertisement. Magazine and newspaper advertisements are seen in a more competitive context, that is, editorial articles and other advertisements on the page compete for the reader's attention. This forces you to use large headlines, photographs, and logos to compete with other text elements on the page.

But a Web page displayed on the screen of your visitor's computer occupies the entire attention span of your Web site visitor. There's no temptation for the visitor to sneak a look at a competitor's Web page lurking off to the side of your computer. Because you already have a monopoly—albeit a temporary monopoly—on your visitor's attention, you don't have to make text and elements as large as you otherwise would.

2. Strive for Simplicity

Simplicity implies restraint. Simplicity creates unity. Simplicity projects elegance and professionalism and makes your job as well as your visitor's job easier. Let's examine these concepts more closely:

◆ Restraint involves choosing a few signature colors, typefaces, and layouts and using them throughout your Web site. Your goal is to maximize the differences between your Web site and others by emphasizing a few basic choices. If, on the other hand, you clutter up your Web site with a variety of colors, typefaces, links, layouts, and backgrounds, your Web site will not be memorable because it will be difficult—if not impossible—for Web site visitors to identify what sets your Web site apart.

◆ Unity involves making as few changes as possible to the design of your Web site as you add pages to it. Unity involves using the same title, headline, and body copy typeface and background color choices throughout your Web site. Web site visitors are always searching for the meaning of change. An appropriate change might relate the colors used for headlines and subheads on an article to the color of the link that brought the Web site visitor to the article. But an inappropriate change often sends the wrong message to your Web site viewer. If all of your subheads have been black, for example, but the subheads used on one page are set in a different color, Web site visitors might interpret this to mean that the subheads are not just subheads, but they're also links!

◆ Simplicity involves changing one element at a time. When you choose two or more elements, the importance of the change is greatly diminished. Change three elements, and confusion results—the importance of the changed variable is lost in the clutter. Refer back to Figures 3.19 and 3.20, for example. Notice how dramatically different each page appears because just the headline typeface is changed. Imagine how the impact of this simple design change would be lost if the background color of the page and the color of the body copy text were also changed!

Simplicity also implies taking a good hard look at advanced techniques like sound and movement. These can be great when they contribute to your content, but they can also distract from your message. You'd probably be disappointed if you visited a Web site devoted to radio history, for example, and found that you couldn't download audio clips of important radio broadcasts. Likewise, at a visit devoted to television history, you'd willingly wait for video clips of your favorite *I Love Lucy* episode to download or access retrospective interviews with the cast members from *M*A*S*H*.

But extraneous sound and movement—like trumpet fanfares introducing new pages—wear thin very quickly. Likewise, movement is always distracting. If the movement is purposeful—that is, if it helps draw your Web site visitor's eyes to your "special of the day," then movement can be defended. But, spinning gears and text scrolling from right to left along the bottom of the screen are usually so distracting it becomes extremely difficult to concentrate on the content of the rest of the Web page.

Aim for transparency. Use the minimum number of tools and techniques necessary to communicate your Web site's content as quickly as possible. If considering introducing new typefaces, colors, or graphic accents—when in doubt, leave it out.

When in doubt, leave it out!

3. Build Visual Contrast into Each Page

The above discussion is not meant to imply that you should strive for boredom. The context—or visual design—your content appears in is as important as the content itself. Page after page of boring text is a certain turn-off. Here are some of the ways boredom can slip into your Web site, along with some suggested cures:

◆ *Text extending from one edge of the screen to another.* In addition to being too long to be comfortably read, Web pages containing long lines of text lack visual contrast—areas where nothing is happening, which forms a strong contrast with the text. These empty areas make your message look shorter and also provide a resting spot for your reader's eyes as they view each page.

◆ *Solid background colors.* No matter how good something is, too much is often overwhelming. Solid backgrounds—the use of a single background color which extends from left to right across your Web site visitor's computer screen—is boring. Instead, use your Web site's background color to horizontally subdivide your Web site. For example, place navigation links or subheads against a different colored background. This creates zones of interest that not only organize the contents of your Web site but set it apart from your competition's.

4. Provide a Meaningful Hierarchy of Content

The layout of your Web site should reflect the importance of its content. Important content should be easier to locate than less important content. Important ideas should be significantly larger and/or more noticeable than less important ideas. Web site visitors should be able to immediately gauge the importance of each content element by the ease with which it can be located and its prominence on the page where it appears.

The above is easier said than done, of course. Creating a meaningful hierarchy also requires more planning than simply randomly adding text and visuals to your Web site.

5. Choose a Limited Color Palette

The best-looking Web sites and Web pages typically use the fewest colors—chosen from the 216 colors of the platform-safe palette, of course. Indeed, two- and three-color Web sites are not unknown and can be startlingly effective, especially if the colors of the text links are indicated by different shades of the original two or three basic colors.

As you analyze the various Web sites you visit, using the Web Site Impression Sheet and printouts described in Chapter 4, notice how the best-looking Web sites use the fewest colors. Often, the most obvious difference between professionally created Web sites and home-grown Web sites is the number of colors employed. This is especially important if your goal is to project an upscale image, as described in Chapter 8. In this case, you'll want to pay particular attention to the Web sites run by religious and financial institutions attempting to communicate profes-sionalism and trust worthiness (see Figure 3.31).

6. Make Navigation Intuitive, Obvious, and Fast

Hidden content is wasted content. If your Web site visitors can't locate easily the information they desire, they'll quickly move on—even if the information is really there! There are simply too many other Web sites waiting for their attention.

Don't make visitors to your Web site puzzle out the meaning of the icons and graphic links employed at your site. Icons and graphics can add visual interest, but they may also add confu-sion—especially if your goal is to attract an international market to your Web site.

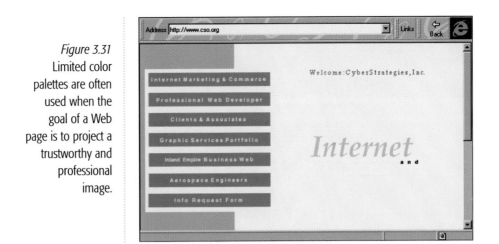

Figure 3.31
Limited color palettes are often used when the goal of a Web page is to project a trustworthy and professional image.

CONCLUSION

This chapter has summarized the basic tools you'll be working with when you design and produce your Web site. By analogy, if you were a newcomer to carpentry, you're at the point where you now know the difference between a hammer, a saw, a chisel, and a plane. To carry the analogy further, you'd also be able to recognize a professional, tight-fitting joint, as opposed to an amateurish joint—characterized by gaps between the pieces of wood and imperfections caused by the hammer hitting the wood instead of the nail.

In Chapter 8, "Identifying and Projecting a Desired Image," we'll look at how you can adapt the tools and techniques described in this chapter to your particular Web site.

Chapter 4

Learning By Observing

Benefit from the Mistakes and Successes of Others

Learning by observing is one of the best ways you can develop your Web site content and design skills. The more sites you visit, the more you'll appreciate the elements that go into a successful Web site—and the better you'll be able to identify problem areas you want to avoid when you create (or improve) your own Web site.

Just visiting Web sites isn't enough, of course. The key to success is to carefully *analyze* the strengths and weaknesses of each of the Web sites you visit and keep track of your impressions and observations. You can do this using the Web Site Impression Sheet in this chapter or, if you have a color printer and screen capture program, you can take, print, and file screen shots (or photographs) of the various Web sites you visit.

SELECTING SITES TO VISIT

Avoid being seduced by the temptation to confine your Web site surfing to the professionally designed sites featured in computer and design magazines or the Web sites of large Fortune 1000 corporations. Although interesting, these may be too sophisticated to show both the dos and the don'ts of effective Web content and design.

Instead, visit a broad spectrum of sites. Analyze Web sites ranging from those from large corporations, colleges, and government bureaus to small and medium-sized sites. Visit sites created by small business owners and independent freelance graphic designers that are just as likely to have important lessons to teach as those created by professional graphic designers creating site for "budget doesn't matter" Fortune 1000 firms. Although nonprofessional Web sites may be less sophisticated, they may be more valuable in showing you what to avoid.

Locating Web Sites

Here are some of the ways you can easily locate Web sites from a variety of both large and small businesses and organizations:

◆   Internet Service Providers. Visit the Web sites of Internet service providers in your area—or any area, for that matter—and locate the page containing links to all of the sites on their site. These lists will likely provide a variety of Web sites representing firms of varying sizes.

◆   Selected categories of Web sites. Another way of identifying a variety of Web sites to visit is to search for lists containing links to a variety of Web sites within a given category and just go through them one by one. Commercial search engines like Yahoo often contain lists of Web sites within a given field: colleges, radio stations, restaurants, engineers by specialty, etc. Try to locate lists containing a variety of professionally created and home-grown Web sites from firms of different sizes.

◆   Magazines and newspapers. Many magazines and newspapers contain listings of the Web site addresses of their advertisers. Magazines often give Web site addresses of advertisers in each issue as well as the Web site addresses of their advertisers on their Web site. Many newspaper ads contain Web site addresses and the classified sections of many newspapers list the Web site addresses of their advertisers. In addition, more and more newspapers are going on-line and listing their advertisers on their Web sites.

◆ Casual encounters. Jot down Web addresses as you notice them on billboards or as their addresses turn up while you are talking to your friends. Because of their complexity, many Web site addresses are hard to remember, so it will pay to take a second or two to jot down the address on a piece of paper.

Check Out More than Home Pages

It is important that you do not confine your analysis of a Web site to just the first pages—or home pages—of the sites you visit. Instead, be sure you check out links to a variety of pages at each Web site. Visitors usually spend more time reading articles, searching databases, and following links to desired data than they do concentrating on the Web site's home page. Indeed, you can usually learn a lot about a Web site by analyzing how consistently the colors, layout, and typography of the home page are maintained throughout the various pages of the site.

Although the home page creates the first impression of a Web site, most of a visitor's time is spent at pages other than home pages.

MAKING THE MOST OF YOUR VISITS

Keep track of the sites you have visited. Once you leave a Web site, it's very difficult to recall its strengths and weaknesses. It's hard to remember the colors, layout, links, and typography employed.

There are three ways to record your observations of the Web sites you visit:

◆ Bookmark or download pages from the Web sites you visit
◆ Use the Web Site Impression Sheet
◆ Print color screen captures of the Web sites you have visited

Bookmarking and Downloading Web Sites

Most Web site browsers—the software you use to view Web sites on the Internet—permit you to *bookmark*, or capture, the address of Web sites you may want to remember. (The browser's menu usually contains a Favorites entry which, when opened, contains an Add to favorites command plus a list of Web sites you have already bookmarked. There are several disadvantages to this approach, primarily that it's very hard to make meaningful side-by-side comparisons of memories. Once you leave a Web site, it's nearly impossible to remember its important characteristics when you visit another site. Another disadvantage of relying exclusively on bookmarks is that you have to go on-line and revisit the Web site to review its strengths and weaknesses—which takes time and may incur additional on-line costs.

Several utilities are available to help you download a Web site to your hard disk so you can review the entire site, or just portions of it, off-line. The disadvantages of this approach is that it is, again, impossible to compare memories and that just a few Web sites can fill up your Web site—especially if they contain numerous graphics. Clearly, these alternatives are not the way to go!

Using the Web Site Impression Sheet

The easiest way to learn by surfing is to photocopy the Web Site Impression Sheet in this chapter and fill out one for each Web site you visit. The Web Site Impression Sheet will make it easy for you to analyze the important elements of Web site design as well as provide a permanent record of the site, so you can refer back to it later.

The Web Site Impression Sheet makes it easy to analyze the strengthens and weaknesses of the important elements of Web site architecture and keep track of how consistently these elements are executed on both the home page and the pages that follow.

Here are some tips to help you make maximum use of the Web Site Impression Sheets:

◆ *Three-hole punch* them and store them alphabetically in three-ring binders for easy retrieval and review.

◆ Be sure you *enter the date* of your visit, and occasionally revisit the site. If major changes have been made, note any important changes on a new Web Site Impression Sheet and file it next to the original.

◆ *Visit the best and worst sites often.* Your impressions of the Web site may change as you gain more experience with the Web and your impressions become more critical.

◆ *Refer to the Index* at the back of this book for explanations of any terms you may not be familiar with.

THE WEB SITE IMPRESSION SHEET

1. Firm or organization posting Web site (describe)   URL (i.e., Web site address):

    Significance of URL:

2. Date visited

3. Contents of opening Screen

    1.
    2.
    3.
    4.
    5.
    6.

4. Is scrolling required to access links?   ❏ Yes   ❏ No

5. Does the opening screen involve you or   ❏ No   ❏ Yes (If "Yes," what? Describe below)
    include a hook, i.e., something to capture
    your interest?

    Rate the importance of the hook on a scale of 1 to 10, with 1 repre-
    senting "poor," "10 representing "excellent".

6. Opening page graphics   ❏ Too large?   ❏ Too small?   ❏ Just right

    Relevance of opening page graphics: (describe below)

7. Does the opening page open,   ❏ Yes   ❏ No (If no, why not?)
    i.e., download, quickly?

8. Is the design of the opening page appropriate   ❏ Yes   ❏ No (If no, why not?)
    to the theme of the Web site or the
    business the firm is involved in?

9. Draw a thumbnail sketch of the opening screen

10. Does the design of the links reflect the site's theme? ❏ Yes ❏ No

11. Are links intuitive? ❏ Yes ❏ No

12. Does the site contain frames? ❏ No ❏ Yes (If "yes," how are they used?)

13. Line length (articles and text features) ❏ Too long ❏ Just right

What technique was used to reduce line length?
(Hint: use your browser's View Source command)

14. Are subheads used to break up long articles? ❏ Yes ❏ No

15. Do links at the beginning of articles permit you
to go directly to subheads within the article? ❏ Yes ❏ No

16. Is full contact information provided,
i.e., telephone, mailing address, fax, e-mail? ❏ Yes ❏ No

17. Are forms used for visitor registration? ❏ Yes ❏ No

18. Are reasons given for visitors to register? ❏ No ❏ Yes (If so, what?)

19. Quality of content

Rate on a scale of 1 to 10, with 1 representing poor, 10 representing excellent. Describe importance of content below:

20. Does the site offer meaningful involvement,
i.e., searchable databases, finance or lease
calculators, custom-chosen views? ❏ No ❏ Yes (If Yes, what benefits does the involvement offer?)

21. What design elements unify the Web site?

❏ Background colors
❏ Text colors
❏ Logo
❏ Links
❏ Typeface choices
❏ Graphic accents

	❑ Text margins
	❑ Size, location, or manipulation of graphics
	❑ Other (describe below)

22. Sketch a typical Web page at this site, indicating links and text placement

23. Links
- ❑ Easy to locate
- ❑ Easy to identify current location
- ❑ Context-specific—i.e., depend on current page location

24. Does the Web site contain valuable links to other Web sites?
- ❑ No
- ❑ Yes (If so, describe what makes the links valuable)

25. Does the site make effective use of color?
- ❑ Yes
- ❑ No (If "no," describe why)

26. Does the Web site employ animation or movement?
- ❑ No
- ❑ Yes (If yes, how is the movement used? How does it enhance your visit? Does it communicate meaningful information?)

27. Does the Web site contain sound?
- ❑ No
- ❑ Yes (If yes, how is sound used? Does it enhance your visit? Does it communicate meaningful information?)

28. Is the Web site useful and memorable?
- ❑ No
- ❑ Yes (If useful, why and how is it useful?)

- ❑ No
- ❑ Yes (If memorable, what makes it memorable?)

29. Did you encounter any problems?

❏ Out of date information

❏ Lack of meaningful content

❏ Bright or distracting backgrounds? (Describe below)

❏ Is the text hard to read? (If so, why? Describe below)

❏ Slow-loading pages throughout site

❏ Oversize pages (i.e., need to use horizontal scroll bar)

❏ Broken links

❏ Typographical errors

❏ Other (describe below)

30. Overall rating of Web site

Rate on a scale of 1 to 10, with 1 representing poor, 10 representing excellent

As a preview of what's to come, let's review some of the questions on the Web Site Impression Sheet. As you continue reading this book, however, the importance of the questions in the Web Site Impression Sheet will become increasingly clear to you, so don't worry if you're not 100 percent comfortable with every question at this point.

◆ In Chapter 6, we'll examine the importance of a Web site's *URL*, or address, and the role it plays in describing and locating Web sites.

◆ *Opening screen* refers to the horizontal image displayed on your computer monitor by your Web site monitor when you first arrive at a Web site. It's important to remember that your browser doesn't show an entire page of your Web site; it just shows a horizontal slice of each page. The opening screen is the first slice revealed—it's the top half of the home page. The opening screen is extremely important to the success of a Web site because it's the point where many continue or go-elsewhere decisions are made.

- The hook mentioned in Question Five refers to the Web site's lead, the presence or absence of a particular product or article that involves the reader by encouraging them to start reading a particular article, rather than just clicking on links at random.

- *Links* refer to text or graphic elements which, when clicked, take you to a different location on the Web site or a different Web site entirely.

- *Frames* permit your Web site to display more than one file on the visitor's screen at one time. Typically, one frame is used for navigation elements, another contains the text and graphics contained on each individual page.

- *Forms* provide a structure for Web site visitors to register by entering their name, e-mail address, and any other information the Web site designer wants to collect from the visitor. These forms can typically be sent by the Web site visitor simply clicking on a Submit button. One of the reasons to capture the Web site visitor's e-mail address is so they can be easily and inexpensively contacted in the future.

- *Content* refers to information, what the Web site visitor takes away from the Web site.

- *Involvement* refers to ways the Web site visitor can customize the experience they have at the Web site by finding out if a desired product is available or by finding out how much it would cost to lease or purchase an automobile or home.

The above are just a few of the many Web site characteristics that determine the success, or effectiveness, of the Web site.

WORKING WITH SCREEN CAPTURE PROGRAMS

An even better alternative is to use a screen capture program. A screen capture program takes a picture of everything appearing on your computer monitor—foreground as well as background elements. Screen capture programs for Microsoft's Windows 95 include Collage from Inner Media (Hollis, NH), or Hijack Pro from Inset Systems (Danbury, CT). Screen capture programs for the Apple Macintosh include SnapJot from XX Systems.

You can store screen captures as files on your computer's hard disk (or, better yet, an external drive such as an Iomega Zip Drive). Or, you can print them directly, without saving them. If you have a color printer, you'll find that printing and filing screen captures of visited Web sites can be the single most important way you can master or improve your Web content and design skills.

If you have a color printer, you'll find that printing screen captures of Web sites can be the single most important way you can master or improve your Web content and design skills.

There is a world of difference between printing screen captures and printing the pages of the Web site you are visiting. Here are some of the reasons a screen capture program is preferable to printing out a Web page from a browser:

◆ When you print a screen capture of a Web page, you print exactly what was visible on your computer monitor, including frames and backgrounds. When you print from the Web browser, however, backgrounds and frames are eliminated. You get just a page, or pages of text and graphics, without the ability to evaluate them in their original context.

◆ When you print a screen capture, you print just the horizontal slice of the Web page visible on the computer monitor. When you print from the Web browser, however, you print the entire page (or pages). This means you lose the horizontal perspective characteristic of viewing a Web page on screen.

◆ Another advantage of taking a screen capture of a Web site is that, if you choose the screen capture program's "whole screen" option, you also capture your browser and—if you leave its menu bar revealed—the address of the Web site. This makes it easy for you to return later to the Web site.

◆ Printing directly from your screen capture program avoids filling up your hard disk with images of Web sites you have visited.

Since pages printed on a color ink-jet printer can be very delicate—the colors may smear if they are in contact with moisture from wet fingers, for example—I have found the best way to store the printed pages is to insert them in clear plastic holders available in most office supply firms. These clear plastic holders are available three-hole punched, ready for insertion in binders.

WORKING WITH A SCREEN CAPTURE PROGRAM

Most screen capture programs operate the same way. You can capture a screen from within the Web browser, or you can start the screen capture program and return to your Web browser.

◆ To capture a screen from within a Web browser, load the browser before going on-line. Then, to capture a screen, press the hot key combination that captures the screen. The default hot key for my screen capture program, for example, consists of holding down the left **Shift** key while pressing the **F10** key. (You can usually choose any combination of keys to start the screen capture sequence.)

◆ Alternatively, you can switch to the screen capture program and start the capture sequence from there. Most screen capture programs allow you to specify the *countdown*, or amount of time that elapses, between the time you start the capture sequence and when the screen capture takes place. This gives you plenty of time to return to your Web browser.

After taking a screen capture, you can either print it out or save it to your hard disk.

Note that the printed colors may not match the colors shown on the screen of your computer. Do not be concerned with the difference because, at this point, you are more concerned with the relative choice and placement of colors rather than replicating exactly what you saw on the screen of your computer.

Working as Efficiently as Possible

Here are some lessons I've learned from experience:

◆ To save money, avoid the temptation to print screen shots larger than necessary. Images between one-quarter and one-third the size of the page are large enough to reveal the strengths and weaknesses of each Web page's content and design. Larger images use more ink, increasing supply costs unnecessarily. You can always print individual pages at larger size if you want to analyze them in greater detail.

◆ Be consistent the way you take screen shots. Choose either *landscape* (horizontal) or *portrait* (vertical) printing, but don't mix the two. Few things are as frustrating as having to constantly reorient the binder in order to view its contents.

◆ Include all necessary information. Some screen capture programs allow you to add the date the image was printed on the print-out as well as add comments (or a caption). Printing the date helps you track changes in a Web site over time. Adding comments or a caption can remind you what you liked—or disliked—about the Web site.

CONCLUSION

Whichever method you choose, try to devote an hour or two a week to analyzing various Web sites on the Web. Although experience is the best teacher, the experience doesn't have to be your own. By spending time analyzing the work of others, you can profit from their experiences as well as your own.

Section 2

Getting Started

Chapter 5

Planning Your Web Site

Measure Twice, Cut Once

Many approach their first Web site by considering colors, typefaces, or special effects like sound and movement. A much better approach is to begin by planning. You'll work far more efficiently if you base your Web site on your answers to a series of increasingly detailed questions. Every step in the creation and maintenance of your Web site should be based on your answers to the questions first encountered during the planning stage and then reexamined as you advance through the various steps involved in creating and maintaining your Web site.

In this chapter, we'll briefly introduce the twenty basic planning questions of successful Web design and look at some of the ways your answers should influence your decisions as you create your Web site. In the following chapters, we'll examine some these questions in increasing detail and ask other—increasingly detailed—questions.

The following questions are summarized in a worksheet for your use at the end of the first section of this chapter. Feel free to photocopy the worksheet and make as many copies as desired. You might want to invite your co-workers to fill out copies of the worksheet, so you can develop as many ideas and resources to work with as possible. This also encourages enthusiasm and support for your Web site.

Invite your co-workers to fill out copies of the worksheet so you can have as many ideas to work with as possible.

TWENTY QUESTIONS

There are twenty basic questions you'll want to answer before proceeding. Taking the time to carefully answer these questions now will help you avoid wasting your time and energy creating a purposeless Web site that neither supports your firm's goals nor your customers' and prospects' needs later.

Purpose

Form follows function. The content and design of your Web site should reflect both why you are creating it and why people are visiting it. Answering these questions, and those in the following section, will help you focus on the message rather than the medium. Accordingly, start by focusing on the results you want to achieve from your Web site.

1. *What is the primary purpose of your Web site?* Why are you creating a Web site? What kind of results are you looking for? Are you looking for immediate response or paving the way for a more aggressive Web presence in the future? Is your goal to sell a specific product or service, generate floor traffic, communicate with investors and shareholders, or support products that you have already sold? Or are you trying to position your business relative to your competition? Is your goal to reduce customer support costs? If you could communicate only one idea to your Web site visitors, what would it be? How can you substantiate it? What evidence, or information, can you provide?

2. *What are some of your other goals?* List some of the other objectives you would like your Web site to achieve in order of importance. Hint: the easiest way to answer this one is to reconsider the alternatives you considered for Question One.

3. *What action do you want Web site visitors to take?* Do you want them to request further information, visit your place of business, or purchase directly from your Web site?

4. How are you going to measure the success of your Web site? Try to establish ways to quantify the success of your Web sites. Establish a mechanism for tracking the results of your Web sales by identifying incremental leads, sales, and visits that are directly attributable to your Web site.

Successful Web sites are designed to satisfy both results and resources. Success comes to the degree you identify your goals and make a realistic appraisal of the resources you have at your disposal. The alternative is to waste a lot of time and money.

Content

You are only one-half of the equation. Your Web site visitors are the other half. Successful Web sites are outer-directed—they are built around the needs of their visitors rather than the egos and enthusiasms of the Web site creators. Remember: you're not creating a Web site for yourself; you're creating it to satisfy your visitors' needs. Success will come to the degree that you identify your Web site visitors and their needs and then create a Web site that satisfies their needs.

Your Web site will succeed to the extent that your goals and your Web site visitors' needs overlap. Chapter 7 is devoted to describing how to create a "community of information" that includes your goals and the goals of your Web site visitors.

You're not creating a Web site for yourself; you're creating it to satisfy your visitors' needs.

5. *Whom do you want to visit your Web site?* The design and type of information you include in your Web site should reflect the expectations of your customers—and this involves knowing who they are. Are you interested in attracting first-time buyers, repeat buyers, or step-up buyers looking for improved performance?

6. *What types of information are they looking for?* If they are repeat customers, they probably already possess basic buying information and are more likely to be price- or feature-oriented than first-time buyers who are interested in a basic introduction to the field.

7. *What types of information can you provide?* Your goal is to avoid marketing myopia—the feeling that just because you know something, your prospective buyers also know it. Chances are, they don't. Your Web site will succeed to the extent that you expand the market by educating them. From your entire universe of information about your field, your goal is to choose information that your Web site visitors are searching for.

8. *How often do you want Web site visitors to return?* The more you want your Web site visitors to return, the more you'll want to frequently update your site.

9. *How can you build immediacy into your Web site?* Your market is likely to have a short memory. If visitors don't immediately act, they might never act. What incentives can you offer to encourage your market to immediately respond to your offerings? Are there ways you can make your Web visitors feel special and, hence, more likely to respond immediately?

Information is the core of a successful Web site. Success comes from offering your Web site visitors information that supports your goals.

Design

The design—colors, typography, layout, and organization—of your Web site should be influenced by the image you want to project (as influenced by the market you want to attract) as well as the content you're going to include.

10. *What type of image do you want to project?* Do you want to project an affordable or upscale image? Do you want to project a youthful or a more conservative image?

11. *What type of content will be included?* The balance of text and graphics is likely to play a key role in the organization and layout of your Web site. Text-heavy Web sites present an entirely different set of challenges than do Web sites containing numerous images. The type of content you are going to include also influences the production tools you'll need to create your Web site. If you are going to include a lot of photographs, for example, you'll probably want to purchase a scanner or digital camera. If you're going to include only a few, you can probably get by having important photographs converted into digital files at a local service bureau or office support firm like Kinko's.

12. *How much involvement do you want to include?* Are there ways that you can begin to help Web site visitors sell themselves and encourage the sale by helping them prequalify themselves? Tools like financing and lease calculators can save a great deal of your sales staff's time.

13. *What do your competitor's Web sites look like?* It's important that your Web site projects a unique and consistent image, one clearly different from your competitors. The last thing in the world you want is for your Web site to be confused with your competitors—or worse to sell their products!

The design of your Web site should also reflect the resources you have available as well as the resources your Web site visitors are likely to have available. If your visitors are likely to be computer literate or power users, you can safely include more sophisticated graphics, animation, audio, and video that the typical Web browser has.

Production

Before beginning work, it's appropriate to take an inventory of available resources.

14. *What resources are available for creating your Web site?* Is this a project you are doing on your own, delegating to others, or hiring an outside firm?

15. *How much Internet or desktop publishing skills do you, or your staff, possess?* Do you or a member of your staff have desktop publishing experience or are you starting from scratch? If you're starting from scratch, plan on spending some time familiarizing yourself with Web site authoring software.

The design of your Web site and the level of visitor involvement you choose to allow should reflect your time, budget, and hardware/software resources. If your resources are limited, you should start out with a plain and simple Web site, and improve it as your resources improve.

Follow-Up, Promotion, and Maintenance

Web sites do not operate in a vacuum. Their success is based as much on management as on design. The best-looking, most content-filled Web site will not succeed unless it is carefully integrated into your firm's day-to-day marketing and sales activities. Likewise, Web sites do not succeed on their own. Like a garden, a Web site requires constant attention.

Web sites succeed to the extent that they attract repeat visitors—and recommendations from repeat visitors. At the very least, some highly visible aspect of your Web site should change every month. The goal is not to undermine the consistency and image of your Web site, but simply to highlight new content and provide a fresh reason for visitors to take another look at what you have to offer.

Here are some of the questions you'll want to think about before addressing them in greater depth in Chapters 11, 12, and 13.

16. *Who is going to follow-up on comments, queries, requests for information and sales?* The volume of e-mail, for example, is certain to increase as your Web site becomes more and more successful. Successful Web sites are those that begin relationships with prospective clients and customers by making them participants rather than observers.

17. *How are you going to promote your Web site?* To succeed, Web sites need to be promoted. At the very least, your Web site address should be included in every advertisement and on every print communication you prepare—including brochures, business cards, flyers, letterheads, newsletters, postcards, and posters. This will ensure that present customers will become familiar with your Web site address. Does it make sense to send a postcard to past and present customers inviting them to visit your Web site?

18. *Where are you going to list your Web site?* How can you bring your Web site to the attention of search engines? Whom should you notify about your Web site address? What information categories should be listed in your page headers so that search engines can locate your Web site?

19. *What Web sites can contain links to your Web site?* What can you offer them motivate others to include a link to your Web site in theirs? If you are a retailer, can you list your Web site on your vendor's Web sites? If you are a member of an association, can your Web site address be included on their site? Does your local Chamber of Commerce have a Web site containing links to the Web sites of its members?

20. *How are you going to keep your Web site fresh?* What can you do to encourage repeat visits? What types of information is likely to change? How often does new information become available? What types of information at your Web site is appropriate for updating: products, procedures, prices or your commentary on the issues of the day?

The simpler the design of your Web site, of course, the easier it will be to maintain it by making relatively minor changes in its content. Maintenance becomes easy to the extent that your design has been planned to accommodate updating and revision.

Central to most of the preceding discussion, of course, is the question of who is going to do the work. Will the person who creates the Web site also be the one who promotes and maintains it? Is enough time available?

PUTTING THE ANSWERS TO WORK

These twenty questions are by no means the only questions you'll be considering in the coming chapters—and the coming weeks. Additional questions requiring additional answers will come up as we take an increasingly detailed look at developing the content and design of your Web site.

Did you notice that many of the questions are related? For example, the results you want to achieve and the type of visitors you want to attract determines the content and design of your Web site, and the content and design of your Web site, in turn, influence the hardware and software required to create an appropriate Web site.

Other Relationships

The frequency with which you want visitors to return to your Web site, for example, influences your Web site's initial design, the type of information you must include to keep it fresh, and the resources needed to update your site at appropriate intervals.

PLANNING WORKSHEET

1. What is the primary purpose of your Web site?

2. What are some of your other goals?

3. What action do you want Web site visitors to take?

4. How are you going to measure the success of your Web site?

5. Whom do you want to visit your Web site?

6. What types of information are they looking for?

7. What types of information can you provide?

8. How often do you want Web site visitors to return?

9. How can you build immediacy into your Web site?

10. What type of image do you want to project?

11. What type of content will be included?

12. How much involvement do you want to include?

13. What do your competitor's Web pages look like?

14. What resources are available for creating your Web site?

15. How much Internet or desktop publishing skills
    do you or your staff possess?

16. Who is going to follow up on comments, queries, requests
    for information, and sales generated by your Web site?

17. How are you going to promote your Web site?

18. Where are you going to list your Web site?

19. What Web sites can contain links to yours?

20. How are you going to keep your Web site fresh?

Likewise, if one of your secondary goals is to generate revenue by selling advertising space—typically banners along the top of your Web site—the design of your Web site must be able to accommodate the needs of advertisers. In addition, you'll need to include more sophisticated content and update your site more often than if your goal is simply to sell your own products and services. Your desire to sell advertising space will require more sophisticated content and

Figure 5.1
A desire to sell advertising space will influence the design of your Web site.

more flexible design than if you were simply interested in keeping your past customers informed. You will also want to promote your Web site more aggressively and develop involvement devices to demonstrate the success of your Web site to prospective advertisers.

A Word Of Warning

The very success of your Web site can be its undoing, because—unless you're careful—it may generate so much business that you will be unable to follow up on requests for information and to keep your Web site fresh with new and different content.

This is said not to discourage you, but to emphasize once again that a successful Web site does not exist in a vacuum. It is not created, posted, and forgotten about. Rather, a successful Web site and the results it generates require careful nurturing, and this nurturing must be integrated into your everyday marketing and business activities.

CONCLUSION

Instead of starting out by being seduced by the fancy effects that can be included on your Web site, begin by focusing on the basics. As you undertake the various tasks involved in creating your Web site, keep your eye on your answers to the twenty basic questions introduced in this chapter.

Focus on your answers to these three basic questions:

◆ Who do I want to visit my Web site?

◆ What action do I want them to take?

◆ How can I encourage them to take the desired action?

Your answers to the twenty questions in the Planning Worksheet should have provided the foundation for your instinctive answers.

Success on the Web is not a matter of choosing the latest and most powerful hardware and software or the trendiest color combinations and typefaces. As in baseball, Web success comes from keeping your eye on the ball and hitting it where there's a gap in the outfield.

Chapter 6

Choosing a Web Site Address

Your Web Site Address Is Central to Your Success

To succeed, visitors must be able to find you by directly typing in your *URL*—the characters that make up your unique Web site address. Although search engines and links from other sites will point a lot of people to your Web site, many others will have to type in your address in order to visit your Web site. For this reason, it's imperative that your Web site address be as easy to remember and to type as possible.

Your Web site address is as important an aspect of Web site content and design as the specific words and appearance chosen for the titles, headlines, and text on each page of your Web site. Indeed, your Web site address might be considered more important, since it is far easier to change the contents of your Web site than your Web site address.

This chapter describes some of the characteristics of a successful Web site address and outlines how to decide between basing your Web site address on your firm's name or developing alternative approaches.

CHARACTERISTICS OF SUCCESSFUL WEB SITE ADDRESSES

◆ **Short and simple**. Shorter is always better. Short Web addresses are easier to remember and reduce the possibility of typing errors that can trip up potential visitors.

◆ **Descriptive**. Your Web address should preview the content that visitors will encounter when they visit your site. Your name, in itself, may not provide enough of a clue to your Web site's contents to entice visitors to drop in.

◆ **Memorable**. The best URLs combine simplicity and description with an unique element—often a play on words—that helps potential visitors remember your Web site address hours, days, or even months after they first encounter it. Ideally, your Web site address should so easy to be remembered, it will be remembered even if it is heard only in passing in a party conversation or at the end of a radio broadcast heard while driving.

Let's take a more detailed look at each characteristic of the successful Web site address.

Short and Simple

Whenever possible, use the minimum number of letters necessary to identify your Web site. This reduces the chances for ambiguity and typing errors. *Homes & Land Magazine* offers an excellent example. Their Web site permits you to view photographs and descriptions of hundreds of thousands of homes across the United States. Although the name "homes and land" is relatively difficult to misspell, as it's composed of familiar letters, the large number of letters offers increased opportunities for typing errors. In addition, there is the ambiguity of whether visitors should spell out or use the ampersand symbol. Homes and Land skillfully eliminated these potential problems by simply calling their site *www.homes.com*.

Initials and acronyms offer a great way of reducing long names. Foreign Motors West is an automobile dealer outside Boston. It would be a lot to ask visitors to type in *www.foreignmotorswest.com*. Instead, Foreign Motors West wisely chose the far shorter www.*fmwest.com*, which provides a geographic clue to Foreign Motor's location in the Boston metropolitan area.

Descriptive

Your Web site address should describe either your area of specialization or the benefit (or benefits) that customers will enjoy when they deal with you.

Names are often not as memorable as descriptions of the business. For example, Chet's Plumbing and Heating Supply or Smith Motor Sales doesn't really tell very much about either firm or the benefits you'll enjoy when you visit them or buy from them. But, *http://www.cyberfaucet.com* or *http://www.onlymercedes.com* tells you a lot more.

In some cases, the business name does do a good job of describing the contents of the Web site. An example that comes to mind is *www.caboosehobbies.com*. This address leaves little doubt that the site deals with model railroad supplies and not radio-controlled airplanes or slot car racers! And, although long, the words are not easily misspelled. Another hobby shop, Mitchells, located at *http://www.mitchells.com* doesn't do as good a job of indicating that it specializes in model railroad trains—although this may be to the firm's advantage, as Mitchell's also services other hobbies.

Ease of typing and the degree of familiarity of the name can often provide the exception that proves the rule. For example, some names are relatively long, but are so familiar and so easy to type that it doesn't make sense to change them simply for the sake of change. Examples that come to mind include *www.rollingstone.com*, *www.circuitcity.com*, and *www.radioshack.com*.

DOES ANYTHING SOUND FAMILIAR?

The development of an effective Web site address is very similar to the process of choosing a name for your business or organization. In general, names that are short are better than names that are long. Likewise, in general, names that describe what the business does—or the benefits it offers customers and clients—are better than names that glorify the founder. And, in general, the easier the name is to remember, the more it will be remembered!

As has been mentioned, the Web is often a catalyst for a firm to take a whole new look at its marketing identity. It's entirely possible that your search for an appropriate Web site address might be an important first step in creating a new and vibrant identity for your firm and the message or messages it communicates.

A well-chosen name, like Audio Experts, Inc., results in a well-chosen Web address (www.audioexperts.com). Likewise, Easy Heat, Inc. translates into www.easyheat.com, in both cases, letting you know both the product and the benefit offered. Likewise, how could you come up with something better than The Mountain Zone (www.mountainzone.com) for the name of a firm and its Web address to describe a mail order business specializing in mountain climbing books, photographs, climbing supplies, and expeditions? But this is only true, of course, if you get there early enough and register the name (as described later in this chapter)!

Sometimes, of course, it's possible to use a generic description of your business because, if you get there early enough, you can appropriate the field names, as the firms at *www.cameras.com* or *www.hifi.com* have done. If your area of business has already been taken, however, you might still be able to add a geographic or a modification tag to the generic name: hypothetically, *www.bostoncameras.com* or *www.besthifinyc.com*.

Memorable

One of my friends is an author whose name is Crystal Waters. Crystal has written several books on Internet design. If Crystal named her Web site after herself, that is, *www.crystalwaters.com* or *www.cwaters.com*, her address wouldn't be very memorable. It would likely be immediately forgotten. However, typographical errors are something that everyone in communications fears. Thus, Crystal named her Web site *www.typo.com*, which satisfies several objectives: it's short, easy to type, hard to misspell, and signals that the Web site addresses communications issues. Most important, *www.typo.com* is easily remembered. Ten minutes from now, you may have forgotten her name, but you'll probably remember her Web address.

John Towey is a realtor in the Magnolia district of Seattle who wisely chose not to name his e-mail address after himself. Instead, in his twin desires not only to be known as the leading source of real estate in Magnolia but also to develop a memorable Web site address, he came up with *www.mrmagnolia.com*. This is simple, descriptive, and definitely harder to forget than just his first and last name.

EXAMPLES OF WEB SITES WITH APPROPRIATE OR CREATIVE URLS

Firm or organization name	Web site address*	Significance
Boston Symphony Orchestra	*www.bso.org*	Short, (acronym of initial letters of name) alphabetical
E. P. Levine Co.	*www.cameras.com*	Firm appropriates product area
Cathy Lee Curtis (author)	*www.cathylee.com*	Short, but enough to be remembered
Communications Briefings	*www.combriefings.com*	Abbreviated word of secondary importance to primary word, which describes the type of information communicated
Cookin' Audio/Video	*www.cookinonline.com*	*Cookin'* was already taken, *cookinav* was awkward, but *cookinonline* separated retail mall locations from Internet
Chet's Plumbing and Heating, Inc.	*www.cyberfaucet.com*	a) Signals the firm's field of business b) An everyday name becomes memorable
ThunderLizard Productions, Inc.	*www.desktopublishing.com*	Service area (seminars) is more important than the name
The Soil Refinery	*www.enviroww.com*	Emphasizes environmental activities throughout the world (*world wide*)

Pursell's Sta-Green	www.fertilizer.com	Emphasizes the product
Seattle Filmworks, Inc.	www.filmworks.com	Shortened to key word that describes the product
Foreign Motors West	www.fmwest.com	Short and obvious, provides geographic identification
Desktop Publishing and Graphics Magazine	www.graphic-design.com	Takes over a field and appears high in search engines
Cambridge Sound Works, Inc.	www.hifi.com	Generic product description, dominates field
The Audible Difference, Inc.	www.highendaudio.com	Emphasizes area of product specialization
The Audible Difference	www.highendaudio.com	Describes firm's principal business activity
Homes and Land	www.homes.com	Shorter, easily remembered, dominates the field.
Chuck Green	www.ideabook.com	Relates author to his most popular book
Conrad Taylor	www.ideography.co.uk	Emphasizes area of expertise: information design
David Siegel (author)	www.killersites.com	Builds on equity of author's signature book
Leonard Berstein Society	www.leonardbernstein.com	Describes type of products offered
Loon Mountain Area Development Corporation	www.loonmtn.com	Logical enough to be located on the first try, without even consulting a search engine!
Robert Gruttner	www.mediachild.com	Emphasizes the area of expertise as well as projects a contemporary, "with an attitude" position
John Towey	www.mrmagnolia.com	Emphasizes the geographic area of concentration, builds his credibility as "the" source of information
Yankee Magazine	www.newengland.com	Emphasizes geographic area
National Trust for Historic Preservation	www.nhtp.org	Logical abbreviation
Smith Motor Sales	www.onlymercedes.com	Identifies the product sold as well as describes the dealer's position as a Mercedes-Benz specialist
Price Pfister Co.	www.pfaucet.com	Easy to remember and spell, builds on product category
Jeff Rubin	www.put-it-in-writing.com	Simpler and far more memorable than the individual's name
Sametz Blackstone Associates	www.sametz.com	Shortened to key word
The Lebow Group	www.sharedvalues.com	Describes the firm's central philosophy
American Auto Transporters	www.shipcar.com	Short, describes service the firm offers
Boston Acoustics	www.sounsite.com	Describes information that can be found at the Web site
Texas Department of Commerce, Tourism Division	www.TravelTex.com	Emphasizes content
Crystal Waters (author)	www.typo.com	Short, out-of-the-ordinary: likely to be remembered by writers and designers
Laura McCanna (author)	www.webdiner.com	Implies that there are things to buy, served a la carte
Granville Manufacturing Company	www.woodsiding.com	Emphasizes product

Note: For clarity, the http:// prefix has been omitted from all URLs. In addition, whenever you type a URL beginning with www, Microsoft Internet Explorer and Netscape Navigator automatically enter the http:// prefix.

Hyphens OK

Notice that although you cannot include spaces in Web site addresses, you can separate words using hyphens. One firm that takes advantage of this is Rare Earth Hardwoods, Inc., a specialist in providing homebuilders with fine woods. Their Web site address is *www.rare-earth-hard-woods.com*. Another example that comes to mind is S. D. Warren and Company's *www.warren-idea-exchange.com* which builds off their decades of experience providing inspiration and paper samples to graphic designers.

Uppercase letters can also be used in Web site addresses for clarity, for example, *www.TravelTex.com* which is more visually memorable than the same URL set exclusively in lower case letters, that is, *www.traveltext.com*.

The Importance of Establishing Your Own Domain

After you develop a unique Web site address (as described below), it's important that you go through the process of registering it as a domain name. This requires a bit more work than simply attaching your address to the Web site address of an Internet Service Provider, but offers you significant advantages.

◆ *Speed*: To access your Web site, instead of having to remember and enter the Web site address of your Internet Service Provider followed by a tilde (~) and your Web site address, visitors will only have to enter your Web site address.

◆ *Flexibility*: Once you have registered your URL as a domain name, you can change Internet Service Providers without the need to notify clients, friends, prospects, and search engines that you have moved. The identity of the Internet Service Provider hosting your Web site remains invisible when you register your URL as a domain, so you can "invisibly" move your files making up your Web site across the street or across the country.

◆ *Image*: Taking the time to register your Web site symbolizes that you are making a first-class commitment to the Web, instead of taking the easiest route.

CHOOSING YOUR WEB SITE ADDRESS

There are several steps involved in choosing an appropriate Web site address. The following list suggests a four-step approach to choosing the best possible URL for your Web site.

1. *Research*: The first step is to review Web addresses used by your competitors and others in your field of business.

2. *Development*: This is the fun part, where you put on your thinking or marketing cap and attempt to come up with a Web site address for your firm or organization that is short, descriptive, and memorable.

3. *Testing*: Before proceeding further, a reality check may be in order. Try your Web site address out on a few friends and associates and see what they think.

4. *Registration*: Registering your Web site address with an Internet registration organization (e.g. InterNic) ensures that it will be yours, and yours alone.

Research

The starting point for choosing a Web site address is to see what's available in your field. There are a couple of methods you can use for this:

◆ *Trial and error*: Start by going online and typing in your firm's name and variations of your firm name to see if any Web sites appear. (Don't forget to add *.com* at the end!) This is an easy way to see if your firm's name (or initials) has already been taken. Although not foolproof, trying out variations of your business name (and its initials) is a good start. Keep track of rejected alternatives, however, so you don't have to unnecessarily repeat your work.

◆ *Search engines*: Another alternative is to utilize search engines like *Yahoo.com* to find out what others in your field of business are using. The easiest way to do this is to check out Business and Economics and then search the names of firms operating in your field of expertise.

Here's how to use a search engine like *Yahoo.com* to check out the URLs of firms in your line of business by moving from the general to the specific.

Access Yahoo by entering its URL (*http://www.yahoo.com*), or you can usually directly access it through your Internet browser. Start by clicking on Business and Economics, then select the basic activity your firm is involved in. Then, narrow your search by clicking on more and more specific options. Each time you make a choice, you're presented with increasingly detailed options (see Figures 6.1 through 6.3). You'll soon end up with descriptions of businesses like yours.

Notice that as you move the pointer through the various options in each screen, the Web address of each firm appears in the Status Bar at the bottom of your screen, saving you the time and trouble of accessing each link in order to find out its Web address.

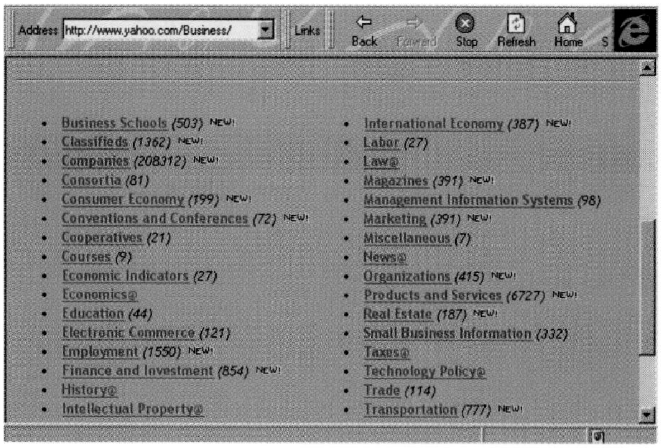

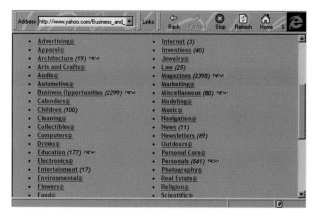

Figure 6.1 After you select Business and Economy, Yahoo presents you with links to various types of businesses.

Figure 6.2 After choosing Products and Services, for example, you can choose from among various types of products and services.

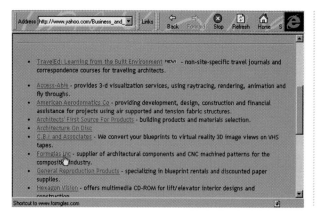

Figure 6.3
Select Architecture, for example, and you can scroll through short descriptions of various firms in the architecture field.

If your firm's name doesn't appear to be already taken, you can safely proceed to the next step, creating a unique name for your firm. Before going on, of course, you might try other search engines, like *AltaVista.com* or *Excite.com* in order to see if they uncover alternatives your first search engine doesn't.

Development

Use the following worksheet as a guide to developing a unique URL for your Web site. Feel free to make as many photocopies of it as you and your co-workers need. You might make several copies of the URL Selection Worksheet and distribute them to your co-workers, for example.

As you work with the URL Selection Worksheet, *free-associate*—that is, avoid self-censoring your ideas as you come up with them. Instead, let your imagination go free.

URL SELECTION WORKSHEET

1. Enter your firm's name

2. What are some of the ways your firm's name
    can be shortened?

3. What happens when you reduce your firm's name
    to a few key words or the acronym composed
    of the initial letter of each word?

4. If your firm's name has already been taken as a
    Web address by someone else, can you simply add
    online to your firm's name (if it is otherwise appropriate)?

5. What is your firm's motto? Are there ways of adapting
    it into a Web address?

6. What field of activity is your firm engaged in?

7. Are there any advantages to incorporating your
    firm's primary geographic location into your
    Web site address?

8. What are some of the ways your firm differs
    from the competition?

9. What is the principal benefit that customers enjoy
    when they buy from you?

10. What is the principal benefit that Web site visitors enjoy when they visit your site?

11. Describe some of the contents that your Web site will contain.

12. How is your Web site different from the competition's?

While in the development phase, it's always a good idea to come up with more than one proposed URL so that if one is taken, you still have several options.

Testing

Before proceeding to the registration phase, be sure you ask your co-workers, clients, and customers what they think of your proposed choices. Their input can provide a valuable reality check to your enthusiasm. If they share your enthusiasm, all the better!

Before proceeding further, you should also go online and type in your favorite alternatives to make sure they haven't already been taken (but didn't show up on any of the search engines).

Registration

The next step is to submit your proposed URL online to find out if it has already been taken. You can take care of registration by yourself by contacting Internic at *http://www.internic.com*, one of many Internet registration services, or your Internet Service Provider can do this for you.

OTHER CONSIDERATIONS

Some other things to bear in mind when selecting a Web site address for your firm appear in the following section.

Act Fast

It's important that you act fast. Because of the explosive growth of the Web, good URLs are going fast. It's to your advantage to choose an appropriate Web site address and register it as soon as possible, before it has been taken by someone else. Accordingly, before you concern yourself with the details of Web design, content, and production, you should develop and register a short, descriptive, and memorable Web site address as soon as possible.

Many airlines, for example, use their initials: Northwest Airlines's Web site is *www.nwa.com*. Evidently, *www.swa.com* was already taken by the time that South West Airlines came on the scene, because their Web site is named *www.iflyswa.com* which you might have to think about, but, once you do, it makes perfect sense. (After all, how often do you get a chance to create a chant out of your Web site address?)

Geography or Product

You might build your URL around specific products, events, or your location. Perhaps you want your business to be known as the best source for a particularly well-known product or service in a given area. For example, *www.saabnyc.com* would be a logical choice if you wanted to be known as the leading Saab automotive dealer in New York City.

Similarly, multiple Web sites can make sense in many circumstances. Let's say you're a concert promoter. You could have one umbrella Web site that describes your firm and the musicians you represent. In order to attract visitors to a Web site devoted to a major upcoming concert, you might create a separate Web site devoted specifically to the upcoming concert, such as (hypothetically) *www.bluesbash98.com*. Needless to say, you'd provide numerous links between this Web site and your primary, ongoing Web site, that is, *www.concertcentral.com*.

Oops

Be careful about the way the eyes plays tricks with words, creating words and letter combinations where none were intended. Beware of Web addresses that inadvertently create words within words. At first glance a Web address for Rogers Audio/Video might be reduced to the partial acronym *www.rogersav.com*. The problem is that visually the address emerges as "Roger Save" (which my accountant keeps telling me to do).

Be particularly careful about unintentional combinations of consonants and vowels that may divide long Web addresses into separate words. For example, notice that there is a tendency to unconsciously read *www.chamberscars.com* as "chamber scars." Perhaps you noticed earlier, how your eye focuses on the "finyc" in the hypothetical *www.besthifinyc.com* mentioned above. Or, you may read it as two words: "best" and "thifi," because you are accustomed to reading *th* together and linking *th* to the following vowels.

Support

Most important of all, as described in Chapter 10, it's important that you support your Web site address throughout all of your marketing materials and broadcast advertising. Your ads, brochures, business cards, letterheads, and newsletters should all prominently feature your Web address. The more exposure your Web site address gets, the greater the number of visits it will enjoy, especially if your address is short, descriptive, and memorable.

CONCLUSION

Your Web site address is one of the most important decisions you make when setting up a Web site. Although many people will encounter your Web site by using search engines and links from other sites, many more will have to remember your URL and enter it by typing it into their Internet browser.

Test the appropriateness of your present or proposed URL by reviewing how it stacks up against these criteria:

◆   *Short.* Is your URL as short and easy to type as possible?

◆   *Descriptive.* Does your URL do a good job of describing the content visitors will find when they visit?

◆   *Memorable.* Is your URL easy to remember, even if your name or your firm's name isn't? Is it distinctive or humorous?

Unlike other aspects of Internet marketing, your choice of Web site address is one of the few decisions you make early on that you should plan to live with for a long time. Because of the fluid nature of electronically posting information and design on the Web, it is easy to change the content and appearance of your Web site as your design and content skills improve. It is far harder to change a Web site address, however, once it has been chosen, registered, and promoted. Although there are ways you can work around the problems involved in changing your Web site address at a later date, why put yourself through the unnecessary work? Plus, there would probably be a period of time during the transition when you would lose some of your loyal visitors.

Thus, time spent choosing the right Web site address will be repaid over and over again in the years to come.

Section 3

Initial Steps

Developing Meaningful Content

Working Backwards from Desired Results

Information—content—forms the basis of a successful Web site. An attractive, easy-to-navigate, fast-loading Web site that lacks appropriate content may win awards but is unlikely to produce results. If you're serious about achieving results with your Web site, it's crucial that you create the content necessary to achieve your desired results.

The best way to develop meaningful content for your Web site is to identify the goals you want to achieve and work backwards. This involves the following three steps:

1. Identify the goals you want your Web site to achieve.

2. Describe the marketing obstacles that stand in the way of your achieving those goals. In most cases, this will involve a lack of information on the part of your market.

3. Create the missing links—that is, the content (or information) needed to overcome these obstacles and achieve your goals.

Your mission, in other words, is to concentrate on the *intersection between your goals and your audience's needs.* Your Web site will succeed to the extent that its content and your audience's needs overlap. To the extent that content and market needs don't overlap, your Web site will fail—no matter how attractive or well-promoted it may be or how many bells and whistles (like animation and sound) it incorporates.

> *Your Web site will succeed to the extent that its content and your audience's needs overlap. To the extent that content and market needs don't overlap, your Web site will fail—no matter how attractive and well-promoted it may be.*

It helps to think of your goals and the Web site visitor's needs as two intersecting circles, one representing your Web site's content, the other your desired Web site visitor's information needs. Your Web site will succeed to the extent that you increase the amount of overlap of the two circles.

As you review the various Web sites you have visited by now, and will be visiting in the future, you might try analyzing the extent to which the Web site's goals and the needs of its market appear to overlap.

ASKING QUESTIONS

The best way to increase the overlap between your Web site's contents and your prospect's information and buying needs is to work as concretely as possible, answering the questions in the worksheets provided in this chapter. Abstract thinking doesn't get the job done. The questions in the next three sections will provide the framework you need for developing meaningful content for your Web site. By focusing on the job at hand—the specific Web site you want to create (or improve)—and answering the questions posed in the worksheets in this chapter, you'll probably be surprised how easily you can determine the right content for your Web site.

The questions on the worksheets parallel some of the questions on the Planning Worksheet in Chapter 3. Photocopy these worksheets and use them as idea-starters. Success will come to the extent that your responses become increasingly detailed and specific. However, this time, to help you think more concretely about your responses, the questions are more specific—and each question leads to other increasingly detailed questions.

Identifying Goals

Start by analyzing your goals and what you want your want your Web site to achieve. The first six questions will help you begin to identify the types of information you will need to include on your Web site to attract the appropriate visitors and provide them with the information they need to support your goals.

The more specific your goals, the easier it will be to identify the information necessary to achieve them. For example, many people respond that the purpose of their Web site is to increase sales. However, increased sales is such an open-ended concept that it doesn't really say anything. It doesn't identify who should buy what product or service or begin the process of identifying the information needed to make a sale—let alone, many sales.

Considering Question 2, "What is the immediate, short-term goal of your Web site?" If the immediate goal of your Web site is to sell a book entitled *Confessions of a New Hampshire Web Designer*, the picture completely changes. The more you specify a concrete action you want Web site visitors to take, the easier it becomes to identify the information needed to achieve your desired goal. In this case, content for the Web site could include:

◆ Pictures of the front cover of the book

◆ Comments from reviewers

◆ Endorsements from respected peers (that is, other designers and Web site creators)

◆ Testimonials from satisfied readers

◆ Sample chapter

◆ Specifications: Size, number of pages, hard cover or soft cover, price, shipping information, credit cards accepted, etc.

Similarly, in Question 3, if one of your secondary objectives was to encourage Web site visitors to send you their e-mail addresses so you could inform them of upcoming books or seminars, it would be appropriate to include the following information—or content—on your Web site:

◆ Pictures of the front covers of other books

◆ Brief descriptions of other books

◆ Information about upcoming seminars (dates, content, locations, costs)

◆ Testimonials from previous seminar attendees

GOAL PLANNING WORKSHEET

1. What type of business are you or your firm engaged in?

❏ Consulting

❏ Construction

❏ Education

❏ Entertainment

❏ Financial services

❏ Manufacturing or distribution

❏ Medical care

❏ Publishing

❏ Real Estate

❏ Retail sales to consumers

❏ Transportation and lodging

❏ Other (describe below)

2. What is the immediate, short-term goal of your Web site— what action do you want Web site visitors to take?

❏ Buy a specific product or service (if so, what?)

❏ Attend a concert (if so, what, where, and when?)

❏ Attend more concerts (or plays)

❏ Join an organization

❏ Renew their membership

❏ Make a donation to a cause

❏ Increase purchases of other products and services you sell

❏ Subscribe to your magazine or newsletter

❏ Invest their money

❏ Tune in your radio program

❏ Spend more time listening to your radio station or viewing or your television station

❏ Solve problems they are having with their purchase

❏ Other (describe below):

3. What other actions do you want your
    Web site visitors to take?

❏ Increase purchases of other products and services you sell
❏ Recommend your business to their friends
❏ Comment on your firm's performance
❏ Inform the press of upcoming events
❏ Keep investors informed
❏ Request information on future products and services
❏ Request information about upcoming events
❏ Sell advertising space on your Web site
❏ Describe products or services they may be interested in purchasing in the future

❏ Describe a specific product they are interested in obtaining—i.e., specific make and model pre-owned luxury automobile, home, or collectible (describe below):

❏ Send you their resume
❏ Increase admissions or enrollment
❏ Send you their e-mail address (so you can advertise directly to them in the future)
❏ Other (describe below):

4. What are your long term Web objectives?

❏ Continue to supplement other sales activities
❏ Play an increasingly important role in your firm's sales
❏ Replace current sales activities

However, if one of your long-term goals is to sell advertising space on your Web site, this goal indicates the need for different content. In this case, you'd want to play down your specific accomplishments and instead provide increasing amounts of valuable information on topics other than those promoting your books and seminars. Content might focus on industrywide trends, software shortcuts, new-product introductions (even if you don't sell them), profiles of industry leaders, and other nonselling information.

Notice how quickly everything falls into place once you focus on identifying your primary and secondary objectives. Everything comes from knowing what you want to accomplish before beginning work! As you begin to identify specific objectives, it will become easier and easier to determine your Web site's content.

Focusing on an immediate goal, that is, the sale of a particular product or service, plays another role in the success of your Web site. Promoting a particular product or service provides a lead—a starting point for organizing the design and layout of your Web site. In many cases, your "lead" product or service will provide a metaphor or the visual inspiration you need to create a good-looking Web site. Notice how the front covers of most magazines feature a photograph and paragraph introducing a specific article plus teasers describing secondary articles. Likewise, the home pages of most successful Web sites don't just present options, but begin by focusing on a particular event, product, or service.

As you answer the questions in the worksheets, you'll find that subtle differences in goals can cause major differences in the Web site content needed to achieve them. For example, there is a world of difference between the content of a Web site intended to promote a single concert versus a Web site intended to promote a series of concerts. In the former case, a great deal of emphasis would be placed on the specifics of the particular concert (or event). In the latter case, the Web site's content would contain a calendar of upcoming concerts and stress the advantages of buying series tickets, and so forth.

Similarly, if one of your long-term goals is to sell banners or advertising to vendors or others likely to be interested in your customer base, the content of your Web site will probably be much different than a Web site intended to promote a specific event, product, or service.

Finally, if your long-term goals include an increasing percentage of Web sales, you should be prepared to overinvest in the beginning, (i.e., invest more than current or anticipated revenues would otherwise justify) in order to prepare the groundwork for a later increase in Web sales.

Who Is Your Market and What Are Their Needs?

What action do you want Web site visitors to take? What are their needs? What information do they need to take the action you want them to take? Start by analyzing the market, or audience, your Web site is intended to serve. Use the Market Identification Worksheet as a framework for determining your online customer base. Then, determine their information needs in light of the Web site goals you have identified in the Goal Planning Worksheet.

MARKET IDENTIFICATION WORKSHEET

1. Who do you want to visit your Web site?

    - ❏ Potential buyers of your products and services
    - ❏ Previous clients or customers
    - ❏ Donors and supporters of your organization
    - ❏ Potential donors or supporters
    - ❏ Listeners to your radio show (or viewers of your station)
    - ❏ Potential employees
    - ❏ Potential co-marketers
    - ❏ The press
    - ❏ Other (describe below):

2. Where is your market located?

    - ❏ Locally
    - ❏ Nationally
    - ❏ International (describe below):

3. What are the challenges facing your market?

    - ❏ Information overload—too many options
    - ❏ Lack of time
    - ❏ Lack of money
    - ❏ Information
    - ❏ Other (describe below):

4. What solutions or satisfactions do your products or services provide?

    - ❏ Pleasure
    - ❏ Pride of ownership
    - ❏ Increased sales
    - ❏ Reduced expenditures
    - ❏ Saved time
    - ❏ Financial returns on investment
    - ❏ Career advancement

❏ Improved health

❏ Assistance locating a new home

❏ Transportation from point A to point B

❏ Other (describe below):

5. What information should your Web site provide in order to achieve your primary goal?

❏ Market education—reasons they should be interested in the benefits your product or service category offers

❏ Description of the specific benefits your featured product or service offers

❏ Descriptions of the symptoms your product or service cures

❏ Specifications: size, weight, availability, delivery options, set-up instructions, etc.

❏ Other (describe below):

6. What information can you provide to encourage them to act right now?

❏ Ordering information—price, availability, store location, mailing address, financing and leasing options, credit cards accepted.

❏ Limited time price incentive

❏ Limited product availability

❏ Other (free supplies, free shipping, etc.) Describe below:

7. What questions do you get asked over and over again (on the phone and in person)?

Describe below:

1.

2.

3.

4.

5.

8. What information can you provide to achieve your secondary goals?

- ❑ Generic information about the latest trends in your field
- ❑ Commentary about important issues of the day
- ❑ Reviews of popular products
- ❑ Lists of recordings (title, performer, label, etc.) recently played on your program (or on your station)
- ❑ Case histories describing how you helped past clients solve problems
- ❑ Stories describing how your organization reduced suffering or, in some other way, made a positive impact
- ❑ Other (describe below):

9. Where does your market go for information?

- ❑ Magazines
- ❑ Seminars
- ❑ Word of mouth
- ❑ Newspapers
- ❑ Radio and television broadcasts
- ❑ Subscription newsletters

10. How often do you want visitors to revisit your Web site?

- ❑ Once
- ❑ Daily
- ❑ Weekly
- ❑ Monthly
- ❑ Other (describe below):

Each of the previous questions will help you develop a better understanding of the information your Web site should contain. Let's look at these ten questions and see how your response influences your Web site content:

♦ *Question 1*: "Who do you want to visit your Web site?" Your response to this question will help you determine the type and level of detail your Web site should contain. If your primary market consists of first-time buyers, you'll want to include a lot of "How to buy" information that will expand your market by educating potential customers as to what they should look for. If you are concentrating on repeat buyers, however, more detail (features, specifications, etc.) is appropriate.

♦ *Question 2*: "Where is your market located?" If you are targeting a local market and want to encourage visits to your place of business, it makes sense to include a map showing the location of your store or office. A map doesn't make sense, however, if you are selling a book by mail order (indeed, if you are a busy author, you might not want visitors at all!) If you are dealing with a national or international market, your Web site must contain information describing shipping and payment options, currency exchange rates, etc.

♦ *Question 3*: "What are the challenges facing your market?" If you are in a fast-moving, very competitive area, like personal computers, your customers are probably overwhelmed by choices. In this case, your Web site will succeed to the extent that you identify the major options and simplify the buyer's choices. If lack of money is a factor, your Web site should stress creative financing and leasing options.

♦ *Question 4*: "What solutions or satisfactions do your products or services provide?" Your Web site will succeed to the extent that you provide content that translates product or service features into benefits your market can easily understand. Speed, for example, is not an issue if you are selling space on a cruise line, but is if your market is composed of business travelers. Taste and vitamin content are more important to a health-conscious market than a leisure market. By focusing on the real product your market is buying, you can develop Web site content that will appeal to your market's self-interest—instead of your own.

♦ *Question 5*: "What information do Web site visitors need to take in order for you to achieve your primary goal?" If you are primarily interested in first-time buyers, then you should concentrate on explaining the virtues of the product or service category. But, if you are targeting previous customers, you can describe your product or service in greater detail.

♦ *Question 6*: "What information can you provide to encourage them to act right now?" This will depend on how price sensitive your market is in your opinion. Referring to the example above, if your *Confessions of a New Hampshire Web Designer* is a major best-seller, just announcing the availability of your product should be enough to generate sales. If you have a cellar full of books, however, you might want to offer a discount or other incentive.

- *Question 7*: "What questions do you get asked over and over again?" Your responses will help you identify the content, or topics, you should address in your Web site. The more you tailor the content of your Web site to your market's demands for information, the better your Web site will perform. Think about the conversations you and your sales staff have with customers. Inevitably, the same questions and concerns will keep turning up.

- *Question 8*: "What information can you provide to achieve your secondary goals?" If your goals are to increase your market awareness, your goals will be enhanced to the extent you provide the kinds of information that prospective buyers—that is, those not in the immediate market to buy—are likely to need. Information about new products and commentary on current challenges and trends will pave the way for future sales. If your goal is to identify unsatisfied market needs, you'll want to include a questionnaire, or form, which will make it easy for your Web site visitors to provide you with the information you desire in order to adapt your business to a changing market.

- *Question 9*: "Where does your market go for information?" Your Web site's content should mirror the information provided by those institutions or publications your market trusts. By analyzing the influencers of your market, and studying the questions and letters to the editor columns, you'll gain valuable clues to the content your market will respond to.

- *Question 10*: "How often do you want visitors to revisit your Web site?" Again, this depends on the goals you have identified when you filled out your Goal Planning Worksheet. To take an extreme example, if your goal is to sell advertising space, or banners, on your Web pages, you'll want your Web site visitors to return as frequently as possible. The implication of this is that you'll want to provide something new and different as often as possible.

Identifying Obstacles

The final step is to identify the obstacles that stand in the way of your achieving those goals. What information does your market require in order to act in a way that supports your goals? "What's holding them back?", in other words. Use the Obstacle Identification Worksheet to identify some of the reasons your market may not be responding as positively as you'd like.

- *Question 1*: "What are some of the possible reasons you don't sell more of your products or services?" Your responses to this question will help you identify the direction your content should take. If potential buyers don't understand the benefits of your product or service, then you can take an educational, market-expanding approach. If prospective buyers know the benefits of your product or service category, but are buying from others, your content should emphasize the benefits of the specific products and services you offer as well as the advantages of buying from you.

OBSTACLE IDENTIFICATION WORKSHEET

1. What are some of the possible reasons you don't sell more of your products or services?

   ❑ Potential buyers don't understand the benefits your product or service provides

   ❑ Your market is not aware that you offer the product or service

   ❑ Your market is buying the product or service from others, knowing that you are in business

   ❑ Other (describe below):

2. What about price?

   ❑ Price is not a significant factor

   ❑ Your market perceives you as more expensive than the others

   ❑ Others are selling your product or service significantly cheaper— and your market is letting you know about it

3. Who is your competition—i.e., who do you lose sales to?

   Describe in detail, in order of importance

   1.

   2.

   3.

   4.

   5.

   6.

4. Does your competition have a Web site?

   What's it like? (Describe below):

   What do you think are its short-term and long-term goals? (Describe below):

5. What are some of the ways you differ from the competition?

- ❏ Product knowledge
- ❏ Training
- ❏ Years in business
- ❏ Location
- ❏ Service backup
- ❏ Extended warranties
- ❏ History of customer satisfaction
- ❏ Other (describe below):

6. How often do you lose sales (that you know about)?

- ❏ Never
- ❏ Sometimes (10 to 20 percent of the time)
- ❏ Frequently (over 75 percent of the time)

7. What are some of the reasons lost prospects give you after you find they have bought elsewhere?

Describe below:

1.

2.

3.

4.

◆ *Question 2*: "What about price?" Your analysis of the price sensitivity of your market is also a key to creating meaningful content for your Web site. In a price-sensitive market, you'll have to either meet the prevailing prices or provide compelling reasons why the alternatives you suggest are better.

◆ *Question 3*: "Who in particular is your competition—that is, to whom do you lose sales?" Knowing your competition is crucial to your success. Identifying your competition will help you determine the arguments, or content, needed to convince prospects to buy from you.

- *Question 4:* "What are some of the ways you differ from the competition?" Once you have identified your competition, it becomes relatively easy to formulate a strategy and content that will make you appear different and better than them. If they are big and you are small, for example, stress the advantages of buying from a firm that offers personalized service. If they are national, emphasize that you are local.

- *Question 5:* "Does your competition have a Web site?" "What's it like?" Check out your competitor's Web site. What type of content does it contain? What products or services does it contain? What do you think their short-term and long-term goals are? What market benefits and obstacles are they ignoring that you can emphasize in your Web site?

- *Question 6:* "How often do you lose sales (that you know about)?" Your response to this question will decide whether you should emphasize expanding the market by reaching new prospects or if you should concentrate on doing a better job of selling current prospects as well as reselling past customers. If you are closing a suspiciously high percentage of formal proposals, for example, perhaps you are underpricing your services or maybe your business isn't growing as quickly and making as much money as if could if you raised prices and targeted a higher-paying market segment on the Web.

- *Question 7:* "What are some of the reasons lost prospects give you after you find they have purchased elsewhere?" Conversations with lost prospects may provide you with ideas for developing some of your Web site's best content. Their comments will help you identify content your Web site should contain.

PUTTING YOUR ANSWERS TO WORK

Web site design and production begin with content! Design and content become simpler and easier to successfully create to the extent you have identified and developed the content your Web site needs to succeed.

Your responses to the questions contained in the three previous worksheets will provide valuable clues to the content you should include in your Web site. Your responses will identify your market's concerns as well as identify the focal point—or featured product or service—that your Web site should be organized around. Likewise, your responses will provide the secondary, content categories of information that will reinforce your long-term goals.

Indeed, you're likely to be surprised at how quickly your Web site will come together once you have determined its content. Your Web site's content provides the building blocks that only have to be arranged in a pleasant and appropriate way in order to create your Web presence.

Your Web site's content provides the building blocks that only have to be arranged in a pleasant and appropriate way in order to create your Web presence.

At this point, to see just how far you've come, you can probably start to formalize the contents of your Web site by filling out the Web Site Content Planner. Filling out the Web Site Content Planner will crystallize the categories of content that only have to be researched, organized, and written in order for you to move on to the design and production of your Web site.

Needless to say, your first Web Site Content Planner may go through several iterations. The contents you feel are important today may not be important six months or a year from now. But every project needs a starting point and the Web Site Content Planner can help you create that first Web site—or analyze the content of your current Web site.

WEB SITE CONTENT PLANNER

1. What will be your lead—your featured product or service?

2. Why should Web site visitors want to purchase your product or service—or read your feature article?

3. What other categories of information will you provide?

4. Why should prospects want to buy from you?

5. How do you want prospects to contact you, beginning a relationship with you?

6. How often are you going to update your Web site?

DESIGN, CONTENT, AND STYLE

Now that you have identified the content—the information—you want to include in your Web site, it's time to begin writing.

It's important to note that preparing content doesn't require a novelist's skills. Creating Web content, however, does require some different habits than you might presently possess.

Chunking and Organization

More than they'll analyze your every sentence in terms of grammatical (and political) correctness, your Web site visitors will pay attention to, and appreciate, your ability to organize the content of your Web site into logical categories and to simplify complex topics by breaking them into a series of short, easily read chunks of information.

To a greater extent than when writing for print, preparing content for your Web site involves fine-tuning your ability to subdivide information into short, manageable chunks. Long sentences and long paragraphs just don't make it on the Web. Your Web site content will succeed to the extent that you break your message into numerous short topics. One of the easiest ways to do this is first to write down everything you want to communicate and then go back through your first draft and insert subheads every two or three paragraphs.

These subheads will not only provide visual interest for your Web page, breaking up the monotony of screen after screen of same-sized text, the subheads will also make it easy to insert links inserted at the start of each article. These links will provide visitors with a quick overview of each topic as well as permit visitors to go directly to the information they desire. (See Figures 7.1 through 7.3.)

One of the best ways to organize your Web site content is first to write down everything you want to communicate, and then go back through your first draft and insert subheads every two or three paragraphs.

As this process illustrates, once you have determined your content, it will be much easier to choose the design that best accommodates it.

As you develop your Web site content, remember that it is harder to read from the screen than from a sheet of paper. Habit and the nature of the Web both play an important role in this. (Not only have most people spent more time reading magazines and newspapers than reading from a screen, it's more visually tiring to read from a screen.) Your Web site will succeed to the extent that you write and design the content of your site to compensate for these handicaps.

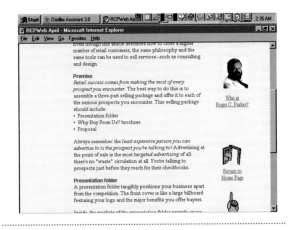

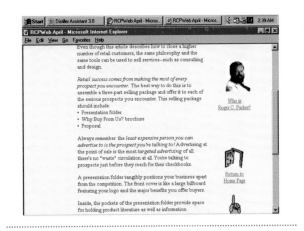

Figure 7.1 Without subheads, even Web sites containing lots of white space aren't very inviting.

Figure 7.2 Simply breaking your topic into short, two- and three-paragraph chunks, each introduced by a subhead, goes a long way towards making the text inviting.

Figure 7.3
Grouping the subheads together as links at the start of the article provides visitors with a quick overview of the contents of each article and makes it easy for them to go directly to a desired topic.

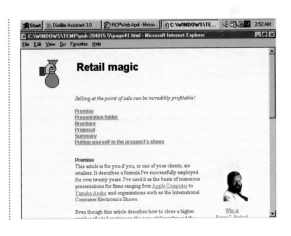

Your concentration on Web site content is likely to provide yet another benefit: Your content decisions will probably provide you with information that will help you decide on the appearance, or design, of your Web site by helping you choose a motif, a recurring theme, that will unify your site.

Web sites succeed to the extent that they reflect their market's goals and concerns. The earlier you identify your market's hot buttons, the easier it will be to choose the visuals that will most appeal to them.

Developing a Style

As you prepare content for your Web site, think about the desired tone of your Web site. Tone refers to the "voice" or "attitude" your Web site projects.

As a starting point, think about your favorite writers of non-fiction. What are the characteristics they have in common? What do you like about their writing? Ask any group of readers, and two terms are likely to come up: credibility and empathy.

◆ *Credibility* refers to the ability to build trust by communicating information without judgment. Chances are, you don't like authors who talk down to you. Well, neither do your Web site visitors. Your Web site visitors are interested in information without condescension or pretense. Web site visitors aren't interested in being reminded that they never quite finished their Master's... or are otherwise made to feel stupid. They simply want to know how to invest their money wisely, buy a car stereo, book a cruise, or set the clock on their VCR.

◆ *Empathy* refers to your ability to identify with your reader and their problems. Your Web site will succeed to the extent that you write from your Web site visitor's perspective, focusing your attention on the problems they face, and speak (that is, write) the language they speak. Ideally, the tone of your Web site should be: "I'm one of you, but I've solved this problem before."

From this perspective, you can see that you don't have to be a "writer" as much as a living, breathing human being, which—hopefully—you already are! Your goal is not to impress your Web site visitors as much as it is to share and simplify the knowledge you have that will solve their problems, offering solutions that advance your goals.

A Word about Files...

Pay particular attention to the placement of the content files that you will be preparing before you begin to assemble your Web site. Everyone is likely to develop their own strategy, but it is extremely important that you follow a consistent naming and placement strategy.

Instead of storing files intended for your Web site in folders associated with your word-processing program, or any other default location, place them in a "Web site contents" folder. This will make them easy to locate when it's time to assemble your Web site.

Similarly, adopt a consistent file-naming system. Identify the contents of each word-processed file as logically as possible, so you don't have to open the file to see what it contains.

CONCLUSION

There's no secret to developing content for your Web site. By this time, if you have filled out the worksheets, you probably have a good idea of the content most appropriate for your site. At this point, you can begin to prepare the word-processed files containing the information that supports your goals and your market's needs and locate and prepare the visuals necessary to support your words.

A successful Web site is a win/win proposition. When done right, you succeed to the extent you resolve your market's problems. Success comes to the extent that your Web site content overlaps your market's needs. Design—colors, layout, typeface decisions, etc.—is secondary to the appropriateness of the content you provide.

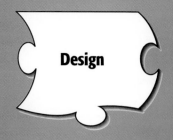

Chapter 8

Design

Designing Your Web Site

Using Color, Type, Layout, and Movement to Reinforce Your Message and Project an Appropriate Image

The design, or appearance, of your Web site is one of the most important decisions you make when creating a Web presence. The design you choose for your Web site creates the emotional environment your message appears in. Design creates a subconscious but extremely strong tendency for visitors to immediately accept or reject your ideas.

Design, by itself, cannot compensate for poor content. But, design *can* either reinforce or undermine your Web site's message. No matter how well planned and meaningful your Web site's content, your Web site will suffer if its design is inappropriate to the image you want to project or the image your Web site visitors expect. Your Web site also suffers if its design makes your message hard to read.

HOW DESIGN WORKS

Design plays an emotional as well as a practical role in the success of your Web site. Here are some of the ways design functions:

- *Design plays an emotional role* in that the colors, type, and layout of your Web site send out visual signals that influence how relevant or interesting your Web site visitor feels your message is likely to be. This influences how receptive your Web site visitor is likely to be to your ideas. Just as you'd feel more comfortable with a doctor wearing a freshly starched uniform, you'd probably be less trusting of a doctor wearing a ripped and torn Grateful Dead T-shirt with ketchup stains on it and a chain instead of a belt.

- *Design plays a pragmatic role* by determining how easy it will be for Web site visitors to locate and understand your message. Your Web site visitors are unlikely to stick around long if the colors, layout, and movement incorporated in your Web site become so dominant they make it difficult to locate your navigation tools and to read and remember your message. Design also plays an unwanted role when the colors you choose are so bright they make your Web site tiring to read or when you employ sophisticated techniques that lock out potential Web site visitors whose hardware and software cannot take advantage of the design sophistication built into your Web site.

Successful design should be both appropriate and transparent. Design should be *appropriate* to both the image you want to project and the image your market identifies with. Design should be *transparent* to the extent that your Web site visitors can concentrate on the contents of your Web site rather than consciously notice the colors or typefaces you have chosen.

Personal preference should play a very minor role in your color, typeface, and layout choices. You're not designing your Web site for yourself; you're designing it for your target market. What you like or dislike isn't as important as what your target market likes and will respond to. Similarly, although you should always consult your peers and co-workers, their preferences, too, may or may not represent your target market's preferences.

You're not designing your Web site for yourself; you're designing it for your target market.

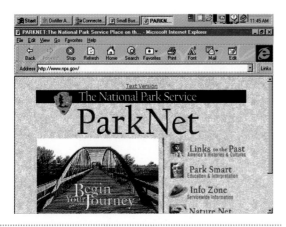

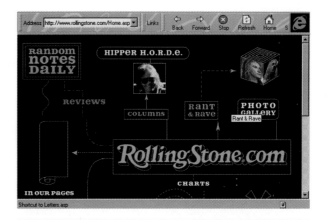

Figure 8.1 The image presented by the home page of the National Park Service's Web site is appropriate to both its subject matter and the interests of those who want to learn more about our national heritage.

Figure 8.2 Rolling Stone's image is equally appropriate to its young, contemporary, counter-culture audience.

Choosing an Appropriate Image

Two more ideas have to be added to your Web project. (These ideas are represented by the two remaining overlapping circles introduced in Chapter 7.) The content you want to communicate must overlap in some way with your Web visitor's needs. And the image you want to communicate must in some way represent the image your customers expect.

Visitors do not consciously think about and agonize over your Web site's image. Rather, they will respond to your Web site's image in an instant and on a purely emotional way. Just as you make snap judgments about new people you meet on the basis of their appearance and handshake, your Web site's image must be appropriate to the expectations of your visitors.

If your Web site is promoting an upscale product or service, your color, type, and layout choices are likely to be totally different than if you are targeting members of the MTV generation or the so-called Generation X. Compare Figures 8.1 and 8.2.

Imagine what would happen if you reversed the two images, so that the National Park Service's Web site used the colors, layout, and typography of *Rolling Stone* magazine! Total chaos would result…and neither Web site would be respected.

Design and Efficiency

Design also plays a pragmatic role in determining the speed (or efficiency) with which you create your Web site as well as the speed with which your Web site responds. If the design of your Web site is too complicated, you may not have time to include all the content you want or to update it frequently. Likewise, the effectiveness of your Web site will suffer if the colors and layout hinder

QUIZ YOURSELF

Take a few moments to analyze the different ways color, type, and layout are used in the National Park Service's and *Rolling Stone* magazine's Web sites using the Design Analysis Worksheet. Use the worksheet below to note the differences you observe. Refer back to this worksheet after you finish reading this chapter and see if you can identify some other differences.

In addition to noting the effective or ineffective use of color, type, and layout, be sure you evaluate the appropriate or inappropriate use of movement as you analyze various Web sites. As you'll see later in this chapter, movement can play a major role in communicating your message.

You might want to photocopy the Design Analysis Worksheet and use it while you and your staff analyze the design of the various Web sites you visit. Start by identifying the image the Web site was designed to project and judge how effectively color, type, layout, and movement each contributes to, or undermines, the desired image.

DESIGN ANALYSIS WORKSHEET

(On a scale of 1–10, rate how well you feel each of the following Web sites acheives its goals.)

Web site and desired image	Color	Type	Layout	Movement
National Park Service	How effectively used?	How effectively used?	How effectively used?	How effectively used?
URL: *http://www.nps.gov* Apparent desired image: antique	How ineffectively used?	How ineffectively used?	How ineffectively used?	How ineffectively used?
Rolling Stone magazine	How effectively used?	How effectively used?	How effectively used?	How effectively used?
URL: *www.rollingstone.com/home* Apparent desired image: youthful	How ineffectively used?	How ineffectively used?	How ineffectively used?	How ineffectively used?
Site name:	How effectively used?	How effectively used?	How effectively used?	How effectively used?
URL: Apparent desired image:	How ineffectively used?	How ineffectively used?	How ineffectively used?	How ineffectively used?

Web site and desired image	Color	Type	Layout	Movement
Site name: URL: Apparent desired image:	How effectively used? How ineffectively used?	How effectively used? How ineffectively used?	How effectively used? How ineffectively used?	How effectively used? How ineffectively used?
Site name: URL: Apparent desired image:	How effectively used? How ineffectively used?	How effectively used? How ineffectively used?	How effectively used? How ineffectively used?	How effectively used? How ineffectively used?
Site name: URL: Apparent desired image:	How effectively used? How ineffectively used?	How effectively used? How ineffectively used?	How effectively used? How ineffectively used?	How effectively used? How ineffectively used?
Site name: URL: Apparent desired image:	How effectively used? How ineffectively used?	How effectively used? How ineffectively used?	How effectively used? How ineffectively used?	How effectively used? How ineffectively used?

Design and Efficiency

Design also plays a pragmatic role in determining the speed (or efficiency) with which you create your Web site as well as the speed with which your Web site responds. If the design of your Web site is too complicated, you may not have time to include all the content you want or to update it frequently. Likewise, the effectiveness of your Web site will suffer if the colors and layout hinder your visitor's ability to quickly access desired information.

Thus, in order to succeed, your design must be both appropriate and practical from the production, accessibility, and maintenance points of view. An overly elaborate Web site with a design too difficult to be easily updated is equally wrong. If a Web site is too hard to update, it is unlikely to be updated, with the result that visitors will quit returning because they're tired of seeing the same old content.

DEVELOPING A UNIFYING LOOK

Ideally, as you work with the various tools at your disposal—primarily color, type, and layout—you'll achieve a "look" that projects the image you want to project.

This image should become a metaphor, a visual symbol for your Web site, one that sets it apart from competing Web sites and that communicates a message. It should also visually represent its premise, its Big Idea, the payoff, the major benefit your firm offers your prospects and customers.

As you'll see in the "Movement" section of this chapter, the power of symbols is virtually unlimited. Flags represent symbols on a national level, the White House symbolizes the power of government; the car you drive, the clothes you wear, and the neighborhood where you live similarly symbolize your values. A room filled floor to ceiling with books symbolizes something entirely different about the occupant than the same room plastered with posters from x-rated movies—even if the same individual had lived in both. You'd also approach what they said a bit differently!

The Central Organizing Concept

Your Web site's look should reflect the central organizing concept of your Web site: the primary message it projects. This message can be one of competence, entertainment, or fantasy. It can be an image of seriousness or frivolity.

What's important is that the image remain consistent from page to page. Few Web design transgressions are as jarring as images that change from page to page. All too often, a very strong and well-designed home page leads to pages created using different colors, typefaces, and layouts.

Figure 8.3
Once you have visited this Web site, you're likely to be more aware of the "milk mustache" image when you encounter it elsewhere.

This lack of unity seriously undermines the Web site's credibility. Visitors find it very disconcerting when color, type, layout, and use of movement changes from page to page; it's as if they left one Web site to visit another. This often occurs when older pages fail to get updated to a new look created during the life of a Web site.

The Lasting Memory

The best Web sites leave visitors with a single lasting memory, an idea that represents the meaning of the Web site. Like an effective billboard, a strong central organizing concept creates an image that just won't go away. More important, successful Web sites can reinforce your firm's advertising in other media, by reminding them of the firm's central marketing idea (see Figure 8.3).

Often, movement, as discussed later in this chapter, is used to emphasize the Web site's central idea. Movement permits you to orchestrate the presentation of your idea to your Web site visitors, so the ideas build upon each other like themes in a symphony, until your customer reaches the inevitable conclusion that you wanted to communicate.

CHOOSING AND USING THE RIGHT COLORS

Color can either assist or hinder the success of your Web site. This is particularly true if:

◆ Too many colors are used.

◆ The wrong colors are used.

◆ The colors distract, rather than enhance, legibility.

In the following sections appear some ways to make sure you choose and use color as effectively as possible.

REPETITION WITHOUT BOREDOM

One of the challenges you face, after having identified a symbol or metaphor for your Web site, is to balance the need to make your symbol noticeable yet avoid it becoming so noticeable that it overwhelms the message on each page. You also have to balance the need to repeat your symbol and yet avoid boring your Web site visitors.

Placing the same symbol on every page isn't enough; you need to introduce variety to keep the idea from getting so stale that Web site visitors will overlook it. Options include varying the size, location, and color of the symbol as it appears on the different pages of your Web site (see Figures 8.4 and 8.5).

When appropriately handled, the symbol subliminally communicates your message without your customers being aware of it.

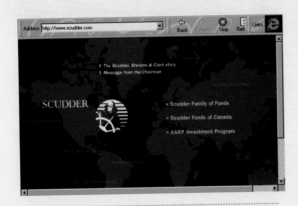

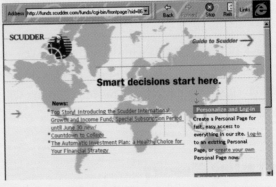

Figure 8.4 The image that unifies your Web site doesn't have to dominate every page of your Web site: It just has to be there! Scudder's "master at the helm of your financial future" symbol appears relatively small on the Scudder home page, for example, but is extremely noticeable because it appears white against a dark background.

Figure 8.5 On pages with a light background, the "master at the helm" symbol appears darker.

Too Many Colors

Although color is free, this shouldn't be interpreted to mean you should use as many colors as you possibly can in your Web site. The fewer colors you use, the better.

The emphasis added by color is in inverse proportion to the number of colors used. Limiting the number of colors used emphasizes each of the colors and makes the messages they communicate more dramatic. If you're using just three colors on your Web site, for example, the addition of a fourth color will be immediately noticed. But, if you're using ten colors, Web site visitors will be likely to overlook the addition of an eleventh (see Figure 8.6).

The emphasis added by color is in inverse proportion the number of colors used. Limiting the number of colors used emphasizes each of the colors and makes the messages they communicate more dramatic.

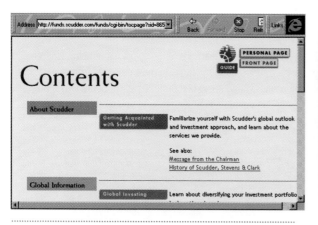 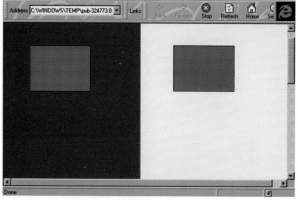

Figure 8.6 Notice how clearly the four colors employed on the Scudder Web site emerges. (Note the Scudder "Helmsman" symbol at the upper right.)

Figure 8.7 Colors appear brighter or darker according to the background they're placed against.

Colors and Backgrounds

It's important to note that colors gain or lose strength from the backgrounds they appear against. Colors take on the characteristics of their backgrounds, that is, colors placed against light backgrounds appear lighter than colors placed against dark backgrounds (see Figure 8.7). Text, especially, is influenced by background colors.

When choosing backgrounds for your Web site, attempt to choose backgrounds which offer the maximum options for text and graphic accent colors. Avoid choosing background colors so bright or so dark they limit your options or detract from the characteristics of the colors you want to emphasize.

When used with discretion, textured or patterned backgrounds can help you emphasize your foreground colors. Often, adding a small amount of pattern, or "noise," to the background mutes the starkness of a solid color.

Use of the Wrong Colors

Success comes not only from limiting your use of color but also from choosing the right colors. The wrong colors can torpedo even the best Web sites. There are two types of wrong colors:

◆ Colors may project the wrong image. Colors come with images that often reflect cultural biases.

◆ Some colors fight with each other. When equal areas of two strong, dominant colors are placed in close proximity to each other, they fight for dominance, often tiring out the Web site visitor in the process.

Notice how some of the examples below work, while others are immediately rejected.

Visitors to your Web site are likely to accept or reject your message based on similar reactions to the colors you employ. Notice how painfully wrong some of the colors are relative to the message they are supposed to reinforce. In most cases, the colors are at distinct odds with the message, undermining both the message and the credibility and presumed professionalism of the firm sponsoring the Web site.

Figure 8.8 Are you ready for some kind and gentle dreams?

Figure 8.9 Maybe kinder and gentler animals live here!

Figure 8.10 Experience the ambiance of restrained, understated elegance.

Figure 8.11 People will camp out all night to take advantage of prices like these!

Figure 8.12 The quiet, blissful, pure, restful peace and quiet is enough to put you right to sleep.

Figure 8.13 Our favorite time of the year rolls around once again.

Figure 8.14
This is one business that doesn't take "no" for an answer!

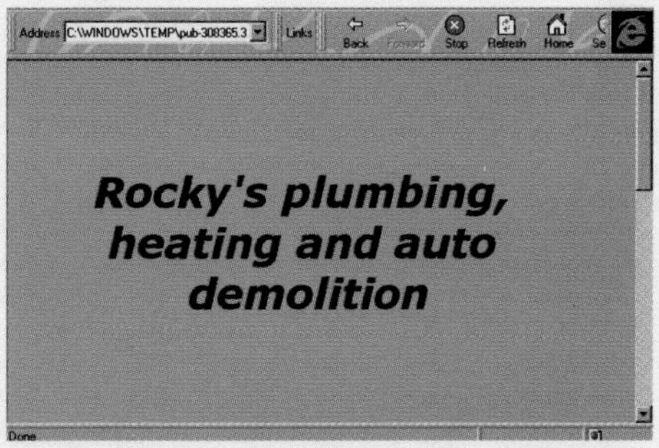

◆ Other colors are hard to read. Bright colors, especially bright-colored backgrounds, can greatly discourage Web readers. Sufficient foreground/background contrast must be present in order for your message to be read.

Colors May Project the Wrong Image

Colors carry with them strong emotional connotations. These connotations relate to seasons, holidays, geography, and income/status. Confusion and, ultimately, rejection of your message is likely to result when you choose colors without regard for their subliminal emotional messages.

The images that colors carry with them are often culturally based. We grow up associating Christmas with red and green, and the Chamber of Commerce from the many Southwest states help us associate adobe architecture with yellows, tans, and oranges.

Strong Colors Often Fight Each Other

There are two types of colors: advancing colors and receding colors. Advancing colors, like yellows, reds, and oranges, stimulate a different portion of the eye than do receding colors like blues, greens, and tans. Strong colors do not work well for backgrounds, as the background becomes too visually hot for visitors to stare at for long time periods of time. The presence of too many strong colors almost burns your eyes. In addition, when equal amounts of strong, advancing colors are used in close proximity to each other, they compete with one another, canceling the other out, distracting your customer.

Figure 8.15 Web sites quickly become tiring when too many strong colors are used in close proximity to each other.

Figure 8.16 When advancing and receding colors are used in proper balance, unnecessary graphic accents are removed, and black is shaded to gray, the key words set in red emerge with far greater impact and less visual fatigue.

Figure 8.17 When the previous gray text is replaced with full-strength black, the colors used in the Web site begin to compete with each other.

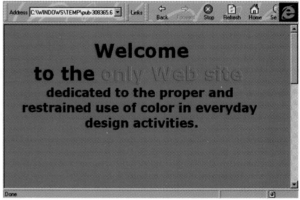

Figure 8.18 If the previous shaded background is replaced with a full-strength blue, we're back where we started with fighting colors.

A better alternative is to use receding colors for your Web site backgrounds and use strong, advancing colors for the foreground text and graphic accents. You can also make use of shades of colors for text and backgrounds. Instead of using 100 percent shades of color, experiment with shades (or tints) of the various foreground and background colors. Sometimes black is too strong, but gray works perfectly!

Colors that Distract, Rather than Enhance, Legibility

Always strive for maximum foreground/background color contrast. The closer the color of the foreground text is to the background color, the harder it will be to read the text. This, of course, is another reason for using tinted or shaded backgrounds rather than full-strength color backgrounds.

Red text against a pink background is as difficult to read as green text against a light green background or brown text against a tan background. The combination of black text against dark background colors tends to be especially difficult to read. Maximum legibility occurs when black type is laced against a white background, and visuals often appear best when placed against a white background (especially if a slight shadow is added to help separate them from the background). White backgrounds can quickly become tiring, however. That's why panels of a contrasting color are often used along the left or right edges of the page to offset the whiteness of a pure white background.

Figures 8.19 through 8.22 offer good examples of good use of color.

Always respect your reader's right to an easy, transparent, reading environment and strive to provide sufficient contrast between text and backgrounds.

Figure 8.19 The introduction to the Sierra City site uses colors appropriate to the region and the relaxed atmosphere it provides visitors.

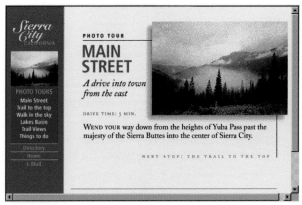

Figure 8.20 In this, and the following illustration, note the way the restrained background allows the content–the photograph–to dominate the Web page. Note, also, the way the color of "next stop" repeats the color used in the background panel to the left of each page.

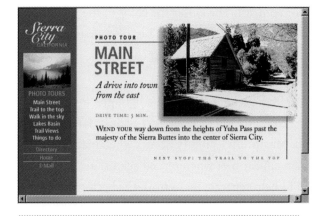

Figure 8.21 After reading the introduction, you'll be impressed by the ease with which you can read the text and enjoy the photos as they appear, one after another.

Figure 8.22 If the colors and page layout were any busier, they would detract from the message contained in the photographs.

Color Palettes

Success usually comes from selecting a limited color palette, a limited number of colors that are used throughout your Web site. The more carefully you choose these colors, the better your Web site will turn out. Your goal is to identify a series of colors that work well together, projecting the right image, while remaining far enough apart in color so as to avoid confusion (see Figures 8.23 and 8.24).

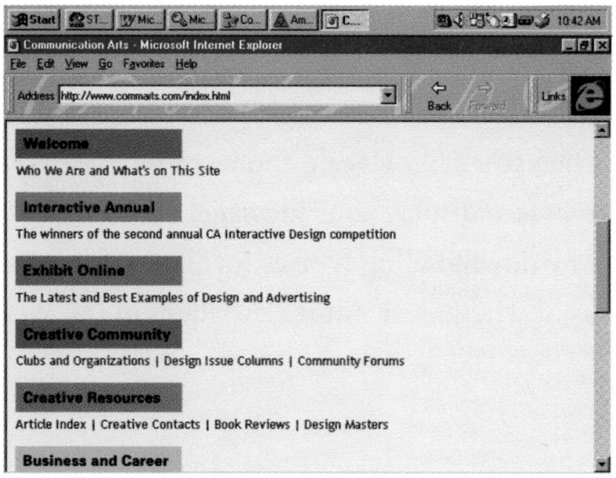

Figure 8.23 There is something almost painfully perfect about the way *Communication Arts* magazine uses a limited color palette for navigation links.

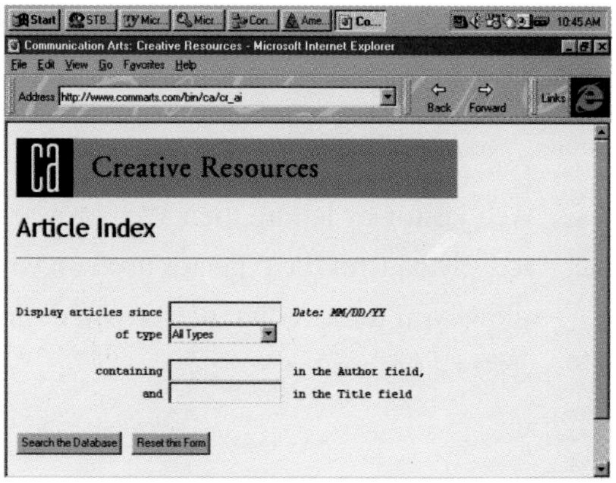

Figure 8.24 Note the way the single color on the linked page repeats the color of the link which accessed the page.

There are numerous books available from Rockport Press and North Light Books which contain palettes of prechosen combinations of colors that reflect desired moods. These books are generally available in the larger bookstores or by mail. You specify the desired mood or image you want to communicate, and the book shows various combinations of colors that can be used together to project that mood. You'll have to cross-check these recommendations, of course, to make sure that the colors you choose are within the 216 browser-safe color spectrum, of course.

Two such titles are *Color Harmony* and *Color Harmony 2* published by Rockport Press. These slim guides can save you dozens of hours of trial and error creating palettes.

THIS WEB SITE HELPS YOU CHOOSE COLOR PALETTES

If you want to visit a virtual clothing store and try out a nearly infinite variety of foreground and background colors, visit the Color Center at http://www.hidaho.com/colorcenter/cc.html. At the Color Center you can instantly view any combination of text and background colors by clicking on them (see Figure 8.25). You can also experiment with a variety of textured and patterned backgrounds available for downloading.

Figure 8.25 At the Color Center Web site, you can try out thousands of different combinations of foreground and text colors, in order to come up with the color palette that best suits your needs.

CHOOSING AND USING THE RIGHT TYPEFACE

After color, the typeface you use for graphic text plays a major role in the appearance of your Web site and the image it projects. As discussed earlier, you can delegate choice of typeface to the Web visitor by letting their Web browser's default typeface display your message. Or you can actively control the typeface used on your Web site by downloading type as formatted files. This allows you to use any typeface you desire, regardless of whether or not it's installed on the Web visitor's system.

Typeface Alternatives

Each typeface projects its own image. You can choose typefaces that project a classic or elegant image, or you can choose a clean and contemporary image. If desired, you can choose to project an image with an "attitude" by choosing a contemporary, deconstructed, typeface.

In general, *serif* typefaces—typefaces with tiny finishing strokes on the ends of each letter—create a more classic or elegant image than sans serif typefaces, which are simpler in design and lack the finishing strokes. Because of their simplicity, sans serif typefaces often project a more contemporary image.

Script typefaces offer yet another variation. Script typefaces resemble stylized handwriting and can be used to impart an elegant image. Finally, there are grunge typefaces which can be used to communicate a trendy image. (Bearing in mind, however, that what is trendy today rapidly becomes old-fashioned.)

TYPEFACE CHOICE AND IMAGE

In the examples that follow (Figures 8.26 through 8.36), note how differently you approach the same message set in each of the different typefaces illustrated. In addition, note how the legibility—or ease with which you can read each message—differs depending on the typeface the message is set in. Notice how the details of some typefaces get lost in the background, while the message remains legible when set in other typefaces.

Also, note that typeface samples in Figures 8.26 through 8.36 were all set the same size. Notice how much larger some typefaces appear than others, even when set the same size.

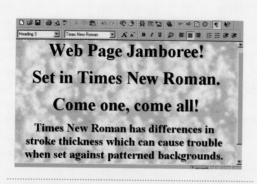

Figure 8.26 Although Times Roman is one of the most frequently used Web browser default typefaces, the significant differences in the thickness of each letter works against its legibility. Notice how the thin portions of the letters tend to disappear against the background.

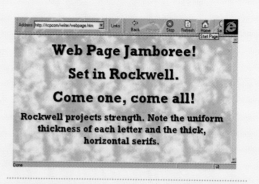

Figure 8.27 Compare Times Roman to Rockwell, and notice how the thick, uniform thickness of each letter helps this typeface to project an image of strength as well as to emerge clearly against the background.

Figure 8.28 Caslon projects a quieter, more subdued image than Times Roman, partly because of its lower x-height—the height of lower case vowels like a, e, i, o, u, and x. Because the thickness of the letters is more uniform, the words emerge clearly against the background.

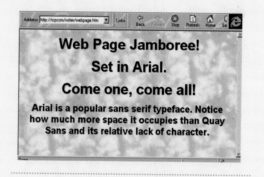

Figure 8.29 After Times New Roman, Arial is the most popular Web browser font. Note how the words are somewhat difficult to read, however, because of the uniformity of the letters.

Figure 8.30 Quay Sans projects a more contemporary, easier-to-read image than Arial. It also allows more words to fit in a given amount of space.

Figure 8.31 Gill Sans is another highly readable sans serif typeface. If you look carefully, you can see that several of the letters resemble the shape of serif typefaces.

Figure 8.32 Maiandra, from Galapagos Design, is a sans serif typeface which projects an easy-to-read, informal image.

Figure 8.33 Comic Sans is an excellent choice for projecting an informal image without sacrificing readability or legibility. You can download it for free from Microsoft's TrueType Web site, http://www.microsoft.com/truetype.htm.

Figure 8.34 Droplet, distributed by Monotype, projects an attitude all its own. Notice how the designer has created several irregular letters without sacrificing legibility.

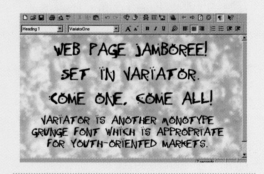

Figure 8.35 VariatorOne, also distributed by Monotype, projects an even more extreme case of trendy design.

Figure 8.36 Sanvito, from Adobe, is a script font which remains readable even against the busiest backgrounds.

Working with Type

Figure 8.37
Only a few words
set in a distinct
typeface are enough
to communicate the
designer's intended
image. Chances are,
you wouldn't want
this designer to cre-
ate an invitation for
a formal fund raiser
or party.

Type and color go hand in hand. Sometimes, in order to emphasize the typeface design even more, you can run the type in shades of black and gray against a white background.

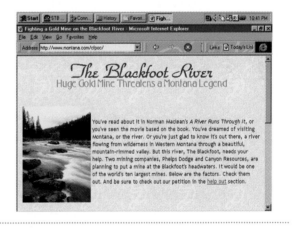

Figure 8.38 A powerful image results from the combination of a grunge typeface combined with stark black, white, and gray.

Figure 8.39 It takes just a few words set in a distinctive typeface to create a distinct image, regardless of the typeface used for the bulk of the message. Note the role that color plays in reinforcing the image established by the typeface.

Making the Most of the Control you have

One of the most important techniques you can develop is to become comfortable combining a few significant words in small graphic files, set in a distinctive typeface, with files of fast-loading downloadable text. This option offers the best of both possible worlds: The short distinctive phrases establish an image, while the bulk of your message downloads quickly (see Figure 8.40).

Although you sacrifice some control over the final appearance of the Web site, (the bulk of your message will appear in either Times New Roman or Arial, or any other typeface your Web site visitor has chosen as their default typeface) the Web site will project a distinctive image and download quickly (see Figure 8.41).

In Figure 8.41, the left-hand color panel and the formatted graphic text will create an easy-to-read, professional image, regardless of the typeface or type style specified in the Web visitor's browser.

CHOOSING AND USING THE RIGHT LAYOUT

Layout refers to the placement of the text and graphic elements on your Web site. Success, as always, comes from making the right choice and applying it consistently.

Well-organized Web sites project an image of control and professionalism. Randomly organized elements project an amateurish and last-minute approach that undermines your firm's credibility and presumed ability to satisfy the prospect. (The only exception, of course, is Web sites that are designed to appeal to artistic or youthful audiences.)

Framing Pages With Space

The biggest challenge that Web designers face is reducing line length, that is, building in space to the left- and right-hand edges of each page. Pages filled border-to-border with text are extremely difficult and disheartening to read. Here's why Web pages with long lines of text are boring and difficult to read:

◆ *Long lines of text require too many left-to-right eye movements.* Visitors to your Web site scan two and three word groups as their eyes move from left to right. If the lines are too long, they have to make several scans per line, which is very tiring.

◆ *Long lines of text make it easy to get lost.* It's too easy for Web site visitors to inadvertently return to the beginning of the line they have just finished, or they might inadvertently skip down two lines. In either case, the result is the same: confusion and a good chance that the Web site visitor will move on to an easier-to-read page.

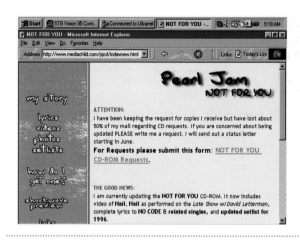

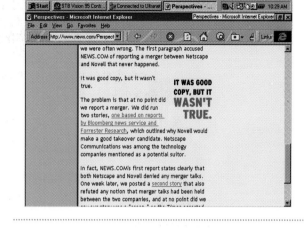

Figure 8.40 Best results are often obtained by using a few short words and phrases as a graphic file set in a distinctive typeface, combined with text that downloads fast and is formatted by your visitor's browser.

Figure 8.41 This Cnet example shows how a graphic text file, used as a formatted tag, can be used in combination with quickly downloading live text to achieve an attractive, easy-to-read image.

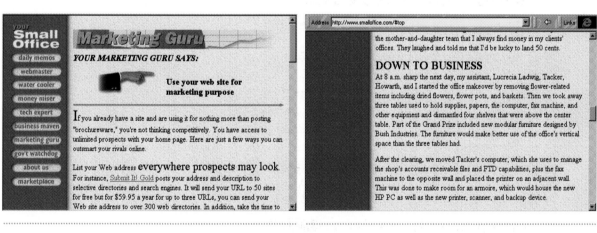

Figure 8.42 Small Office Computing offers an excellent way to reduce line length while organizing links to other features. Links are placed to the left of the text, in a contrasting color which brightens the page yet doesn't interfere with text legibility.

Figure 8.43 As you continue reading the article, the frame to the left remains to provide color and contrast, while reducing line length.

◆ *Pages filled with long lines of text are boring.* This is because there is no variety; the screen is filled with words without a place for readers to rest their eyes. The Web site looks as though it's going to be hard to read because there's nothing else to attract the eye.

Tables and frames make it easy to avoid Web sites filled with page after page of long lines of text (see Figures 8.42 and 8.43).

In Figure 8.42, notice how the horizontal line unifies the column of text with the colored border behind the navigation links.

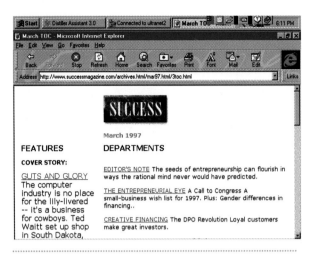

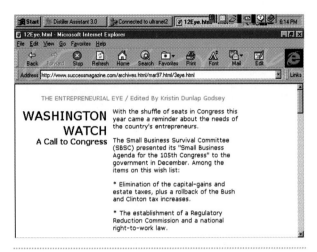

Figure 8.44 The left edge of *Success* magazine's nameplate aligns with the left margin of the Departments, organizing the page into a primary text area plus a secondary sidebar area for short features.

Figure 8.45 Consistent text placement, emphasized by the flush-right on column headline placed to the left of the text column, unifies the various pages of *Success* magazine's Web site.

A colored frame is not necessary to reduce line length and organize a Web page, of course. The publication's nameplate and *sideheads*, subheads placed to the left of the text, can be also be used to organize a page. The result in these cases is the same: reduced line length that permits rapid reading and scrolling plus the appearance of an easy-to-read publication (see Figures 8.44 and 8.45).

In Figure 8.45, note the impact of the single line, set in a second color, which is enough to emphasize the department and editorial byline, without detracting from the simplicity of the page.

Alignment

Another approach is to place the text and graphics in the center of your screen, where they are surrounded by plenty of breathing room. Again, this works best if the centered alignment is established on the home page and continued through every page of the Web site (see Figures 8.46 and 8.47).

Making the Most of Navigation

Links play a major role in Web sites by breaking up long expanses of text into organized, manageable, bite-sized chunks. Instead of telling everything you know about a subject, you'll also do better by providing information in chunks—surrounded by plenty of breathing room—which readers can access as desired (see Figures 8.48 and 8.49).

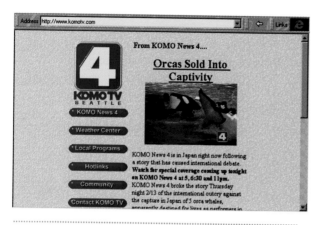

Figure 8.46 Seattle's KOMO-TV centers its links and lead articles with plenty of space, allowing fast downloads and fast scrolling to desired information. Notice, also, how the limited color palette projects a professional image and adds impact to the photograph.

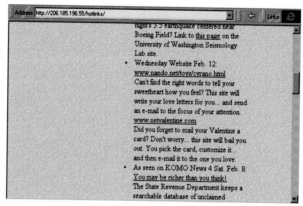

Figure 8.47 Notice how the text remains the same width after visitors have scrolled past the links. The Web site's integrity would be seriously weakened if the text column suddenly got wider after the links ended.

Figure 8.48 Notice the many links offered by this Radio Shack page. Links at the top access different departments, links along the left (which mimic the pegboard displays found in many Radio Shack stores) access different price levels of gifts.

Figure 8.49 When you scroll down through the various product offerings, notice how brief the captions are. This allows more products to be shown at a time. Links under the products, however, allow you to access in-depth information as desired.

As these examples show, links do more than allow Web site visitors to access different pages. Properly used, links are active design tools that permit you to design cleaner, simpler pages which combine a high information content with an open, inviting look.

Links are active design tools that permit you to design cleaner, simpler pages which combine high information content with an open, inviting look.

MAKING THE MOST OF MOVEMENT

Movement is the last—and often most ignored—aspect of design that deserves mention.

Unfortunately, movement is rarely used effectively in Web site design. Movement is often confused with animation and gimmicky special effects that distract, rather than enhance, the Web site's message. Here two examples of the successful use of movement that involves the Web site visitor, leading them by the hand towards the overwhelming message that the Web site is designed to communicate.

The first example uses movement to emphasize the disappearing act our nation's historic buildings are facing (see Figures 8.50 through 8.53).

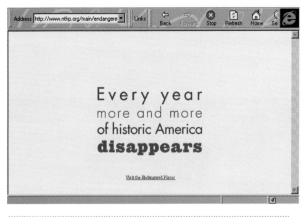

Figure 8.50 When you visit the National Trust for Historic Preservation's site, you'll find that the eye-catching, single red word "disappears" forms a strong contrast with the blue text, but…

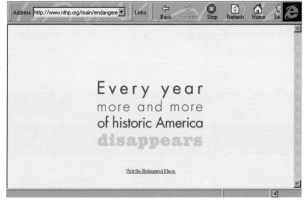

Figure 8.51 …Almost immediately, the word "disappears" itself begins to disappear.

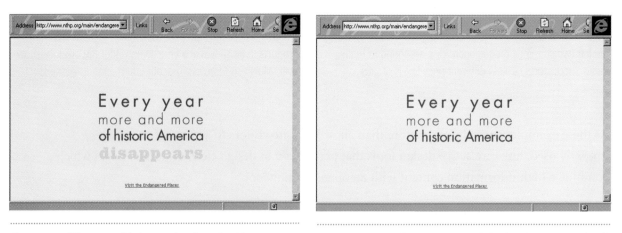

Figure 8.52 "Disappears" fades to a barely noticeable gray…

Figure 8.53 …and is soon gone, reinforcing the message that if we don't act now, it will soon be too late.

Building Towards a Climactic Statement of Your Web Site's Central Message

The second example builds to a different, equally-effective climax that reinforces the Web site's primary message (see Figures 8.54 through 8.58).

Figure 8.54 Visitors to the Mercedes Benz Web site are led through a procession of images that emphasize the importance of symbols.

Figure 8.55 These symbols quickly flash on the screen in about the time it takes readers to grasp the meaning of each.

Figure 8.56 Example after example of symbols rapidly follow each other.

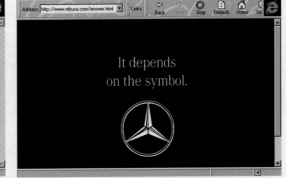

Figure 8.57 Suddenly, you're presented with a statement...

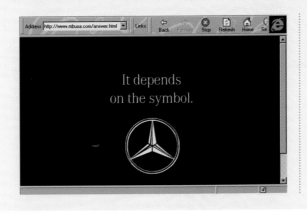

Figure 8.58 ...which leads to the conclusion the procession was building to!

Synergy

Note the similarity as well as the synergy of the techniques used in the above two examples. Here are some points to look for:

♦ Short passages of graphic text were used. This gave the designers full control over the appearance of the few words that appear on the Web visitor's monitor. In the first example, note how this technique permits the four lines of text to be equal in length by modifying the weight (or thickness) of the letters as well as the letter spacing. Using graphic text in the second example allows the use of an elegant serif typeface, even if the Web visitor has specified a different default typeface for their Web browser.

♦ Notice how the active, or text and visual areas, of both illustrations are relatively small and centered in the screen. This allows them to be surrounded by plenty of space which focuses the Web visitor's eyes on their message.

♦ Note the simple background colors used for each of the screens. The use of either a black or white background creates a neutral ground for the important message to emerge against.

Fear of Simplicity

Clutter and change are the biggest obstacles to the development of a strong image. Your goal in choosing the right colors, type, layout, and movement for your Web site is to create unity throughout your Web site, not to provide eye candy unless eye candy is appropriate.

It takes a lot of courage to use only a few colors and typefaces throughout your Web site. It takes even more courage to avoid the temptation to introduce change for the sake of change.

Remember that although you are likely to be familiar with every page on your Web site, few of your visitors are likely to pay critical attention to every page. Most of them will choose only those pages that offer the content they desire. In addition, because you're creating it, you're likely to spend a lot more time with your Web site than your visitors who are only visiting it.

The best Web sites reflect a marvelous synergy between image and simplicity. A few, carefully chosen, carefully colored visuals meet and project exactly the right image and lead the Web site visitor to exactly the place where the information they desire is located (see Figures 8.59 through 8.61).

Figure 8.59 Tower Record's home page invites you in by combining the right image with simplicity and a single, high-impact second color.

Figure 8.60 Unity is maintained by repeating design elements.

Figure 8.61 Later, the harshness of the top of the home page is softened by a muted color palette of links to various types of music.

PUTTING KNOWLEDGE TO WORK

Now that you are familiar with the basics of color, type, layout, and movement, it's time to begin work choosing the design for your Web site.

Use the Design Goals Worksheet below to review your goals, identify the market you want your Web site to attract, and define the characteristics of the image most appropriate for your target market.

You may want to photocopy the Design Goals Worksheet and use it as it was intended, that is, a guide for your own work. But you can also fill it out and give copies to your staff or outside designers who will be working on your Web site. The more detailed information you gather in writing, the better your Web site will turn out!

After your Web site is completed, you can use the Design Goals Worksheet to review how closely your Web site fulfilled its original design intentions.

DESIGN GOALS WORKSHEET

1. Name three of the most memorable and noteworthy Web sites (from a design point of view) you have visited.

   Name   URL (Web address)

   1.

   2.

   3.

2. What are some of their color, typeface, layout, and movement characteristics?

   Site A (name):

   (You may want to refer back to them while answering these questions.)

   Use of color (please describe):

   Use of type (please describe):

   Use of layout (please describe):

   Site B (name):

   Use of color (please describe):

   Use of type (please describe):

   Use of layout (please describe):

Site C (name):

Use of color (please describe):

Use of type (please describe):

Use of layout (please describe):

Use of movement (please describe):

3. What are the age and sex characteristics of the visitors you want your Web site to attract?

    ❏ Male ❏ Female ❏ Both

    ❏ 9–15 ❏ 16–24 ❏ 25–34
    ❏ 35–44 ❏ 45–54 ❏ 55 and over

4. What are the desired income characteristics of the Web site visitors you want to attract?

    Household income:

    ❏ Under $25,000 ❏ $25,000 to $49,000
    ❏ $50,000 to $99,000 ❏ Over $100,000

5. What are some of the attitudes that describe the Web visitors you want to attract?

    ❏ Cost conscious/frugal
    ❏ Conspicuous consumers
    ❏ Risk-taking
    ❏ Security conscious
    ❏ High-profile, i.e., desire attention
    ❏ Low profile, i.e., desire anonymity and quiet

6. Describe some of the characteristics of the image you want to project:

    (Select as many choices as you desire)

    ❏ Youthful
    ❏ Trendy
    ❏ Tradition oriented
    ❏ Counter-culture
    ❏ Healthy and healthful

       ❏ Patriotic

       ❏ Seasonal (if so, which season?) _____

       ❏ Stable and conservative

       ❏ Reassuring

       ❏ Affordable

       ❏ Expensive

       ❏ Pragmatic

       ❏ Excitement and risk-taking

       ❏ High-tech lovers

       ❏ Low-tech/mechanically-oriented

       ❏ Professional

       ❏ Craftsman/works with hands

       ❏ Quiet

       ❏ Flamboyant

7. What colors are you considering using in your Web site?

       ❏ Background

       ❏ Titles and headlines

       ❏ Text

       ❏ Links

       ❏ Current link

       ❏ Visited link

8. How do you plan to use color to unify or code the different sections of your Web site?

       ❏ Headline and title text

       ❏ Navigation links and graphic accents

       ❏ Backgrounds

       ❏ Other (describe below)

9. Where do you plan to use graphic text?

       ❏ Section Titles

       ❏ Navigation links and/or buttons

       ❏ Headlines

       ❏ Subheads

       ❏ Initial caps

       ❏ Section intro's

       ❏ Pull-quotes

       ❏ Sidebars

       ❏ Captions

10. What typefaces are you considering using for graphic type?

    ❏ Serif (Which typeface?)

    ❏ Sans Serif (Which typeface?)

    ❏ Script (Which typeface?)

    ❏ Decorative (Which typeface?)

11. How will you align the various text elements of page architecture?

    ❏ Centered
    ❏ Flush-left/ragged right
    ❏ Random

12. How will you emphasize subheads?

    ❏ Contrasting type face
    ❏ Contrasting type size
    ❏ Contrasting type style
    ❏ Placement (describe or illustrate below):

13. How will you use graphic accents to reinforce your image?

    ❏ Page backgrounds
    ❏ Table backgrounds
    ❏ Separating text and graphic elements
    ❏ Connecting text and graphic elements
    ❏ Section dividers

14. What layout techniques will you use to project a desired image?

    ❏ White space
    ❏ Frames to organize links and background colors

15. Where will you place navigation links?

    ❏ Top of each page
    ❏ Bottom of each page
    ❏ Left side of each page
    ❏ Right side of each page

Chapter 9

Involvement

Involving Your Visitors

Encourage Them to Participate
Rather Than Just Observe!

Successful Web sites involve their visitors. Instead of just sitting back and passively reading your words, involvement encourages visitors to seek out the information you want them to have and clarify any additional information they need to make a positive buying decision. Involvement encourages and makes it possible for visitors to move from being aware of your product to the actual purchase.

Meaningful content, transparent design, and intuitive navigation are only the beginning. Equally important are registration forms and e-mail links that make it easy for your visitors to request additional information. Responding to requests for information forges a one-to-one relationship with Web site visitors, giving them a sense of familiarity while providing the information they need. Responding to information requests also makes it easier for you to fine-tune the contents of your Web site as you maintain it so that it will become increasingly compatible with the information needs of your target market.

High-involvement Web sites encourage visitors to define their needs, pre-qualify their ability to buy, and, moving them through the buying cycle. Increasingly, as the technology needed for secure credit-card transactions on the Web becomes available, the goal of more and more Web sites will be complete involvement, that is, the ability for visitors to purchase your product or service directly from your Web site.

RELATING CONTENT, NAVIGATION, AND MAINTENANCE TO INVOLVEMENT

The content, design, and navigation structure of your Web site are important aspects of visitor involvement. Remember that few visitors will want to thumb through every page of your Web site as they might the pages of a magazine or newsletter. Instead, the navigation structure of your Web site should make it easy for them to quickly locate the desired information. Thus, the first step towards enhancing your site's ability to involve visitors is to review its content and accessibility. Ask yourself question like the following:

◆ Does your Web site provide the content your visitors desire?

◆ Does the design, that is, appearance, of your site enhance or hinder its content?

◆ Is it easy for visitors to locate desired information?

One of the easiest way to ascertain answers to the above questions is to ask your friends and co-workers to access your Web site and watch them as they visit the various pages on it. Observe their reactions and note how easily they can locate desired information. Often, you can learn more by observing them by asking them questions—since many people may not want to openly criticize a friend or co-worker's work to their face.

Addressing Frequently Asked Questions

One of the easiest ways you can augment your site's involvement power and help visitors presell themselves on your product is to include a glossary describing important terms used to describe your product or service and the problems they solve. Another popular option is to include a page answering Frequently Asked Questions (FAQs). These pages enhance your firm's credibility and save time by answering questions you and your sales staff get asked over and over again.

Remember: *nobody ever wants to feel dumb!* By providing the basic information that first-time buyers need, you can simultaneously expand the market for your products as well as enhance your credibility as a source to be trusted.

A Web site that provides meaningful content, but is too advanced for its market, is certain to fail. Always struggle to overcome the myopia of "everybody knows that!" Chances are, everybody *doesn't* know the information you take for granted because you deal with it every day. In most fields, you're the expert and your prospects don't know nearly as much as you do.

In the remainder of this chapter, we'll review the various stages of involvement you can build into your Web site, in the order of increasing sophistication.

REGISTRATION

Registration is the easiest form of involvement. You can encourage registration by providing visitors to your Web site an electronic form for their e-mail, phone number, and postal mailing address, which they can fill out online and submit to you. A registration form offers you many advantages:

◆ *Indicates interest:* It allows you to identify your potential buyers and add them to your serious prospect pool for later follow-up via direct mail, phone call, or a visit to their home or office (depending on the type of product or service you're offering). In direct marketing terms, this is referred to as *lead generation.*

◆ *Helps visitors sell themselves:* Registration can advance visitors along the buying cycle when it helps overcome objections by building familiarity and making it easy for you to address objections that may be keeping your visitors from purchasing.

◆ *Tracks your Web site's performance:* Your registration form should include space for visitors to indicate what brought them to your Web site. Did they find you through a search engine, a link to your site from another site, or locate your Web site address in an advertisement, brochure, or newsletter?

The information that registration forms provide make it easier to follow up on specific questions as well as improve your site. Registration forms make it easy for visitors to provide a lot of valuable information in a simple, structured way.

Registration versus Contact

It's important to recognize the difference between registration and contact:

◆ *Registration* involves your Web site visitor filling out a form and providing specific responses to specific questions.

◆ *Contact*, on the other hand, involves non-structured responses, that is, simply providing easy ways for visitors to your Web site to contact you by phone, fax, or e-mail.

Both have their place. *Registration* based on forms encourages visitors to respond because your registration form provides a framework for their response. The simpler you make it for visitors to respond, the more likely that they will respond. You can reduce the time it takes visitors to register by providing spaces for name, street, city, state, zip code, and other contact information plus radio buttons and check boxes for specific information, as described below. *Contact* is an unstructured response and is unlikely to provide as much information. Visitors will be less likely to submit the same information via e-mail than they would on a registration form since there is no structure for their response. As a result, you're less likely to receive all the information you desire.

Registration and contact also differ according to where your Web site visitors are in the buying cycle. Visitors are more likely to contact you if they are in the desire or purchase stages of the buying cycle—where they have specific questions—although visitors may register at any point depending on the incentive you offer them.

The simpler you make it for Web site visitors to respond...the more likely visitors will be to respond.

Designing a Registration Form

Response will increase to the extent you keep your registration form as short and simple as possible. Long registration forms appear like a lot of work, which discourages visitors from filling them out. Edit your questions to the minimum and condense space whenever possible.

AVOID "REGISTRATION TYRANNY"

Do not make registration a precondition for viewing your site's content. Registration should be a voluntary act, a *reward* visitors offer you in appreciation for your site's content–a reward to you for doing your job well.

Asking visitors to register too early in the game is a sure-fire way to scare them away from your site. Registration implies commitment, and commitment should be earned, not demanded.

Make registration voluntary–although you should do everything possible to make it as attractive a proposition as possible.

Provide radio buttons and check boxes whenever you can. These are easier for visitors to fill out and also easier for you to compile the results. Instead of placing short, one- or two-word radio buttons and check boxes on separate lines, combine several on one line. Use subheads to organize the questions and break up your registration form into several short segments instead of one long "assignment."

Be sure to conclude your registration form with a "Thank you!"

DECIDING WHAT TO ASK

Every Web site's registration form is likely to be different, depending on the information and action desired. The following information, however, provides some general guidelines you can adapt for your Web site.

It's useful to begin by stating in your registration form, as well as on the page that leads to it, that the information visitors are providing is for your firm's use only and will not be shared, sold, or traded to other firms. (Of course, having said that, make sure you live up to your promise!)

Note: use subheads to organize your registration form, breaking your questions into manageable bite-sized chunks. Number each question in each section, but to make your questions appear as few in number as possible, begin renumbering each section with Question One.

REGISTRATION FORM

Part One: Introduce yourself

Last name _____ First name _____ Middle initial _____

Position _____ Firm _____

Street _____

City _____

State _____ Country _____ Zip or Postal Code _____

E-mail address _____ Phone _____ Fax _____

Part Two: Background

1. What brought you to our Web site?

    ❑ Search engine   ❑ Advertisement   ❑ Link from (name of Web site): _____

❑   Other (please describe):

2.   What parts of our Web site did you find *most* useful?

❑   Topic A   ❑   Topic B   ❑   Topic C

❑   Topic D   ❑   Topic E   ❑   Topic F (other, please describe): _____

3.   What parts of our Web site did you find *least* useful?

❑   Topic A   ❑   Topic B   ❑   Topic C

❑   Topic D   ❑   Topic E   ❑   Topic F (other, please describe): _____

4.   What additional topics do you wish we had covered in greater detail? (Please describe)

Part Three: How can we help you?

1.   Would you like us to inform you via e-mail about upcoming promotions, special events, and money-saving opportunities?

❑   Yes   ❑   No

2.   Are there any questions we can answer for you at this time?

❑   No   ❑   Yes (If "yes," what are they?) _____

3.   Is there any special product or service we might be able to locate for you?

❑   No   ❑   Yes (If "yes," what are they?) _____

End your registration form by thanking visitors for taking the time to fill out this registration form and submit it to you.

Resist the urge to make your registration form any longer than it has to be by asking too many additional questions, unless you absolutely have to know the answers. The shorter the registration form, the greater the number of Web site visitors who will use it. Registrations will drop off quickly if you ask too many questions.

Encouraging Registration

One of the first questions you should ask yourself is: *"What can I offer to encourage registration?"* Registrations will quickly increase if you provide a reason for Web site visitors to send you their names and addresses. Here are some ideas:

◆ *Offer a premium,* such as a printed copy of a back issue of one of your previous newsletters or a special "White Paper" containing helpful information, such as software shortcuts, a "hot list" of current interest to your visitors, that is, radio stations around the country featuring programming they're likely want to tune to while driving or a list of upcoming events, or a complimentary admission to an upcoming event. The more meaningful the reward, the higher your rate of registrations.

◆ *Save them money* by promising to notify them via e-mail of upcoming promotions, sending them money-saving content or providing them with a password to access pages of your Web site containing special savings reserved for just "friends" with access to the page.

◆ *Offer a free sample*—for example, offer to answer a question or send a sample of the product you're selling.

◆ *Perform a service,* such as answering questions or searching for a product they're interested in locating, that is, a white low-mileage 1989 Mercedes-Benz E-300 Coupe or a special book, model, or recording. Offering to search for a specific product not only enhances your professional image, but opens communication with visitors when you call them after discovering a low-mileage 1990 model they might be interested in. (In addition, once you know the product or service a Web site is interested in, you can search for those products at auctions or from the inventory of other dealers in your area.) Another valuable service you can offer is to promise to notify visitors when you add new content to your Web site. This saves your visitors the trouble of visiting your Web site to encounter only prior information.

◆ *Enhanced content.* Another option is to include special information on your Web site that can only be accessed by those who register. This might include longer, more in-depth versions of the free articles, buying tips, or up-to-date product information and savings displayed earlier.

◆ *Award a prize.* Create a contest, perhaps based on awarding every n'th registrant a special prize, perhaps a copy of a book or special report you've written. Or, perhaps you can persuade one of your vendors to donate a prize to be given away at a special drawing.

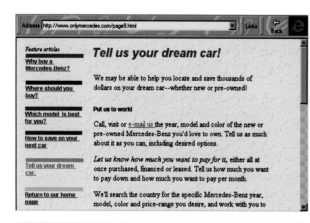

Figure 9.1 Smith motors invites visitors to let them know what model and year of pre-owned Mercedes-Benz you'd be interested in hearing about.

Figure 9.2 The Jelly Belly company offers free jelly beans to visitors who register at their site.

E-mail Synergy

Nearly everyone who visits your Web site is likely to have an e-mail account. E-mail makes it easy and inexpensive for you to communicate with your Web site visitors. The only expense you'll incur will be the time you, or a member of your staff, devotes to responding to e-mail each day.

Airlines have been in the vanguard of taking advantage of customized e-mail to build close, personalized relationships with their prospects. Many airlines offer e-mail-based last-minute travel opportunities to those who register. In most cases, when a visitor to their Web site registers, they can specify a number of nearby airports where they might be willing to depart from for short, impromptu round trips. After registration, each Wednesday the airline sends them a list of travel bargains for travel leaving the next Friday or Saturday and returning Monday or Tuesday (see Figure 9.3).

This is an excellent example of the way the Web offers a win-win situation for everyone: Airlines can fill empty seats and travelers with flexible lifestyles can take trips they could never otherwise afford. It's not unusual for a round trip that would cost $700 or more during the week to be available for just $89 on a last-minute basis!

The question you have to ask yourself is: "What kind of last minute products and services can I promote via e-mail?"

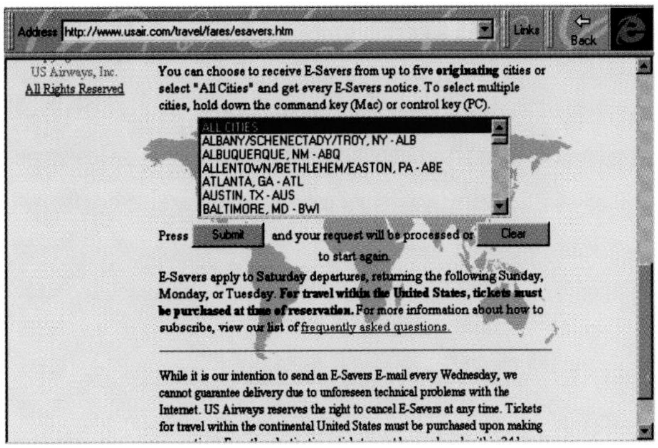

Figure 9.3
After submitting a list of airports close to your home, USAir will send you e-mail Wednesday mornings advising you of travel bargains for the coming weekend.

Acknowledgment

Regardless of the information that you request and receive from Web site visitors, you should always acknowledge receipt of the form, even if no immediate response is indicated. Every contact you have with a prospect is a step towards building a relationship with them. Every contact you have with a customer reinforces that relationship.

> *Every contact you have with a prospect is a step towards building a relationship with them. Every contact you have with a customer reinforces that relationship.*

Many Web sites send an acknowledgment that your registration form has been received, a reassuring touch that keeps visitors from worrying that their registration form and request for further information didn't arrive safely.

Involvement Leads to Maintenance

Registration forms that encourage visitors to rate the value of the information provided on your Web site and identify areas of concern left untouched, will help you fine-tune your Web site so that it will become increasingly helpful to future visitors.

Thus, "Maintenance," discussed in Chapter 13, plays a cause-and-effect relationship with content and involvement. The more involvement and interaction your Web site offers, the more time visitors will spend at your Web site and the more tempted they'll be to return. But *returning visitors don't want to encounter the same content*. Thus, the more frequently you update the content of your Web site, the more involvement you offer visitors. Each return visit reinforces your Web site visitor's relationship with you, advancing them towards the purchase or replacement phases of the buying cycle.

CUSTOMIZING SITE CONTENT

Perhaps the most important way your Web site can advance visitors along the buying cycle is to allow them to become their own sales representatives and sell to themselves. This is done by allowing visitors to customize the content of your Web site on the basis of the information they want to view.

What's Available?

Many Web sites contain far more pages than even the most determined visitor is likely to have time to visit. Imagine how long it would take you to view a photograph and description of every home listed by regional real estate firms like John L. Scott or Windemere in the Pacific Northwest or Coldwell-Banker across the country! Realtors have found it far more efficient to limit the homes they show visitors to Web pages by just showing them homes that meet each visitor's unique and specialized criteria.

Instead of forcing you to scroll through tens of thousands of pages of listings, the Web sites of most realtors permit you to specify criteria like:

◆   City and state

◆   Distance from downtown (that is, within city limits or within a given number of miles)

◆   Number of bedrooms and bathrooms

◆   Price range

Pages containing a photograph of the home and a description of its important characteristics typically contain an e-mail link to the listing realtor. Often, an e-mail to that person in the afternoon results in a return fax containing detailed information the next morning or a mailed package containing more information about similar listings in the area within a few days. This Web site involvement saves both you and the realtor time and the mutual frustration of driving around an area only to view homes that don't satisfy your criteria (see Figures 9.4 through 9.6).

Be Your Own Travel Agent!

Another way that the Web can help you avoid the hassle of waiting on hold, listening to instrumental music while waiting for a service representative to assist you is to permit you to schedule your own trips. This is especially useful for what-if travel planning, that is, vacation trips where time and departure/return dates are more flexible than business travel. Web travel searching also eliminates the commitment that passenger service representatives force upon you by requiring you to specify a day and time of departure.

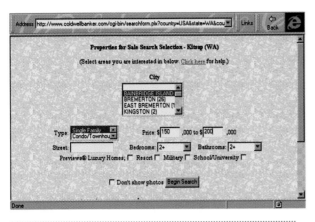

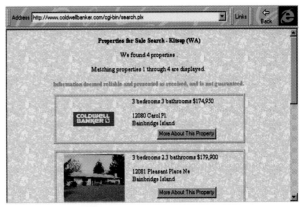

Figure 9.4 Like many realtors, Coldwell-Banker invites you to preselect homes on the basis of desired location, size, desired amenities, and price range.

Figure 9.5 Usually, you're presented with brief, fast-loading descriptions of homes that might meet your requirements.

Figure 9.6
Clicking on one of the descriptions takes you to a larger picture of the home and detailed information plus an e-mail link to the listing real estate agent .

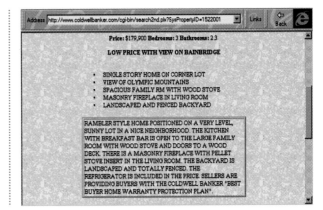

The Web sites of most airlines allow you to preview their flight and time options at your leisure, without any commitment (see Figures 9.7 and 9.8). This gives you a far better idea of your options than forcing you to focus on a specific day and time.

After scheduling the first half of your trip, simply repeat the procedure to determine the most convenient schedule for your return.

Note that, instead of limiting you only to flights on a given airline, the Web sites of many airports contain a similar search mechanism that allows you to view your options on all of the airlines that serve that airport.

Other airlines not only allow you to schedule your own travel, but allow you to choose the seat that's most comfortable for you, that is, perhaps a bulkhead seat (see Figure 9.9).

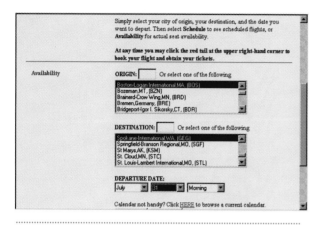

Simply select your city of origin, your destination, and the date you want to depart. Then select **Schedule** to see scheduled flights, or **Availability** for actual seat availability.

At any time you may click the red tail at the upper right-hand corner to book your flight and obtain your tickets.

Availability

ORIGIN: [ ]   Or select one of the following

Boston-Logan International,MA, (BOS)
Bozeman,MT, (BZN)
Brainerd-Crow Wing,MN, (BRD)
Bremen,Germany, (BRE)
Bridgeport-Igor I. Sikorsky,CT, (BDR)

DESTINATION: [ ]   Or select one of the following

Spokane-International,WA, (GEG)
Springfield-Branson Regional,MO, (SGF)
St Marys,AK, (KSM)
St. Cloud,MN, (STC)
St. Louis-Lambert International,MO, (STL)

DEPARTURE DATE:
[July ▼] [31 ▼] [Morning ▼]

Calendar not handy? Click HERE to browse a current calendar.

Flight Schedule
Boston-Logan International,MA, (BOS)
to
Spokane-International,WA, (GEG)
on Thursday, July 31, 1997

Flight	Departs	Arrives	Day	Stops	Eqp
NW 1762	BOS 0600A	MSP 0758A	0	0	757
NW 0611	MSP 0920A	GEG 1023A	0	0	727
NW 1762	BOS 0600A	MSP 0758A	0	0	757
NW 0619	MSP 1150A	GEG 1251P	0	0	D93
NW 0305	BOS 0800A	MSP 1006A	0	0	D10
NW 0619	MSP 1150A	GEG 1251P	0	0	D93
NW 0083	BOS 0830A	SEA 1127A	0	0	757
NW 7305	SEA 1240P	GEG 0133P	0	0	M80

Figure 9.7 Northwest Airline's Web site makes it easy for you to specify departure and arrival cities, time of day, and date of proposed travel.

Figure 9.8 After specifying departure and arrival cities, you're presented with a list of flights that meet your criteria.

Figure 9.9
After you have chosen a flight, some airlines, like Delta, even describe the type of aircraft usually assigned to the flight and show you its seating chart!

Is This Really What I Want?

Many Web sites allow you to preview your product, such as preview interior/exterior colors or—as described in Chapter 7—view the stage from your seat.

The Web sites of many automobile manufacturers, for example, permit you to "build your own car" by choosing the precise combination of interior and exterior colors you desire, and then view the finished car from a variety of perspectives (see Figures 9.10 through 9.12). You can decide whether black or tan leather with a red exterior on your dream convertible.

Figure 9.10 You can "build your own" car at the Mercedes-Benz USA site. Start by choosing the desired model and desired exterior and interior colors.

Figure 9.11 Next, try out different combinations of colors.

Figure 9.12
Finally, view your
dream car at large
size and, if avail-
able, print it out
on your color ink-
jet printer.

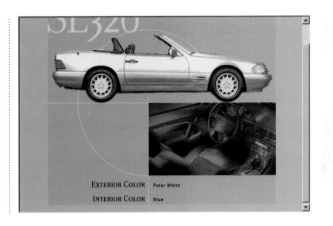

Can I afford it?

Many Web sites include mortgage, financing, and leasing calculators that allow visitors to find out how much it will cost to purchase the product. This further prequalifies and presells the Web site visitor, eliminating wasted time, and in many cases can help the visitor "sell themselves up" by convincing them they can afford a better car or home than they thought they could.

These calculators generally allow you to play what-if games by showing how monthly payments will vary depending on your down payment, the length of the loan, and the impact of interest rates (which will depend on your credit rating). (See Figure 9.13.) Other calculators will even include insurance and taxes into your analysis, increasing your ability to prequalify and presell yourself.

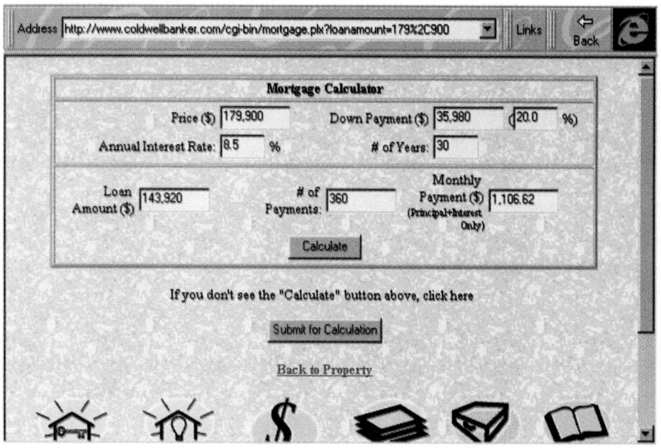

Figure 9.13
After choosing a desired house, Coldwell-Banker's mortgage calculator permits you to try out different financing scenarios, with different down payments, interest rates, and duration of loan.

Is it in stock?

As your Web site begins to attract visitors who are fairly advanced along the buying cycle, you can build immediacy into your Web site by allowing them to check the status of their purchase, ascertaining whether the product they desire is in stock or has already been sold.

This approach makes sense when quantities are limited—that is, only one seat A-1 can be sold for any performance and there's only one 23C on any given airline flight. Making it possible for visitors to click on a desired seat location and reminding them that it can be sold at any moment is an easy way to encourage immediate action. Nobody wants to be left out after they have made a decision to buy!

Newsgroups

Another way of increasing visitors' involvement in your Web site, and encouraging them to return, is to create a newsgroup. A newsgroup can serve as a bulletin board where visitors can post messages to each other or address areas of common concern.

Newsgroups offer many advantages, although administering them can occupy a lot of your time. One of the advantages is that you can quickly gain visibility among your peers and those whose requests you need in order to succeed. Thus, newsgroups are excellent involvement vehicles for consultants and others in service businesses who want to be perceived as authorities. Your ongoing analysis of the submissions to your newsgroup will also make it easy for you to identify trends and keep abreast of changes in your field.

A final advantage is that your Web site will take on a life of its own, reducing the amount of information you need to develop because your visitors will be providing information. Canceling this out, of course, is the time required for you to monitor submissions to your newsgroup and

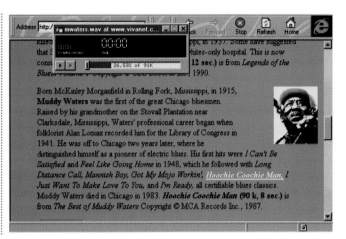

Figure 9.14
Web sites, like
those of Muddy
Waters as well as
of many music
labels, stores, and
performers, allow
you to hear as well
as read about your
favorite music.

keep it on track (avoiding potentially embarrassing or libelous submissions). A newsgroup may be hard to start up and monitor, but it is certain to raise your visibility in your field as well as create numerous public relations opportunities for promoting your Web site.

Adding Audio, Video, and Virtual Reality to Your Site

Since the Web permits you to include audio, and increasing numbers of home machines include sound cards and stereo speakers, you can also include sound on your Web site. If you own a radio station or a record store, you can allow visitors to your Web site to preview cuts from new recordings or previews of upcoming concerts (see Figure 9.14).

If the product or service you're offering is appropriate, you might consider adding video clips to your Web site. Video clips might take the form of short introductions by your key staff members or pictures of your product in use. Alternatively, you could include virtual reality in your Web site, allowing visitors to view your product in a three-dimensional fashion.

Virtual reality is perhaps the closest step towards a purchase that it's possible to take without asking your visitors to leave their home or office. Virtual reality puts Web site visitors quite literally in the driver's seat, allowing them to look out the window of a car they're considering, or drop their eyes down to the gauges and picture themselves adjusting the volume on the radio or selecting another CD (see Figures 9.15 and 9.16).

Although your business may not presently need or have the necessary resources to accomplish some of the techniques described above, it's never too early to begin thinking about the future. Advances in technology are occurring at an exponential rate, and what's a dream today is likely to be taken for granted tomorrow.

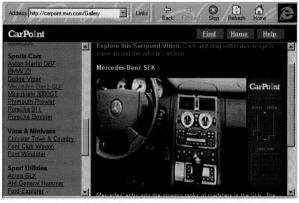

Figure 9.15 Web sites like Car Point at the Microsoft Network allow you to gaze—in either direction—out the window of a car that interests you.

Figure 9.16 Alternatively, you can gaze down and focus on the climate and radio controls, or select a different compact disc.

Purchase—The Ultimate Involvement

The ultimate expression of Web involvement, of course, is to complete a purchase over the Web. As the technology for secure transactions over the Web improves, more and more purchases will take place. The primary stumbling block is the hesitation of many consumers to provide credit card numbers over the Web…even though the same individuals have no compunction about giving their credit card to an anonymous waiter or waitress in a crowded restaurant hundreds of miles from home. Also, fear of credit card theft is somewhat excessive because of the upper limits of loss by theft that many credit card companies offer. Insurance is also available.

One option, if your market is concerned about the security of credit transactions, might be for them to get a second credit card with a low credit limit and use it only for Web transactions.

At present, many firms have found that the easiest way to encourage purchases is to include toll-free ordering numbers so that credit card information can be provided over a telephone. Faxed information is also an option.

Applying These Lessons to Your Business

Use the following Involvement Worksheet to review how "involving" your Web site is and identify ways of making it more so.

Remember: The more your Web site involves your Web site visitors, the easier it will be to advance them along the buying cycle by building their enthusiasm and providing necessary information to address possible objections.

INVOLVEMENT WORKSHEET

1. Does the structure of your Web site make it easy for visitors to directly access desired information?

    ❏ Yes ❏ No (If "no", what can you change to make it more involving?)

2. What information are you interested in obtaining from your Web site visitors?

    1.

    2.

    3.

    4.

    5.

    6.

3. What can you offer to motivate visitors to register?

    ❏ Offer a premium (describe below):

    ❏ Provide opportunities to save money (describe below):

    ❏ Answer questions or search for specific products (describe below):

    ❏ Allow access to enhanced content (describe below):

    ❏ Award a prize (describe below):

4. How can you acknowledge and/or reward visitors who register?

5. What types of promotions and last-minute specials can you promote via e-mail?

6. What are some of the other ways you can use the e-mail and postal service addresses of Web site visitors who register?

    1.

    2.

    3.

    4.

7. How can visitors customize the content of your Web site to suit their interests and needs?

    ❏ Searchable databases

    ❏ Product previews

    ❏ Product availability

    ❏ Financing information

    ❏ Newsgroup (describe below):

    ❏ Audio, video, or virtual reality (describe below):

8. What assistance or service can you offer Web site visitors by the use of return e-mail or the postal service?

9. How close to actual sales do you want your Web site to take visitors?

10. Does my firm's product or service lend itself to sales over the Internet?

    ❏ Yes (describe below):

    ❏ No. If "no," what can you do to make your products or services more attractive to Web buyers?

Chapter 10

Producing Your Web Site

Working as Efficiently as Possible

Now that the planning, content, and design phases of your Web site have been taken care of, it's time to address the actual production of your Web site. Production involves management issues as much as it involves hardware and software. After all, the hardware and software don't operate themselves…someone has to take your vision—your Web site's goals and plans—and actualize them.

Whether you or someone else produces your Web site, its success has less to do with software mastery than being provided time to do the job right. Web production is extremely time-consuming and tedious. The smallest details are very important. It's important that adequate time be provided for producing and fine-tuning your Web site before it's finally posted.

Not only is it important that you work as efficiently as possible, but your Web site has to operate as efficiently as possible. It's important that your Web site be easily accessible to the greatest possible number of visitors.

WHO SHOULD DO THE WORK?

Let's start by looking at one of the fundamental questions of Web page production: "Who's going to do the work?" This is one of the biggest Web decisions you face. Let's analyze some of your options:

◆ You can do the work yourself.

◆ You can assign Web production duties to someone on your staff.

◆ You can hire an outside *firm*.

Each option offers its own combination of advantages and disadvantages. Let's look at these in detail.

Doing the Work Yourself

Producing your own Web site offers several advantages. First, there are no costs involved—whether outside costs or the hidden costs of taking some of your staff's time away from their regular activities—especially if their activities produce immediate revenue, that is, sales. Second, you don't have to communicate your goals or your vision of your Web site to someone else. You can simply do it without trying to explain what you want to accomplish or how you feel the Web site should look when completed. You have the information and the vision, so there's less to go wrong from the communications point of view.

The disadvantages of doing it yourself is that it take time and there may be a strong learning curve involved if this is your first Web site. Questions you have to ask yourself include:

◆ Do I really have time to master another computer skill in addition to keeping up with my day-to-day management tasks?

◆ Will I be able to produce my Web site during the day, while I'm fresh, or will I have to do the work weekends and in the evenings—at the expense of my family life?

◆ Do I have the tools necessary to do the job? Or, am I going to have to invest in additional hardware and software?

◆ How much of a software learning curve do I have to master before I can do a credible job producing my Web site? Do I have the time to master yet another computer program?

What these questions boil down to is the reality that there are only so many hours a day to work, and—in many cases—other marketing and management tasks are likely to go unfulfilled, or your personal and family life may be compromised, if you decide to do all of the work yourself. This may, or may not, be acceptable, but you should at least be aware of the trade-offs that Web site production involves.

Delegating Web Production to your Staff

Another option includes delegating Web production to an employee. This option offers many of the same advantages and disadvantages as already examined. No additional obvious costs are involved, yet the hidden costs can quickly mount up.

Although some of your staff members may volunteer to produce your Web site, the questions remain:

◆ When will they do the work?

◆ Do they have the skills necessary to do the work?

◆ Are the necessary tools on hand or do I have to make a sizeable investment, that is, the same question you have to answer before deciding to do the work yourself.

Negatives include the twin *c*'s of control and consistency.

You may lose a lot of control by having an employee produce your Web site, especially if they are doing it in addition to their full-time responsibilities. If they're working for free—especially if they're producing your Web site on their own time—they'll likely be producing the Web site to satisfy their own creative desires (while enhancing their portfolio and resume). As a result, the resulting Web site may not reflect your goals and vision as much as it reflects their goals and vision.

Second, since there are only just so many hours a day for your employees or for you, how much revenue will you be losing if they work on your Web site instead of prospecting for new business or satisfying existing customers? If they work at night, will their performance during the day suffer—either because of burn-out or stress.

Most important, can they commit to consistency? A Web site, as discussed further in the Maintenance chapter, should not be considered a one-time event. Rather, a Web site should reflect an ongoing commitment. Your Web site should be frequently updated. In addition, there will likely be numerous follow-up duties that the Web site requires. Can a single employee commit to keeping up with their regular tasks—the job you hired them to do—as well as undertake a whole new set of responsibilities?

Finally, assuming that an existing employee successfully produces, follows up, and maintains your Web site, will they expect additional compensation? And, if not, after their urge for creativity has abated, will they be less enthusiastic about performing Web follow-up and maintenance chores?

Working With Outsiders

What should you do if an analysis of your time and your staff's time indicates that you don't have the time to devote to creating and maintaining your Web site? The answer involves determining what resources are available in your area. In most cases, your resources include:

◆ *Freelance Web designers.* These range from part-timers augmenting their full-time income by working evenings and weekends to professional designers who have left agency positions to work on their own.

◆ *Graphic design studios.* In most cases, these firms have migrated to Web site creation from a background in print production. Design studios differ from advertising agencies in that they concentrate on design and production and rarely get involved in placing advertisements.

◆ Many *Internet Service Providers* offer Web design and production services in addition to renting time on their computers to post your Web site. Sometimes these services are promised for free, or at reduced cost, as a service to clients whose Web sites they post.

One of the problems you'll want to guard against is subsidizing someone else's learning curve. Many freelancers and design firms have far more experience in *print* design and production than they do in Web design and production. Make sure that the firm you decide to work with actually has the Web experience they claim. You don't want to lose revenue while the people you are paying are learning their trade.

Be sure to speak to current and past clients of the freelancers or design firms you're interested in. Asking for the names of previous clients is as important as asking for the names of current clients, because you'll want to find out why the clients left the designer or firm.

Request the Web addresses of at least ten—preferably more—Web sites they have created. Spend quite a bit of time on the Web sites, analyzing them not only from the point of view of content and design but also from the point of view of speed. Slow-loading Web sites are a certain giveaway that the firm puts special effects (fancy Java applets, for example) before content!

Most important, try to ascertain the amount of input you'll have in the design of your Web site. Try to find out how willing the design firm is to listen and implement your ideas and suggestions—or massage them into workable alternatives. Be wary if the designer's attitude reflects a "we know all" prima-donna approach. And, whenever possible, try to visit the office or production facilities. One of the last things you'll want to do, if you value your hard-earned dollars, is to spend too much subsidizing the overhead of an overly image-conscious agency.

Finally, find out who owns the Web site after it is posted. Specifically, will you be able to take over its maintenance after it's been posted or hire a less expensive freelancer to keep it up to date?

These are all questions best answered before you sign on the dotted line!

HIRING THE RIGHT PEOPLE

As when purchasing services from any outside firm, there are several questions you'll want to answer up front in order to ascertain the competence and compatibility of the various outside vendors in your area before you commit to hiring anyone.

Use the Outside Vendor Worksheet as a guide to choosing the right production staff. Use your office photocopier to make as many copies as necessary and take them with you as you interview the various freelancers, graphic design firms, and Internet Service Providers in your area.

OUTSIDE VENDOR WORKSHEET

Name of firm _____

Contact _____ Phone _____

E-mail _____ URL _____

Date visited/interviewed _____

1. How much experience have they had in Web design and production?

    When did they post their first Web site?

2. What do you think of the Web sites they've created for others:

    A. _____   (comment below)

B. _____

C. _____

D. _____

E. _____

F. _____

G. _____

H. _____

3. Who are some previous clients we can contact?

    Name _____   Phone: _____

    Name _____   Phone: _____

    Name _____   Phone: _____

    Name _____   Phone: _____

    Name _____   Phone: _____

4. What is the price range of Web sites they have created?

5. How do they charge?

   ❏ By the hour? (If so, how much?)

   ❏ By the page? (If so, how much?)

   ❏ By the project? (If so, how much?)

   ❏ Other–describe below. (If so, how much?)

6. Did you meet the people who will actually do the work?

7. How much will it cost to create the Web site you have in mind?

8. How long will it take to create your Web site?

9. How much will it cost to revise, i.e. update, the Web site?

10. How long will revisions take from the time information is provided until the changes are posted?

11. How much input can we have in our Web site's design and content?

12. Can we take over the maintenance of the Web site after it has become established?

Of the questions, Question 6 is one of the most important. Make sure that you meet and feel comfortable that you can work with the individuals who'll actually do the work on your site. Often, agency principals get the business, then turn you over to overworked staff members who aren't as interested in your satisfaction as is the agency sales staff.

Question 12 can also be a bit tricky. Like photographers who claim ownership of the negatives of the photographs they have created, some designers claim permanent ownership of their Web sites and do not look favorably on others maintaining Web sites they have created. Be sure to specify in writing your right to take over and maintain your Web site at your discretion.

Templates and Frameworks

One option you might consider is locating a midpoint between doing the work yourself and hiring an outside individual or firm to do the entire job themselves. Let's face it: You go to a dentist to take care of an occasional filling you or a member of your family might need, rather than investing in eight years of dental school yourself. Similarly, you probably take your car to have its oil changed, rather than doing the job yourself—even though you probably could do it if you wanted to.

Similarly, you might want to hire a specialist to create the design-intensive initial stages of your Web site and have them provide you with templates for you to complete on your own.

These templates should contain the crucial elements of Web page design:

◆ A carefully chosen *color palette* that defines foreground and background colors plus internal (that is, body copy) text links

◆ *Key illustrations*, such as an image map

◆ *Navigation icons*, specifying size, shape, color, and location

◆ *Typeface styles* defining headline, title, subhead, body copy, and caption typeface, type size, type style, and colors

◆ *Page layouts* which define the placement of margins, text, and visuals

Your job, after receiving the empty templates will simply be to insert the content you write into the appropriate locations of each page and post to the Web site. This alternative offers a lot of advantages:

◆ You receive a first-class job without investing hours in mastering basic design issues like color, type, and layout.

◆ You avoid the learning curve of mastering drawing and image-manipulation software programs like Adobe Photoshop and Illustrator.

◆ You eliminate routine production costs, as opposed to one-time creative costs, by receiving a framework for placing the text and graphic elements yourself.

◆ By working just on selected aspects of your Web site, you gain the experience you need to take a more advanced role in maintaining your Web site yourself at a later date.

For many firms, professionally designed templates offer the best of all possible worlds. You save money and pick up important skills while getting online as quickly as possible. You invest your money at the point of highest possible return, that is, in quality up-front design, yet save money (and gain an important sense of satisfaction) by doing the routine production work yourself.

WHAT HARDWARE AND SOFTWARE DO YOU NEED?

You can create Web sites with a wide variety of software programs. You may already own the hardware and software necessary to produce your Web site. In this case, you'll simply have to learn how to use it differently.

Software

Since HTML consists of tags placed before and after text elements, production can be very simple. Many successful Web sites have been created with the text editors included with the Apple Macintosh or the Microsoft Windows operating system. (The Windows 95 text editor is called the Notepad; the Apple Macintosh equivalent is called Note Pad.) Although text editors can work, they're a bit less than elegant and you will probably choose an option that offers more flexibility and ease of use. One major frustration is that these operating system text editors do not include a spell checker, which puts the onus on you to make sure every word is correctly spelled!

If you own recent copies of the office suites published by Corel, Lotus, and Microsoft, you can use the word-processing programs that come with these programs to create your Web sites. These programs make it easy to create tables to precisely position text, add background colors, and add hyperlinks permitting Web site visitors to move from location to location within a single page as well as a Web site—or link to other Web sites. The built-in spell checkers found in these word-processor programs further simplify your work. In addition, most word processors contain templates and suggested color schemes for you to choose from. Moreover, when you select a Web page template, you can apply style tags by highlighting the text and directly applying a style, rather than going to the trouble of applying tags to the various levels of headings and body copy in your Web site.

Dedicated Web page authoring programs like Adobe PageMill, Microsoft Publisher, FrontPage, and others make your job even easier. Depending on the program you select, these offer advantages like:

◆ *More template designs* allowing you to choose the image most appropriate for your Web site

◆ *More clip-art options*, including animation effects like letters being placed into envelopes to indicate e-mail links

◆ *Automatic verification of links*, to avoid orphaned pages, that is, pages that do not contain hyperlinks leading to them

◆ A *visual display of your Web site's structure* so you can visually verify its layout

◆ *Automatic conversion of imported graphics* to the proper file format, that is, JPEG or GIF

- *Drag-and-drop* convenience: Most Web authoring programs permit you to simply place text and visual elements on the page and the program will create the tables in the background that lock the elements into position.

- *To-do lists*: Programs like FrontPage 97 and 98 make it easy to keep track of the tasks you have to perform while creating your Web site. Instead of jotting tasks down on an easily lost, and often difficult to read, scrap of paper, you can monitor and review your progress as you produce your Web site.

- *Downloading time.* Many Web authoring programs contain a feature which will estimate the time it will take to download large images and complicated pages at various modem connection speeds.

- *Associated programs.* Many Web authoring programs, like FrontPage 98, come with image enhancement programs which allow you to manipulate scanned photographs and create transparent backgrounds (so a circle, for example, doesn't appear against a square background). These programs can save you the cost of purchasing additional software that you might not already own (see below).

Before finalizing your choice of a Web site authoring program, you'll probably want to try out several designed for the computer platform you'll be working on. Programs differ in the ease and obviousness with which they perform these, and other, procedures.

If you are coming to Web design and production from a print background, you may or may not want to continue working with your existing page layout software program. You may find that your page layout program is better optimized for print—it offers more typographic refinements than needed for Web use and is less smoothly integrated with important Web commands.

One of the areas where you may want to embark into new territory is to invest in more powerful illustration and image manipulation programs. Programs like Adobe Photoshop and Corel PhotoPaint, for example, make it easy to manipulate scanned images so that you can eliminate distracting backgrounds. You can also correct the color balance of scanned images as well as experiment with various typographic effects, such as layering text over photographs.

Hardware

Assuming that you already have a modem connected to, or installed in, your computer, there probably isn't anything else required for Web use. The faster your modem, the faster you'll be able to post your Web site and improve it as you fine-tune and maintain it.

Assuming that you have a reasonably fast computer, that is, a 486-66 at minimum or any Pentium, you're more likely to have to add a second phone line to your home or office than invest in other hardware. Because you're likely to be online more than previously, while updating your Web site and responding to e-mail from visitors, you may find that you are tie up single phone line offices more than is acceptable, disrupting revenue-producing phone calls and faxes from customers and prospects.

KEEPING FILE SIZES SMALL

While producing your Web site, it's important that you keep file sizes as small as possible. Remember: Each graphic element on your Web site is a separate graphic file that is downloaded as needed. The smaller the file size, the faster the file will be downloaded. Here are some of the techniques to bear in mind when including graphics—whether the graphic files contain text, illustrations, or scanned images—in your Web site:

◆ *Import images at the size they'll be used in,* rather than resizing an image in your word processing or Web authoring program. Remember that images that are resized in a word processing or Web authoring program are stored in the program at their original size, even though they appear smaller when viewed. File size is greatly reduced when the images are resized before placing in the program.

◆ *Crop images as tightly as possible* to avoid having distracting borders before resizing and placing on your Web page. Why pay the downloading time penalty for information which you don't want your Web site visitor to see?

◆ *Silhouette images.* Likewise, you can reduce the file size of scanned images by eliminate distracting backgrounds—like skies—unless they're important to the story of the photograph. This technique can greatly reduce file size.

◆ *Finally, reduce the bit depth—or amount of color information—*contained in scanned images. This can greatly reduce file size without affecting image quality. This is often a trial-and-error procedure, that is, you reduce the color depth until the loss of color quality becomes noticeable. Note that complicated photographs containing a lot of colors, like a city skyline, are likely to be more forgiving of reduced color depth than photographs containing large areas of a few colors, that is, an automobile against a home painted a single color.

These techniques can be used in combination with each other, of course. Don't just resize an illustration before placing it on your Web site; manipulate it by resizing it, silhouetting the important parts, and reducing its color depth (see Figures 10.1 and 10.2).

Remember, just as it's acceptable to hire an outside design or design firm to create templates for your Web site, you can also shop for a-la-carte illustration and image manipulation services.

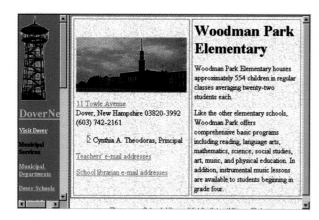

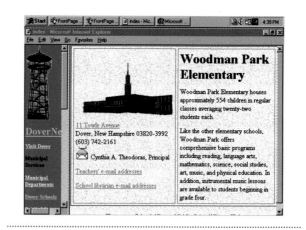

Figure 10.1 Since the emphasis in this photograph is on the building, the sky doesn't really communicate much information even though it contains a lot of color information which inflates the file size and increases download time.

Figure 10.2 Silhouetting the school and eliminating the sky focuses the Web site visitor's attention on the school and also reduces file size, which decreases download time.

If you're only going to be adding one or two new images a month, for example, it doesn't make sense to purchase a scanner and image manipulating software—plus go through the learning curve of mastering it. It might make far more sense for you to concentrate on creating the content—concepts, information, and words—of your Web site and hire others to perform the graphics-intensive aspects of Web site production. After all, lots of people know Adobe Photoshop inside and out, but nobody knows your business like you do! Strive for a division of labor that allows you and the members of your local design community to work at an efficient division of labor, so that you each work at the highest and most efficient level.

Lots of people know advanced software programs like Adobe Photoshop inside and out, but nobody knows your business like you do!

FINE-TUNING THE DETAILS

Web site production is a matter of detail. Small details can make a major difference. When allocating time for Web site, be sure you leave time to fine-tune production details that aren't obvious enough to be design decisions the first time around. Many of the details that spell the difference between good and great only become visible when viewed on the monitor of your computer using your Web browser. These changes are often not obvious when seen using your Web authoring software.

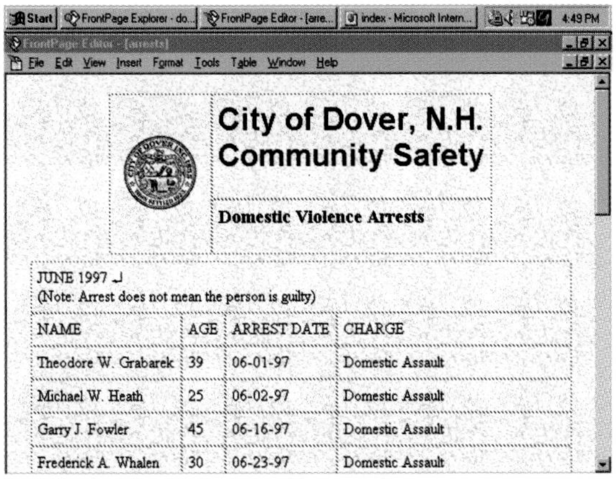

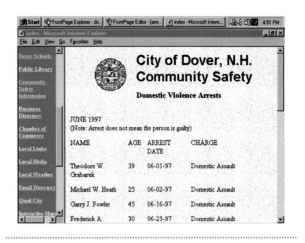

Figure 10.3 Seen in the context of the Web authoring software's table gridlines, the size of the Dover seal appears appropriately sized.

Figure 10.4 However, when viewed using the Web browser—the view your Web site visitor will see—the Dover seal appears dwarfed by the adjacent words.

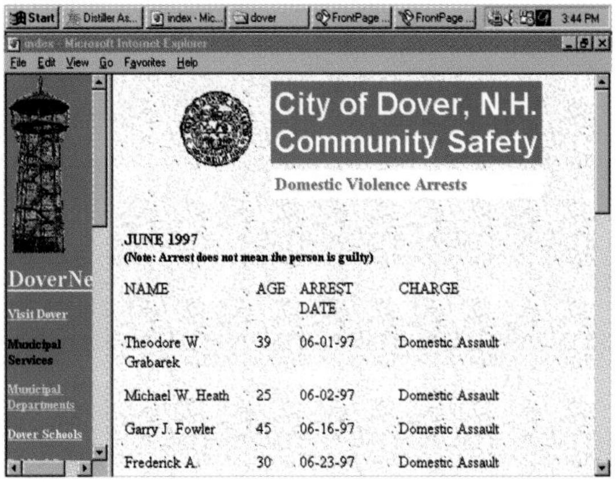

Figure 10.5 Using a colored background to highlight the headline and aligning the seal with the top and bottom of the headline creates a sense of proportionality.

For example, consider the on-the-fly improvements made to the Dover, N.H. Web page. In the first example, the Dover city seal (not an animal) was sized to fit in a cell equal in height to the headline of the table. Although appropriate when viewed in the context of the cells of the table, the seal looked too small when viewed without the table gridlines providing a visual frame of reference. The seal looks much better enlarged to the point where its size equals the height and depth of the adjacent words (see Figures 10.3 through 10.5).

Organizing the Rows in Tables

Another example of table fine-tuning involves adding lightly colored backgrounds to guide the reader's eyes across the table. Having such lightly colored backgrounds, readers can focus their attention on one row at a time (see Figures 10.6 through 10.8).

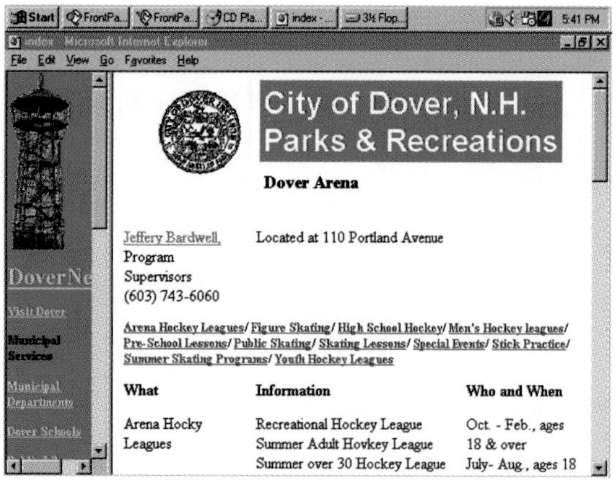

Figure 10.6 Without colored backgrounds, it is difficult for readers to keep track of information in the various columns of a table.

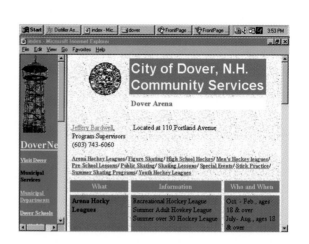

Figure 10.7 Adding a full-strength background actually makes the text harder to read instead of easier to read, defeating the goals of easier reading and enhanced legibility.

Figure 10.8 Reducing the saturation of the background color organizes the table and restores text legibility.

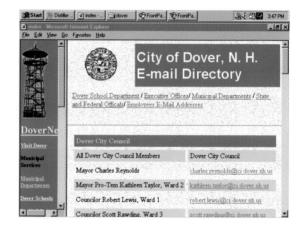

Figure 10.9 The first table separated the individuals' names from their e-mail addresses.

Avoiding Accidental Redundancy

A final example of fine-tuning at the production stage is to unintentional repetition.

The first time the table was created containing names and e-mail links, the e-mail links were isolated in a column by themselves (see Figure 10.9). Upon further reflection, the result of a good night's sleep, it became obvious that there was really no need to provide the e-mail address since Web visitors could send e-mail to the individual by simply clicking on the name! This simplified the table and created more space to surround the table, drawing attention to its contents (see Figures 10.10 and 10.11).

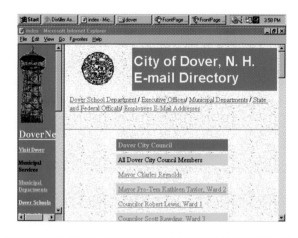

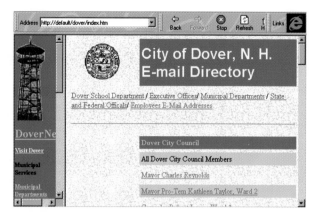

Figure 10.10 The revised table creates an e-mail link out of the individual's name, eliminating the need for a separate, redundant, column. However, the lack of alignment with the heading presents a disorganized image.

Figure 10.11 Simply aligning the table with the heading, however, projects a far more orderly image.

The moral is clear. *Never post a Web site the day you create it!* Always let some time elapse between the time you create it and the time it goes live. Review your work and try to get a good night's sleep. Inevitably, you'll awaken and view your Web site from a fresh perspective, noticing slight refinements that—together—can add up to major improvements in the impression your Web site will make on customers and prospects. Once you train yourself to look for them, you'll probably notice many cases where unintentional redundancy has crept in.

PUTTING KNOWLEDGE TO WORK

Use the Production Worksheet on the next page to determine the individual or individuals best suited to creating and maintaining your Web site.

PRODUCTION WORKSHEET

1. How much time do you have available to create and maintain your Web site?

   _____ hours during the day

   _____ hours evenings and weekends

2. Do you have experience creating ads, brochures, and newsletters using your computer?

   ❏ No ❏ Yes (if so, describe)

3. Does anyone on your staff already possess computerized page layout skills?

   ❏ No ❏ Yes (if so, describe)

4. How much time can they free up to create, produce, and maintain your Web site?

   _____ hours during the day

   _____ hours evenings and weekends

5. Are they likely to expect added reimbursement for creating and maintaining your Web site after the initial thrill has worn off?

   ❏ No ❏ Yes/maybe (If yes or maybe, how much?)

   After developing their Web design skills, what is the possibility they will move on, leaving you without anyone to maintain your Web site?

6. Do you currently own any software programs suitable for creating Web sites?

   ❏ Yes (If yes, which ones? Describe below)

   ❏ No (If no, how much will it cost to acquire them?)

7. Do you own the right hardware?

   ❑ Yes ❑ No   Computer with a fast modem

   ❑ Yes ❑ No   Image scanner

   ❑ Yes ❑ No   Image enhancement software

8. How many hours a day is your computer used for non–Web associated functions, i.e., word processing, accounting, inventory, payroll, etc.

   _____ hours a day

   _____ hours a night

9. Is the computer you intend to use for Web site creation located at home or in your place of business?

   ❑ Home   ❑ Office   ❑ Home office

10. Have you researched freelance design resources in your area?

    ❑ No ❑ Yes (if yes, what is their range of prices?)

    Who seems to do the best work in your area?

    Have you contacted any of their past and present clients? If so, who? What did they have to say about co-operation and pricing? How were unexpected problems resolved?

11. Have you researched graphic design firms in your area?

    ❑ No ❑ Yes (if yes, what is their range of prices?):

    Who seems to do the best work?

    Have you contacted any of their past and present clients? If so, who? What did they have to say about co-operation and pricing? How were unexpected problems resolved?

12. How much will your Internet Service Provider charge to design and maintain your Web site?

    _____ to _____

    Are you satisfied with the quality of their work?

    Have you contacted any of their past and present clients? If so, who? What did they have to say about co-operation and pricing? How were unexpected problems resolved?

    How much will they charge to create and maintain your Web site?

13. How willing are the various freelance designers and design firms to create a template for your Web site and help get you started?

    Firms willing to help:

    a)

    Initial charge: $

    Follow-up consultation (per hour): $

    Scanning and image-enhancement (per image): $

    b)

    Initial charge: $

    Follow-up consultation (per hour): $

    Scanning and image-enhancement (per image): $

    c)

    Initial charge: $

    Follow-up consultation (per hour): $

Scanning and image-enhancement (per image): $

d)

Initial charge: $

Follow-up consultation (per hour): $

Scanning and image-enhancement (per image): $

e)

Initial charge: $

Follow-up consultation (per hour): $

Scanning and image-enhancement (per image) $

Firms *not* willing to help on an a-la-carte basis:

a)

b)

c)

d)

e)

14. Approximately how many scanned images will be included in your first Web site?

15. Approximately how many additional scanned images will be added each month?

16. What determines whether a change is "minor"?

17. Who will pay for minor revisions to the first draft of your Web site, i.e., fine-tuning tables, minor resizing of illustrations, and minor text edits?

   ❏ You pay for all revisions

   ❏ You pay for revisions beyond a certain point or number (describe below):

18. Will you be provided with a colored printouts of your Web site before it is published on the Web?

   ❏ Yes ❏ No

19. Will the design firm charge extra to post your Web site after creating it?
   ❏ Yes ❏ No

20. Did you, or the individuals producing your Web site, do everything possible to reduce file sizes so that your Web site is as fast-loading as possible?

   ❏ Yes ❏ No

21. Did you allow enough time to elapse between production and posting so that you can view your Web site from a fresh perspective?

   ❏ Yes ❏ No

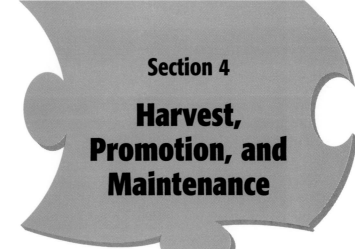

Section 4

Harvest, Promotion, and Maintenance

Chapter 11

Follow-Up and Closure

Follow-up

Converting Interest into Action

An unsupported Web site does more harm than good. When visitors to your Web site register or contact you via e-mail, they expect an immediate response. If this response isn't immediately forthcoming, they are likely to feel short-changed. They'll definitely remove you as a possible source of the product or service they're interested in. Worse, they're likely to tell their friends and associates about your failure to perform. They might even post your Web site's nonperformance on a newsgroup or gripe about it in print.

Follow-up and closure illustrate how important it is to integrate your Web site into your firm's ongoing sales and marketing activities. Follow-up and closure may not be creative functions, in the sense of choosing typefaces or making color choices, yet solving follow-up and closure issues may require just as much planning and monitoring. Indeed, you may have to be even more creative, in problem solving in order to identify, delegate, and monitor follow-up and closure activities.

The amount of follow-up and closure that your Web site requires are likely to be closely related to the stage in the buying cycle where most of your Web site visitors are presently located. More and more follow-up and closure activities are likely to be needed as you target your Web site to appeal to visitors as they approach the purchase, augmentation, and replacement stages of the buying cycle. Your ability to delegate follow-up responsibilities may ultimately become as important to the success of your Web site as your ability to write compelling paragraphs or choose appropriate typefaces and colors.

The following are some of the management issues you should be prepared to address before your new, or improved, Web site goes online.

WHAT TYPES OF WORK HAVE TO BE DONE?

The first step in integrating your Web site into your firm's ongoing sales and marketing activities is to identify the various tasks that must be accomplished.

Creating Staff Awareness

Many Web sites fail to perform to their potential because they are not supported by everyone that a prospect may encounter via e-mail or on the phone. The worst thing that can happen is for a prospect to call with a comment or to request information based on information read at a firm's Web site and receive a "Where did you read that?" response.

Accordingly, your first task is to ensure that everyone on your staff views your Web site at least once a month—more frequently if your Web site is updated more frequently—to review its content and become familiar with the information provided. An added benefit of this scrutiny is that, by encouraging your staff to access your Web site, you'll be made aware (sometimes painfully!) of typographical errors. More important, as your sales staff familiarizes itself with your Web site, they'll probably help you improve it by providing suggestions for new content.

Answering Questions via E-mail

You may be surprised by how much e-mail your Web site generates. Plus, the Web is an extremely fast-moving environment. It exists to provide immediate gratification. The Web and e-mail have trained your market to expect immediate results. Your Web site is likely to generate disappointing results if visitors who submit questions or comments via e-mail have to wait a week or two to receive a response. Overnight or same day responses will pay off in enhanced credibility for your firm and a higher level of enthusiasm by Web site visitors—which will result in faster progress along the buying cycle.

Thus, *someone* has to be made responsible for responding to questions submitted by e-mail. And, in order to succeed, on-the-job time has to be made available for the individual to perform this task. It's neither fair nor reasonable to expect this important function to be done from home during evenings or on weekends. As a business owner, *you* enjoy the right to work evenings and weekends without additional compensation, but you shouldn't expect the same devotion from your employees.

Accordingly, when you delegate this important task, make sure that you provide time for your employee to do the work, make sure they have the knowledge and resources necessary to do it, and reward them for their efforts.

Responding to Requests for Brochures and Further Information

Similarly, someone should be ready when requests for brochures and additional information begin to roll in. Requests for information should be treated with just as much respect as individuals receive when you meet them face-to-face or they visit your place of business.

Thus, once again, delegation is the order of the day. One person should be given responsibility for fulfilling requests for brochures and further information. This individual's job description should emphasize that their role is to advance the buyer along the buying cycle from the desire and comparison stages to the buying, augmentation, and replacement stages.

Never place requested information by itself in an envelope and drop it in the mail. This creates the image of a cold, uncaring, impersonal firm. Instead, include a personalized covering letter signed by an individual (ideally, the same individual who will later follow up by telephone— see below).

Telephone Follow-Up

A follow-up telephone call is appropriate a short time after a question has been answered or additional information sent. This action personalizes your Web site and reinforces the relationship by permitting your visitor to associate a name and a voice with your Web site.

Whenever possible, the same person who answered the original e-mail or sent the requested materials should make follow-up phone calls. This creates continuity and encourages enthusiasm. Delegating follow-up responsibilities to one person encourages that individual to take more pride in the job. It also results in a closer relationship between the prospect and the firm.

Compiling Mailing Lists

As your Web site begins to generate more and more registration forms, something has to be done with the names and addresses. The names and addresses that are received have to be massaged into a useful form. This involves several tedious but accuracy-based tasks:

◆ *Start by assembling "broadcast" e-mail lists* so you can easily prepare one message and send it to everyone who has registered or submitted a question.

◆ *Assemble individualized e-mail address lists* so you can easily send personalized e-mail to individuals on the basis of their type of request or position in the buying cycle.

◆ *Create postal mailing address lists.* These will allow you to send postcards or catalogs via the postal service to prospects and buyers. If your business has been in business a long time, it's extremely important that you merge, or integrate, your existing mailing list with the mailing lists generated from Web activity. The last thing in the world you want to happen is to have duplicate (or triplicate) entries caused by Web-based requests for information or sales, coming from the same individuals whom you have dealt with in the past or who also visit your place of business.

As you can see from the above, what seems simple at first glance can quickly become complicated. Someone with a good eye for detail should be in charge of maintaining your electronic and traditional mailing lists. Because of the detail-orientation of this task, you might want to hire a part-time freelancer to concentrate on just this activity, ensuring that it gets done no matter how busy your firm gets.

Closing Sales

More and more work will be required as your Web site advances prospects from the awareness and desire stages to the purchase stage of the buying cycle. Sales fulfillment will begin to occupy more and more time after visitors to your Web site start buying copies your book, enrolling in your seminar, or purchasing whatever product or service your Web site was designed to sell.

Web sales may force you to change some of your business habits, for example:

◆ You may find that you have to acquire the ability to process credit card orders, which, for many small businesses, is not as easy as it sounds. Credit card sales may become more and more important as the Web expands your market beyond your traditional area.

◆ You may need to install a toll-free 800 telephone line so that individuals who don't' trust the Web will be able to call and give you their credit card information verbally. Or, someone at your firm may have to call the prospect and seek this information.

◆ Indeed, telephone sales may become more important, as often a follow-up phone call will be enough to push a prospect over the edge and encourage them to actualize their desire by purchasing your product.

Regardless of the form that order fulfillment takes, someone is going to have to do the work, and that someone should do the work enthusiastically instead of viewing it as extra work that has been placed on their plate.

Fulfillment can be extremely demanding if your Web activities expand your market beyond your firm's original geographic territory. Chances are, your first order may come from outside your country, requiring you to quickly familiarize yourself with international currency exchange rates and international shipping options and import/export regulations. Indeed, after your Web site has been active for a while, as part of your maintenance chores, you may have to revise your registration premiums and ordering instructions to accommodate the Web's international flavor.

Monitoring Job Performance

Delegation is one-half of success; the other half is monitoring and evaluating. It's not enough to delegate responsibilities to someone; it's equally important that their performance be carefully monitored to ensure that Web site visitors are receiving the same caring treatment that in-person prospects and customers receive.

Accordingly, your management tasks are likely to increase as you delegate Web tasks to others. It is absolutely imperative that Web site visitors receive prompt and courteous service! The whole point of your Web site is to promote your firm and to sell products. Your entire Web effort is in jeopardy if your firm doesn't promptly answer e-mail and fulfill information requests and sales.

TRACKING RESPONSES

Tracking responses to your Web site is as important as fulfilling information requests and filling orders. Your Web site should be a source of more than just revenue; it should be a source of information about your market and what attracts your market. The information you gather by tracking responses will permit you to identify those Web site addresses where promotional efforts pay off and those that can be abandoned because they fail to produce results.

Ideally, because of the importance of tracking the sources of registrations, information requests, and sales, these activities should be separated from information and order fulfillment.

The most important question you should track is "What brought visitors to this Web site?" By analyzing registration forms and providing scripts for telephone follow-up, you should be able to determine which of your Web promotional efforts are paying off the best in terms of increased Web traffic. Did most of your visitors locate your Web site by using a search engine, or was your own advertising more effective? Or did they reach your Web site by being linked from another site? These are questions of first-rank importance.

Conversion into Sales?

It's important to remember that Web traffic isn't as important as sales. Sales pay the rent and help you meet your payroll. Thus, it's important to analyze how, and what percentage of registrants and information-seekers eventually purchase from you. *Quality* of response, *not quantity* of response, is what counts. Here are some of the questions to ask as you track this valuable information:

◆ *Which promotional efforts lead to the most registrations?* By tracking the transition of registrants as they progress along the buying cycle, you should be able to identify which promotional efforts result in the most registrations.

◆ *Which promotional efforts lead to the most sales?* What percentage of visitors who ask questions or request further information turn into buyers? Are these high-profit or low-profit sales?

◆ *Is your Web site actually generating new customers and prospects?* By cross-checking the names and addresses of registrations and Web-generated sales with your existing mailing list, you should be able to determine whether or not your Web site is succeeding in attracting new business.

DELEGATION

Having identified the tasks to be performed, created a method to monitor the execution of these tasks, and evaluated the results your firm enjoys, it's time to get down to specifics and ask the who, what, when, and where questions. The more specifically you answer these questions, the more easily you can implement your follow-up and closure program.

◆ *Who will do the work?* Which employees are best suited to follow-up and closure? What information and skills are required?

◆ *What are the specific tasks to be done?* The more specific you can be, the more likely you are to achieve the results you desire. What information should be communicated? What should be included in a mailing envelope? What questions should be asked on follow-up telephone calls?

◆ *When will your staff get the time?* Time must be set aside to respond to Web questions and requests for further information without interfering with your present business, ignoring your present customers.

◆ *How quickly should your staff respond?* It is important to put a time limit on responses, so that they don't pile up and get ignored in the rush of everyday business.

◆ *When will the work be done?* At home or after hours? E-mail can be answered anytime, from anywhere, as long as all responses go to the firm's e-mail address. By providing "flex time" to allow employees to work at home answering e-mail, you may convert an extra chore into a welcome opportunity for change. When work is done at home, however, it's doubly important that the names and addresses of Web site visitors be entered into the proper databases at work.

◆ *How will your staff be rewarded?* Employees are unlikely to appreciate extra work without extra reward. Is there some way you can reward employees for generating additional sales from your Web site?

◆ *Who will monitor employee efforts?* It's important that standards be set and maintained. You'll want to make sure that e-mail and requests for information are consistently fulfilled within the time frame you have determined.

A successful Web site is as much a management creation as a creative endeavor. The more successful your Web site becomes, the more work it is likely to generate. You can ensure the success of your Web site efforts by being prepared to handle this work *before* your Web site attracts more prospects and buyers than your firm can handle.

PUTTING KNOWLEDGE INTO ACTION

Use the Follow-up and Closure Worksheet on the next page to get an idea of the amount of sales and marketing support your Web site is likely to require as it becomes increasingly successful.

FOLLOW-UP AND CLOSURE WORKSHEET

1. How are you going to keep your staff aware of the contents of your Web site?

2. Who will respond to questions submitted by visitors?

3. Who will respond to requests for literature and additional information?

4. How quickly will questions and requests for additional information be fulfilled?

5. Who will make sure that questions and requests for information are quickly acted upon?

6. Who will compile the information provided on registration forms?

7. Who will follow up on fulfilled information requests, attempting to convert interest into a sale?

8. Who will maintain your firm's mailing list and integrate Web-sourced names and addresses with names and addressed compiled from other sources?

9. Who will be in charge of fulfilling orders that originate on your Web site?

10. Who will monitor the fulfillment of orders originating at your Web site?

11. Where will you and your staff find the time to follow up information requests and close Web-based sales?

12. How will you compensate your staff for their added responsibilities?

Chapter 12

Promoting Your Web Site

Attracting New Visitors to Your Web Site

Suppose you gave a party, but forgot to send invitations? No matter how good the appetizers were, there would likely be quite a few left over at the end of the night. The same principle is true of your Web site.

Your work has just begun when you complete your Web site! After posting your Web site and delegating follow-up and closure to the appropriate individuals—or scheduling time for follow-up and closure yourself—you have to promote your Web site and make sure that visitors show up.

No matter how appropriate your Web site's content or design, its success depends on your ability to attract an ever-growing number of first-time visitors. Following are some of the ways you can promote your Web site, *internally* in your place of business and through your own advertising as well as *externally* by getting others to recommend your site or by encouraging them to link your site to theirs.

INTERNALLY PROMOTING YOUR WEB SITE

The easiest and least expensive way you can promote your Web site is by making sure that its address appears everywhere possible. Everywhere possible includes all your print communications, including:

◆ Business cards

◆ Bookmarks and other premiums (pens, mouse pads, coffee mugs, etc.)

◆ Letterheads, envelopes, mailing labels, and faxes

◆ Brochures and catalogs

◆ Newsletters

◆ Product packaging

◆ Invoices and instructions

On a temporary basis, you can add your Web site address to some printed materials on an as-needed basis, such as including your Web site's address in the header or footer of your letterheads. As you prepare newsletters and reorder business cards, packaging and invoices, however, your Web site address should be a permanent part of the design.

E-mail Signature

One of the easiest and least expensive ways you can promote your Web site address is to include it as part of your e-mail signature. The signature is the footer, or closing information, added to each of your e-mail messages. Typically, signatures contain your name, your firm's name, and a description of your firm's service or philosophy accompanied by your phone number and e-mail address. You should also always include your Web site address.

Although you may find that much of your e-mail originates from your Web site, you'll want to promote your Web site address to everyone you send e-mail to. Adding your Web site address to your e-mail signature reinforces your Web address to those who already know it and also ensures that it will appear in postings to newsgroups (described later in the chapter).

Handouts and Inserts

You might even consider creating a small, inexpensive, "Web tips" mailer or handout—containing a list of Web sites likely to be of interest to your market—that you can distribute to your customers and prospects in person or mail to them. You and your staff should present it to everyone with whom you have a sales contact. This simple mailer can also be inserted in invoices your firm sends out. You can also include it with all correspondence—inviting recipients who already have a copy to pass it along to a friend.

This handout/mailer can be as simple as a bookmark-size sheet of heavy paper printed or photocopied on both sides in your office. By keeping it to bookmark size, you can print several copies at one time on a single sheet of paper and cut them apart. One side should feature your Web site address and a brief description of its contents, the other can describe either surfing tips or Web sites of possible (but noncompeting) interest to your market.

Promoting Your Web Site in Your Advertising

In addition to adding your Web site's address to all your print communications, you should make sure that all your firm's advertisements contain your Web site. This includes display advertising (advertising mixed in with other ads on the editorial pages of your newspaper) as well as your classified advertising. Your Web site's address should also appear on your firm's billboards and be mentioned on your firm's radio ads.

Needless to say, the shorter and more descriptive your Web site address, as described in Chapter 4, the easier it will be for your customers and prospects to remember your Web site address.

You might even consider placing a few trial ads in the classified section of your newspaper inviting readers to your Web site. Let's face it: It's more cost-effective. Instead of going to the expense of listing every reduced-price item in the newspaper, place a teaser ad in the newspaper inviting prospects to visit your Web site and get the whole story.

Finally, the classified sections of many magazines and newspapers contain listings of suppliers in each area. Sometimes these listings contain just street addresses and phone numbers; in other cases, the listings consist of just Web addresses. (Sometimes these listings are free to advertisers elsewhere in the issue; other times the listings are open to anyone. Try listing your Web address there—but be sure to track the responses you get so you can decide if it is worth the cost or not.)

REGISTERING YOUR WEB SITE

The next step is to register your Web site with the various search engines. Search engines, such as Yahoo, Excite, and AltaVista, to name just a few, can be extremely valuable in bringing new visitors to your Web site. These visitors can be considered qualified, because the visitors have sought you out by searching for Web sites that contain their desired content.

Contacting Search Engines

There are several ways you can register your Web site:

◆ *You can do the work yourself.* Registration information is available at the Web sites of many search engines. The service is typically free, although you have to make sure you follow the detailed instructions.

◆ You can *hire someone else* to inform the search engines of your Web site's address. Often, firms will promise to immediately send your information, properly formatted, to twenty or more search engines within a very short time.

◆ *Some Internet Service Providers will offer to register your Web site free*—or for a reduced fee. They may also list your Web site on the page containing links to their clients.

As is so often true, you get what you pay for. If you decide to contract the work to others, find out how many search engines they will contact and when they will do the work. Whether the work is supposed to be done free or for a fee, ask for references from services they have listed.

Regardless of the registration method you choose, be sure you check the search engines after a reasonable amount of time to make sure your site has, indeed, been properly indexed.

After a reasonable amount of time, check the various search engines and make sure your firm's Web address appears in the proper location.

Note that submitting your Web site address to a search engine doesn't automatically mean it will be listed. Some services list every Web site submitted, others are more selective in their listings. Eligibility for listing varies, and repeat applications may be necessary to become listed the way you want to be listed. For this reason, you may want to study the descriptions of sites listed as well as visit some of the sites themselves in order to get a better idea of the preferences and requirements of each search service. Persistence pays off, as does carefully following the instructions each service requires.

Meta-Indexes

Meta-indexes are similar to search engines, except that they are more subject-specific, that is, they contain only links of Web sites pertaining to a particular subject category or confirming to certain (often arbitrary) submission guidelines.

Some meta-indexes are geographically oriented, while others target industry classifications or enthusiasts. Your Web site can benefit greatly if you can locate and be included in a high-visibility meta-index that attracts your target market.

Keywords

Instead of waiting for you to come to them, many search engines go out and actively search the Web, looking for key words and phrases that describe the contents of your Web site. There are several locations in your Web site where these key words can appear.

◆ *Meta tags.* Meta tags are the words that appear in the header, or top, of your Web site's home page. Often, meta tags only list the software used to prepare your Web site. You can augment or replace this information with information that provides a better description of your Web site's content. This will ensure that your Web site will be properly indexed when it appears in the search engine's listings. The more accurately you describe your Web site, the higher the priority—or the earlier in the list—your Web site will appear.

◆ *Title tags.* Similarly, if the software program you are using to prepare your Web site permits access to HTML tags, you can provide descriptive phrases in each page's title tags. In addition to higher visibility to search engines, title tags also appear in the status line of the Web browser used to access your site. Instead of "Page 3," visitors to your Web site will see "FAQ's—Frequently Asked Questions—About Home Theater," or "The Advantages that AC-3 Offers." Finally, when visitors to your Web site bookmark a page to return to, a meaningful description will appear in their favorites list.

ADVERTISING YOUR WEB SITE

Charity begins at home—and so does Web site advertising and promotion. One of the easiest ways to promote your Web site is always to provide up-to-date and appropriate, valuable content and to encourage Web site visitors to bookmark it—or add it to their favorites list so they can easily return to your site without having to type in your Web site address. If visitors value the contents of your Web site, they will certainly respond to your request to bookmark your site.

Remember: just because you always bookmark sites you want to return to, not everyone is as organized. Similarly, the power of suggestion is very strong. Just as telephone calls to public radio programs increase when the music stops and the on-air personality begs listeners to call in, Web site visitors may not think of bookmarking your site until you remind them to. So consider adding banners to a few pages inviting visitors to bookmark your home page, or—alternatively—specific pages of your site so they can return and get the latest information.

Cybermalls and Other Forms of Paid Advertising

The location of your Web site can be its own advertising. Many *cybermalls* have been established. These contain the Web sites—or links to the Web sites—of numerous firms grouped geographically or by product or service.

The advantage of these cybermalls is that—like their physical brethren on the outskirts of cities large and small—they attract buyers. Prospects who might otherwise never visit your Web site will encounter it when they visit a cybermall. The questions you have to ask yourself, however, include:

♦   Can I afford placing or linking my Web site in a cybermall?

♦   How much traffic will the cybermall really generate?

♦   Will the additional Web traffic justify the additional cost?

♦   Where will my Web site appear in the mall? Another way of asking this is: "How visible will my Web site be to mall visitors?"

Like anything else, the best way to evaluate cybermalls—after visiting them yourself, of course—is to contact the Webmasters of firms that are already there and ask them what their experiences have been. A little detective work can go a long way towards separating claims from reality.

Banner Advertising

Numerous Web sites don't sell any products or services themselves; they simply serve as advertising vehicles for other Web advertisers. Search engines like Yahoo fit into this category. These Web sites revenue comes from advertising revenues—particularly short advertising messages displayed in frames located over the information contained on each page. These banners can remain static, or they can rotate every few seconds while the viewer reads the information on the page. Or, different banners will appear each time the page is accessed.

The typical banner advertisement makes a statement and then includes a link to the advertiser's home page.

Other Web sites sell banners to complement their own commercial endeavors. Audio/video stores, for example, can sell advertising space to their vendors, and the Web sites of health clubs can sell banner advertising to manufacturers of exercise equipment or apparel appealing to health-conscious individuals. Automotive dealers can sell advertising space to after-market accessory makers or oil companies. You'll frequently encounter banners for banks and mortgage lenders on a realtor's Web sites.

In addition to advertising on other Web sites, there are also many e-zines—online Web publications that are either associated with print publications or created from scratch. These range from free publications that online readers have to register in order to read, to subscription publications readers have to pay for. E-zines offer further opportunities to purchase banner advertising. The value of these publications as an advertising medium increases to the extent that their readership overlaps your target market.

At present, there is a lot of confusion about the value of banner advertising. This is because there are so many ways to rate hits, or the number of times a Web site is accessed. After contacting the various sites and requesting the costs of banner advertising, you'll have to consider whether the possible rewards will outweigh the costs. Hint: as is true of most aspects of advertising, most banner advertising costs are open to negotiation!

Purchasing E-Mail Lists

A final advertising option is to consider purchasing e-mail lists and promoting your Web site via e-mail announcements to the recipients on the list. This is the e-mail equivalent of the direct mail you suddenly begin to receive after contributing to a favorite charity, joining an organization, or subscribing to a magazine.

The jury is still out on the ethics and legality of sending unsolicited e-mail. Perhaps the best way to approach the subject—assuming that it doesn't become outlawed—is to ask yourself: "How do I feel when I receive unsolicited e-mail?" Do you read unsolicited messages inviting you to make $50,000 at home in your spare time working three hours a week, or do you immediately delete them? Many people, myself included, find that unsolicited electronic e-mail is more annoying than unsolicited mail in my post office box.

At the very least, you'll have to carefully research the firm and its ability to distribute your message to the right lists at the right price. As always, it's a good idea to first contact previous users of the service and find out how happy they were with their investment.

CO-MARKETING

Rather than spending money to attract visitors to your Web site, you might be better off investing time in searching for *affinity market partners*. These are noncompeting firms with Web sites that attract the same type of visitors that are likely to be attracted to your Web site. When you locate an affinity market partner, you simply cross-link your Web sites: You include links to their Web site on your Web site and they'll do the same.

If you're a retailer, for example, it doesn't make sense for you to cross-link your Web sites with a competitor across the street or across town. But, it certainly *does* makes sense to cross-link your Web site with the Web sites of vendors whose products you sell or organizations whose members are likely to be interested in your products. A little creativity can pay big dividends. Audio/video retailers, for example, could cross-link their Web sites with the Web sites of performing arts organizations in their town, with stores selling tapes and compact disks, as well as with local bands.

Cross-linking costs nothing, so you have very little to lose as long as you choose your partners carefully and occasionally check their Web site to make sure your site is properly linked in the right location. And, since your marketing partner is likely to check out *your* Web site to verify that you have included a link to their Web site, you should make doubly sure that you live up to your end of the deal and your Web site *does,* indeed, contain a link to their site.

> *Cross-linking costs nothing, so you have very little to lose as long as you choose your partners carefully and occasionally check their Web site to make sure your Web site is properly linked in the right locations.*

To make your approach to an affinity partner all the more interesting, once you're convinced their Web site can generate significant traffic to your Web site, you can offer to contribute to their Web site by becoming a guest columnist in exchange for another link to your site. You'll find creativity to be as useful promoting your Web site as it is creating your Web site.

TRADE-OUTS AND PARTIAL TRADE-OUTS

When you discover some particularly influential Web sites, you might even consider contributing content to their Web site in exchange for links to your site. As a writer, for example, I will usually reduce my copywriting charges if I want to be visible to visitors of an important Web site if—as partial compensation for my writing—I receive a brief biographical note plus a link to my Web site. Just be sure to *get it in writing* when and where in the publication your Web link will appear and how long it will remain.

SELF-PROMOTION

Once you have added your Web site address to your printed letterheads and your e-mail signature, you can search for opportunities to make your opinion known. Again, the key is to become as visible as possible to your target market. Some suggestions appear in the following sections.

Harnessing the Power of the Press

While developing the content of your Web site, you probably discovered that you know more about your subject area than you thought you did. You may have developed a new perspective on the topics contained in your Web site. If so, consider condensing your thoughts and conclusions into one, or more, press releases that you can submit to the editors of publications likely to be read by your target market.

There is a world of difference between the way readers approach advertising and articles. Readers approach advertising with suspicion and a defensive attitude: "They're trying to sell me something!" Articles, however, especially genuinely helpful articles, are approached with a much more open mind. If the articles are truly helpful, the writer is rewarded with a halo of credibility and respect.

Thus, investigate opportunities where you can submit press releases summarizing the contents of important information at your Web site. Allow the publication's editors to rewrite the information as much as they want, and encourage them to contact you for further assistance. Just be sure to emphasize the importance of their mentioning your Web site address in their reference to the information you submit.

Letters to the Editor

Most magazines and newspapers welcome letters to the editor. More and more, these are accompanied by either the sender's e-mail address or their Web site.

BASING PRESS RELEASES ON VISITOR REGISTRATION FORMS

Don't feel that you have to develop all of the information yourself. You might be able to develop information from the registration forms that visitors to your Web site submit to you. Editors will be impressed that the information and interpretations you are sending are based not just on your ideas but also on visitor input, making your information appear all the more valuable. Needless to say, publicity is a self-fulfilling prophecy; the more you are quoted, the more your Web site will be visited—and the more your Web site is visited, the more information you'll be able to obtain from your visitor's registration forms.

If you have something of importance to share with readers of an important publication, or can develop something important to share, you can quickly promote name recognition and credibility by sharing your thoughts with their readers or Web site visitors. Don't be a wallflower in the back row: Make your feelings known. Just be sure you include your Web site address (inside your message, if possible, but also as part of your signature).

Once you're comfortable writing letters to the editor, the next step is to expand your horizons and consider placing articles in publications likely to be read by your prospects. Again, as you did when preparing press releases, strive to identify areas where you can provide new perspectives, new information, or new interpretations rather than merely brag and boast or blow your own horn. Editors are as quick to see through self-serving promotion as they are grateful for truly useful information and content.

Newsgroup Postings

Once you have added your Web site's address to your e-mail signature, you can begin to investigate opportunities to further increase your visibility by contributing to newsgroups. Newsgroups are the Web equivalent of small-town cracker barrels: they're locations where people gather to share stories and gossip. No matter what field you're involved in, there's probably a newsgroup that will welcome your contribution.

Your visibility and your credibility among potential visitors to your Web site will increase to the extent that your postings to the various newsgroups are meaningful and appropriate. Although the amount of editing—to eliminate blatant advertising—of posted messages varies from group to group, the best type of editing is self-editing. Confine your comments to the subject at hand and let the importance of your message speak for itself. If you make meaningful postings, your credibility will increase and so will visits to your Web site.

PREPARING A PROMOTIONAL PROGRAM FOR YOUR WEB SITE

Use the Promotion Worksheet below to review your various promotional options, prioritize them, and delegate promotional chores to others.

1. Have you added your Web site's address to your e-mail signature?

    ❑ Yes ❑ No

2. Do all of your firm's print communications include your Web site address?

    ❑ Yes ❑ No

    If "no," describe what you have to do to make sure all your advertising contains your Web site's address.

3. Have you considered preparing a simple handout or mailing insert promoting your Web site's address?

    ❑ Yes ❑ No

4. Does all of your firm's advertising contain your Web site's address?

    ❑ Yes ❑ No

    If "no," describe what you have to do to make sure all your advertising contains your Web site's address.

5. Do your home page's meta tags accurately describe your Web site?

    ❑ Yes ❑ No

6. Do your title tags accurately describe the contents of each of your pages?

    ❑ Yes ❑ No

7. Do you invite visitors to bookmark, or add your Web site's address, to their favorites list?

    ❑ Yes ❑ No

8. Does it make sense to place your Web site in a cybermall?

    ❑ Yes ❑ No

Why?

9.   Does paid banner advertising on other Web sites make sense?

☐   Yes   ☐   No

Why?

Which publications? Why?

1.

2.

3.

4.

10. List some possible affinity partners who offer opportunities for cross-linking your Web sites.

Name what makes them appropriate?

1.

2.

3.

4.

5.

6.

11. What are some of the ways you can contribute to publications likely to be read by your target markets?

Title Type of submission (describe):

1. ❑ Press release ❑ Article

2. ❑ Press release ❑ Article

3. ❑ Press release ❑ Article

4. ❑ Press release ❑ Article

12. Are there any newsgroups likely to be read by potential buyers of your product or service?

Chapter 13

Maintenance

Maintaining Your Web Site

Keeping Content Accurate, Up-to-date, and Relevant

As you've probably noticed by now, your job has just begun when you post your Web site! In the months that follow posting your Web site, a great deal of its success will be determined by how aggressively you promote it and how conscientiously you follow up on the leads and sales it generates.

Maintenance is equally important. Stale, tired Web sites are an invitation to failure. Inaccurate or out-of-date information will immediately result in your Web site visitor's pressing their Back key or leaving your site for one that promises more relevant content. After all, how would you respect a greeting card store if you visited it a week after St. Patrick's Day and found Christmas cards on display?

How much would you respect a greeting card store if you visited it a week after St. Patrick's Day and found Christmas cards on display?

There are three primary ways you can keep your Web site alive and fresh:

◆ Keeping information accurate and up-to-date.

◆ Improving your Web site on the basis of visitor comments.

◆ Searching for new ideas at other Web sites.

KEEPING CONTENT UP-TO-DATE

To be effective, it's imperative that your Web site always contain up-to-date content. To determine the amount of maintenance your Web site is likely to require, start by addressing questions like the following:

◆ *Which content is likely to go out of date?* Not all types of content are likely to be time-sensitive; although some content will go out of date, other content can be archived and kept available for future reference at a less visible location on your Web site. One of my favorite magazines used as its tagline: "Every issue is new until you've read it." Similarly, as a result of your promotional efforts, your Web site will be attracting new visitors every day. One of your first tasks is to identify which content can remain and which should be discarded.

◆ *How quickly will content go out of date?* Once you have identified which content is time-sensitive, you'll have to set up a schedule for reviewing its accuracy. If your Web promotes a restaurant, for example, daily specials will obviously have to be changed once a day. If your Web site features up-to-the-minute stock market quotes and analyses, its content should change (at least) every hour. The content of Web sites describing luxury cruises to exotic destinations, however, is likely to have a longer shelf life and can remain in place for months at a time. Keep the frequency of expected change in mind as you plan your maintenance tasks for the upcoming months.

◆ *How often will you post new content?* The amount of maintenance your Web site is likely to require will also be determined by how quickly new content becomes available. Think of how rarely you'd be tempted to buy a day-old newspaper containing yesterday's headlines; the essence of a newspaper is up-to-date news. Similarly, up-to-date content is the essence of Web site. Thus, the rapidity of change in your area should influence how often you update your Web site. The last thing you want to happen is for your Web site visitors to know more about a subject than your Web site reveals you know.

◆ *How often will you review links for accuracy?* One of your most important Web site maintenance tasks involves verifying the accuracy of external links. Even though you have no control over the content or location of external links, *you'll* be blamed if visitors to your Web site can't locate the information you promised. As a result, you should plan to verify each Web link at least once a month.

Keep the frequency of expected change in mind as you plan your time for the coming months.

The Buying Cycle and Content

The content of your Web site should also reflect the various stages of the buying cycle. *The more that you target your Web site to buyers at the Comparison and Purchase stages, the more important it will be to keep its content up-to-date.* Ideally, of course, your Web site should include something for everyone, that is, content for visitors at various stages of the buying cycle.

To illustrate the importance of relating content to the visitors at various stages of the buying cycle, let's examine the suggested content of an audio/video retailer's Web site:

◆ *Introductory articles* describing the features and benefits of home theater components, a glossary explaining the terminology of the field and a page of answers to Frequently Asked Questions will appeal to visitors at the Awareness and Desire stages.

◆ Content stressing the benefits of buying particular audio/video components from *that particular store* will address the content needs of visitors at the Comparison stage.

◆ Information describing the latest and best *components* as well as special limited-time *promotions and savings* is necessary to satisfy and motivate Web site visitors at the Purchase phase.

◆ Articles describing how to properly set up and improve *a home theater system* will satisfy visitors at the Augmentation and Replacement stages and—probably—result in repeat sales and word-of-mouth recommendations.

As you can see, content targeted at visitors at the Purchase phase is more to quickly go out of date—on a daily basis, for example—whereas content aimed at visitors at the Awareness and Desire phases is unlikely to change very frequently. Similarly, content targeting visitors at the Augmentation and Replacement stages is unlikely to change for months at a time.

Successful Web site maintenance involves constantly reviewing its content and making sure that up-to-date content appropriately addresses needs of visitors at various stages of the buying cycle.

Updating Your Home Page

Just as the front cover of a magazine reflects the contents of that particular issue and not the contents of the previous issue, your home page should change to reflect changed content. As emphasized in Chapter 3, the home page of your Web site should begin the sale by promoting one of the major features inside. In addition to content-based home pages, if one of your goals is to project a friendly or informal image for your firm or organization, you might consider updating your Web site's home page on a seasonal basis.

An alternative, warm and fuzzy, seasonally based home page can project an entirely different image than does an all-business home page. This friendly approach will encourage visitors to approach your Web site's content in a completely different frame of mind—even if the season has very little to do with content (see Figure 13.1).

Your site maintenance chores will increase, of course, to the extent that you decide to update your home page on the basis of both content and seasonal themes.

REVIEWING YOUR WEB SITE'S EFFECTIVENESS

The feedback you receive from visitors should influence your maintenance—as well as your promotional—efforts. Changing content is not the only reason to update your Web site. Maintenance efforts should also be influenced by tracking the results of your Web site.

Monitoring the Success of Your Web Site.

In Chapter 9, "Encouraging Involvement," we described how you can use registration forms to find out answers to the following questions:

◆ *Where are visitors coming from?* Are most of your visitors attracted to your Web site by search engines, advertisements, links from other Web sites, or mentions in the press? Once you identify your best and your least-productive sources of Web traffic, you know where to place increasing emphasis and where to reduce future promotional efforts.

◆ *Are there any observable trends* in the amount of e-mail and registration forms received? Are the quantities received increasing, decreasing, or remaining the same? If the number is the same, or declining, you may want to place more emphasis on promoting your Web site.

Figure 13.1
In order to present a friendly image, the home page of the Massachusetts Institute of Technology often reflects a seasonal theme.

◆ *How many sales* is your Web site producing? What is your Web site's closure rate? How many people who register or contact you for further information via e-mail actually end up buying from you? If contact is not leading to sales, you may want to review the content and speed of your follow-up and closure efforts. You might want to personally contact prospects who didn't purchase and find out if they purchased elsewhere or didn't purchase at all.

Success comes to the extent that you maintain your Web site on the basis of evidence and results rather than intuitive feelings about what you and your staff like. Your Web site exists to satisfy your visitors, not yourself.

Listening to Your Visitors

Listening to your Web site visitors involves keeping track of their evaluations of the content of your Web site, as indicated on the registration form, and their suggestions for future content. Pay special attention to your visitors' responses to the following questions:

◆ Which topics did you find *most* useful?

◆ Which topics did you find *least* useful?

◆ What *other* topics would you like to see covered?

Here are two additional ways you can further leverage off of the registration forms you encourage Web site visitors to submit. You can:

◆ E-mail registered visitors lists containing new topics you're thinking of adding to your Web site and ask them to evaluate the importance of the topics.

◆ E-mail visitors and ask them to recommend Web sites they find especially useful and tell you why they like them.

LOOKING ELSEWHERE FOR INSPIRATION

Analyzing the content of your Web site and monitoring comments and results from Web site visitors are only two of the ways you can improve your Web site. You should also look beyond your Web site for inspiration.

For example, you can *constantly review other Web sites in other fields* for new ideas. The goal, of course, is not to copy their contents, but to adapt their content categories to your specific needs. Just as many firms have emulated the airlines' use of e-mail to offer savings for last-minute weekend travel to those who request it, keep your eyes open for ideas you can adapt to your Web site from other fields.

You can also *compare your Web site to others in your field.* Invest time reviewing your competitors' Web sites as well as the Web sites of others in your field. As you do this, ask yourself questions like:

◆ How do your Web site's *content, design,* and *accessibility* stack up in comparison to others?

◆ Pay particular attention to content and design. How does the *amount* and *quality of the information* you offer compare to that offered elsewhere? Again, the goal is not plagiarism but inspiration.

◆ Does your Web site do a better or lesser job in terms of offering something for visitors at *different stages* of the buying cycle?

◆ How does your Web site's *appearance and ease of navigation* compare to others in the field?

As you review the contents of your Web site, strive to relate its content closer and closer to the various stages of the buying cycle. Simultaneously, listen to your Web site visitors and fine-tune your content on the basis of their comments and the ideas you receive by viewing other sites. The more you compare, the easier you'll find it to maintain and improve the contents of your Web site, which will reward you with increased response from visitors at all stages of the buying cycle.

PLANNING FOR CHANGE

Use the following Maintenance Worksheet to identify the tasks needed to keep your Web site up-to-date and identify the individuals who will do the work.

As in so many other aspects of the Web, success comes from management rather than creativity. Results will come to the extent that you build ongoing maintenance into your and your firm's continuing management goals and job descriptions. Evaluations of site content and suggestions for new content won't happen by themselves. Someone has to be given responsibility for the tasks.

If you desire to undertake Web maintenance tasks yourself, you'll have to create the necessary time by delegating other duties to someone else in your organization. Biting off more than you can chew represents a fast road to Web burnout!

Regardless of who does the work, responsibility, time, motivation, and a timetable for completion of various Web maintenance activities will have to be assigned and built into your firm's ongoing marketing efforts.

The Web is a process, not an event. Once launched, it has to be carefully nurtured!

MAINTENANCE WORKSHEET

1. How time-sensitive is your Web site's content? Is it likely to go out of date?

   ❑ Very much   ❑ Somewhat   ❑ Very little

2. Which content is likely to go out of date?   Describe below:

3. How quickly will your Web site's content become obsolete?

   ❑ Daily   ❑ Weekly   ❑ Monthly   ❑ Quarterly

   When? (describe below):

4. How often is new content likely to become available?

   ❑ Daily   ❑ Weekly   ❑ Monthly   ❑ Quarterly

   When? (describe below):

5. How often should you review links for accuracy?

6. How often will you change your home page to reflect new contents or a seasonal theme?

7. Who will be in charge of reviewing and updating content?

8. How much time should be spent on issues relating to Web maintenance? _____ hours each

    ❏ Day ❏ Week   ❏ Month

    ❏ Quarter ❏ Other (describe below):

9. Where can you locate ideas for new sources of content?

10. Who will keep track of information contained on registration forms and e-mail and follow the resulting sales?

11. Who will search other sites for ideas that can be adapted?

12. How much time will be spent searching for inspiration at other Web sites? _____ hours each

    ❏ Day ❏ Week   ❏ Month

    ❏ Quarter ❏ Other (describe below):

13. Who will compare your Web site to others in your field?

14. Where will time be found for these activities and how will those performing these activities be rewarded?

15. Who will monitor those involved in maintaining your Web site?

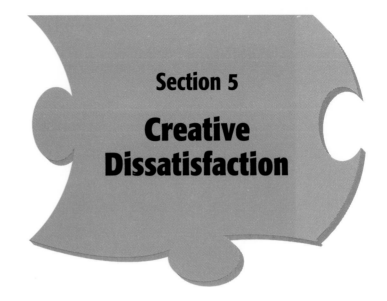

Section 5

Creative Dissatisfaction

Chapter 14

Improving Existing Web Sites

Converting Good into Great, and Great into Outstanding

As you create and maintain your Web site, cultivate a habit of creative dissatisfaction. In addition to continually updating your Web site as new material becomes available, you should search for ways to improve your Web site's design. You should never become so satisfied with the design of your Web site that you consider it finished.

Subtle improvements to the design of your Web site can add up to major improvements in its appearance and communicating power. These improvements typically fall into three major categories:

◆ Reducing the size of text and visual elements

◆ Simplifying your Web site by eliminating unnecessary text and graphic elements as well as unwanted space between elements

◆ Identifying and repairing awkward typography and phrasing

Let's take a look at each of these areas of possible improvement.

We'll end by discussing ways you can take a fresh look at your Web site and provide a Web Site Review Worksheet that summarizes many of the design ideas in this book and will guide you through the review of your existing Web site—or a site you're just about to post on the Web.

REDUCING THE SIZE OF ELEMENTS

Often, text and graphic elements are larger than they need to be to accomplish their function. One of the biggest culprits is beginning your visitor's journey through your Web site with a large image of your firm's logo.

What's wrong with a large logo? Here are some reasons to reconsider the size of your opening logo:

◆ *A large logo doesn't communicate a message.* A large logo may satisfy you, or your client's ego, but it doesn't communicate a message to your visitor who is interested in here and now benefits, not abstractions. There simply isn't any more information value in a large logo than is contained in a smaller logo. A large logo is thus likely to be greeted by a yawn of "so what?"

◆ *A large logo may be redundant.* Although a large logo lets your visitor know which Web site they've entered, they probably already know this because they deliberately accessed your Web site address. In such a case, the logo simplify confirms what the visitor knows.

◆ *A large logo takes longer to download than a small logo.* The larger the graphic, the longer the download time, adding insult to injury by making Web site visitors wait (or pay access time) to receive noninformation they may already know!

   The logo may not be unique. Retail and distribution firms that feature one of their vendor's logos on their home page sacrifice a valuable opportunity to create a distinct image which can position their Web site apart from their competitors. In addition, the same logo may appear on dozens of their competitors' Web sites.

◆ *There's no room for anything else.* Large logos don't leave space for anything else, for example, headlines that begin the buying cycle by involving the visitor. Large logos prevent mouth-watering summaries of the benefits of the product or service offered, or an involvement headline selling a feature article contained on the Web site or describing a limited-time promotion on a specific product or service.

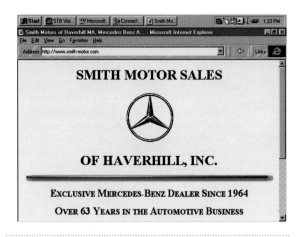

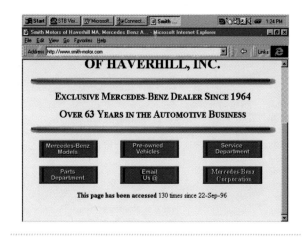

Figure 14.1 Web sites beginning with oversized brag and boast logos offer visitors little incentive to investigate further.

Figure 14.2 Oversize logos are often accompanied by widely spaced, oversize links that require further scrolling.

The biggest problem with a large logo, however, is that it forces Web site visitors to scroll down to reach the navigation links necessary to access the various pages of the Web site. After waiting for a large logo to download, visitors may feel short-changed when they have to scroll down before they can even begin to see what's available on your Web site. This is especially bothersome if they also have to wait for the navigation buttons or icons to download (see Figures 14.1 and 14.2).

Smaller Equals More

By reducing the size of the logo and links, more information can be communicated in the same space. Contrast the above examples to Web sites that use smaller, more tightly grouped elements. Notice how much more information can be accommodated in a single screen when elements are tightly grouped together.

Compare the previous two screens to Figure 14.3's single-screen (that is, no-scroll) example: Notice the many points covered in the monotype example:

◆ The Monotype logo is accompanied by a positioning statement "1897–1997" which is communicated both visually (as part of the logo) and as part of the "Your Font and Software Resource" headline.

◆ There are links to six different categories of information at the Web site, allowing visitors at different stages of the buying cycle to find content of interest.

◆ The Web site projects a restrained, yet distinctive image through the use of a limited color palette plus a two-color background (that is, a right-to-left graduated tint) on the left and a white background on the right.

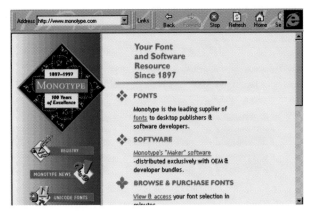

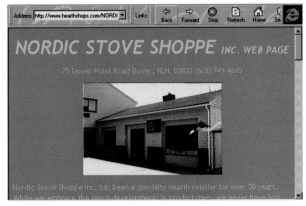

Figure 14.3 Notice how much more information can be communicated when the logo is made smaller, allowing access to more benefits, as in the Monotype site.

Figure 14.4 The firm's address and a picture of the building is only important once the Web site visitors have determined that they want to visit the building and need to be able to recognize it when they reach it.

Home Page Hierarchy and Color

Always construct the first screen of your home page around your Web site visitor's information needs rather than what you consider important. Remember to present information in the order of its necessity to the reader's progress through the buying cycle.

Just as many Web sites begin with an oversize logo, many begin with their name plus their address and a picture of their building. Again, a picture of a business's headquarters building—no matter how attractive—is of little informational value until the visitor has determined that this is a building they might want to visit. Similarly, it doesn't make sense to put the firm's address at the top of the home page because, until the visitor has determined they want to visit the store, there's no reason to include the address at all! (See Figure 14.4.)

Reviewing a Web site after a significant amount of time has passed since its creation offers an opportunity to review not only content hierarchy but also design elements like colors and typography (see Figure 14.5). Colors that make creative sense to Web site design newcomers, like using red and yellow to represent heating with wood, are often later seen to be so bright as to be distractions requiring change.

Adding and Rethinking Links

As you become more comfortable working on the Web, the distinction between a home page and a Web site will become increasingly obvious. A home page will be seen more and more as the Web analogy to the front page of a print magazine. Whereas in the beginning, you might think of

Figure 14.5 Replacing the original firm's overly large name and photograph of the store with a headline and copy more suited to visitors at various stages of the buying cycle broadens the site's appeal.

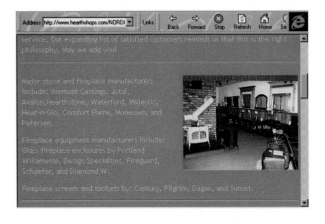

Figure 14.6 Redesigning a Web site often involves adding links originally omitted, permitting you to devote more selling space (that is, content) to the products or services sold.

Figure 14.7 A table containing links to vendors describing the various products a firm sells greatly increases a Web site's selling power.

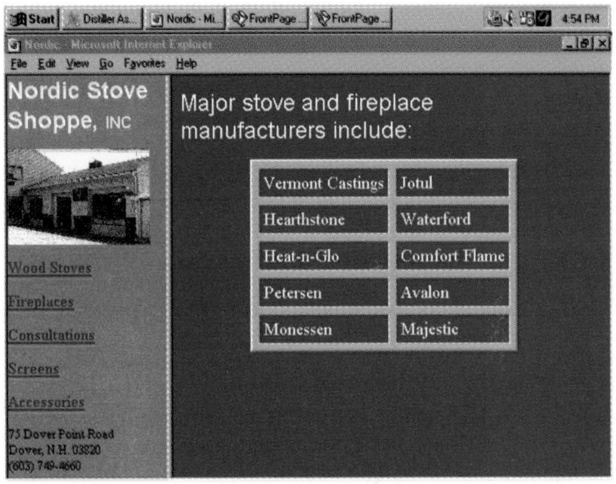

a Web site as a single page that visitors will scroll through, from top to bottom, as you become more cyber-conversant, you may want to revise your concept of the home page to the point where it becomes a single screen that teases visitors into investigating other pages of a Web site.

Notice how the original wood stove shop listed the manufacturers of stoves and fireplace manufacturers and accessories in paragraph form (see Figure 14.6). This eliminated the possibility of describing the various models and benefits of each of the brands. A much better alternative, based on rethinking the function of the home page, however, would emphasize its role as a table of contents containing links to detailed descriptions of the various products sold (see Figure 14.7).

By replacing vendor names located inside paragraphs with a list of products sold permits you to describe the products and their benefits in greater detail. This added detail—or content—would greatly enhance the selling power of your Web site. More important, if co-operative advertising funds were available from the vendors, you could use these to offset some of your Web site's development and administration costs.

SIMPLIFYING YOUR WEB SITE

Simplicity is more than a virtue; it is a necessity if you want your Web site to communicate as clearly and effectively as possible. Every unnecessary word and graphic element on your Web site can interfere with your visitor's progression through the site. Here are some of the ways to simplify your Web site so your message appears as transparent and obvious as possible.

Edit to the Bone

After your Web site has been posted, print it out and go over it with a yellow highlighter. Highlight all unnecessary or redundant words. You may be surprised how many words aren't really needed. For example:

◆ *Avoid restating the obvious.* Notice how much space "Inc." and "Web Page" occupy in the headline of Figure 14.4. "Web Page" really isn't needed. After all, the only way your visitor can encounter your Web page is if they're on the Web! Similarly, the legal status of the firm isn't that important to first-time Web visitors.

◆ *Avoid being chatty.* Unless you want to deliberately project an ultra-friendly image, avoid words like "Welcome to" and other clichés. Instead, go right for the kill and immediately describe the benefit or benefits that visitors will enjoy by remaining at your site and exploring it. You're not in business to make friends as much as you're in business to make sales—immediate sales, before your competitor gets there first!

◆ *Reduce headline and subhead length.* Headlines and subheads should be teasers that attract readers into the text that follows, rather than mini-paragraphs that convey too much information. Try to simultaneously reduce headline length and involve the reader by using the magic word "You" whenever possible. Instead of saying: "We have the largest selection of wood stoves and fireplace accessories on the Seacoast," which is a brag and boast headline with little interest to readers, consider a more involving headline like: "Are you looking for an alternative to high home-heating-oil prices?"

You're not in business to make friends as much as you're in business to make sales—immediate sales, before your competitor gets there first!

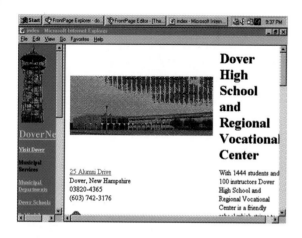

Figure 14.8 Note the awkward multiline headline to the right of the picture of the school, creating unnecessary space above and below the illustration.

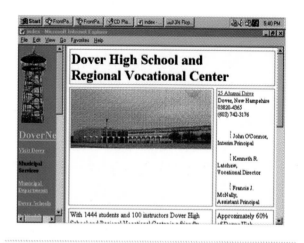

Figure 14.9 Replacing the vertical headline with a horizontal one eliminates the unwanted space above the photograph and creates space to list the school's administrators.

Figure 14.10 Filling the remaining space with e-mail links to the administration and faculty saves further space and also creates an area to include more information about the school and its activities.

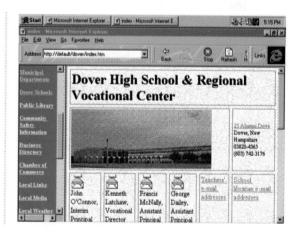

Eliminating Unnecessary Spacing

The appearance of many Web sites can be improved by reducing the spacing between text and graphic elements. Think of the various text and graphic elements of your Web site as the pieces of a puzzle that must rearranged and played with until they fit together as tightly as possible.

Unsightly Web sites are often characterized by large holes between elements. When surrounded by text and graphics, these holes attract attention far out of proportion to their importance. In the series of illustrations that follow (Figures 14.8 through 14.10), notice how the progressive rearrangement of the elements not only simplifies the Web site by providing alignment points but also increases the amount of information displayed in the single screen—reducing the amount of scrolling visitors will have to do.

Reorganizing and Rethinking Links

Look for opportunities where you can group links together into common categories. Web sites that present visitors with ten or a dozen Web links of equal importance tend to confuse visitors by offering too many choices. Instead, analyze your links into categories so that your home page offers a few major options, each of which is subdivided into further links.

Instead of using buttons and icons for every link level, consider using text links placed in tables for secondary link classifications. These conserve space and download quicker.

Another way to speed up as well as simplify your Web site is to replace graphic links with text links placed in frames. Frames permit the screen of your Web site visitor to display two (or more) files. Typically, text links are displayed in a frame placed along one side of the page, while the remainder of the space is used to display content. Replacing buttons and icons with text links saves time and space. Buttons and icons take more time to download than text in frames. This is because the frame containing the text links doesn't have to download every time the visitor accesses a different page (see Figures 14.11 and 14.12).

Archiving Old Content

Another technique for reducing "link overkill" is to archive early content, such as articles which appeared in previous months. Microsoft's SmallBiz site does an excellent job of this (see Figure 14.13). At the end of each month's article, there's a pull-down menu with a scroll bar that allows you to access the same author's articles which appeared earlier.

Simplifying Alignment

Another easy, but extremely significant, way you can simplify your Web site is by rethinking your use of centered text alignment. All too often, centered text and headlines are harder to read than headlines and text set flush-left/ragged-right. This is because visitors have to search for the beginnings of each line. In addition, the space surrounding the lines of text is divided between the left and right sides of the words, rather than concentrated to one side, creating a more crowded page (see Figures 14.14 and 14.15).

Unnecessary Counters

Do you really want to include a counter on your Web site? Why? There are several problems associated with public counters, that is, counters that Web site visitors can view (other than hidden counters for your use own use).

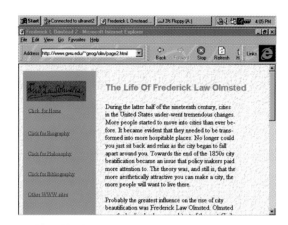

Figure 14.11 The original Web site was slower than the later version because the green panel containing the links had to be downloaded every time a different page was accessed.

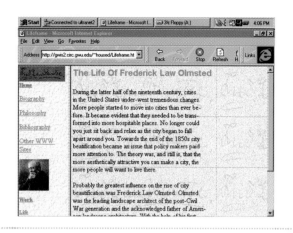

Figure 14.12 Frames simplify and speed up the Web site because the text frames remain constant even when different pages are accessed. Note, also, that the narrower frame with green text links not only reinforces the headline color but also adds a pleasing amount of space to the right of the text.

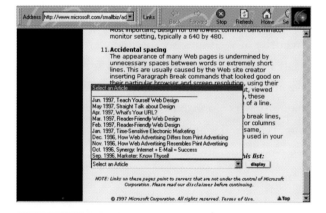

Figure 14.13 Archiving old content by placing links to previous articles at the end of current articles, as found at the Microsoft SmallBiz site, reduces the need for links.

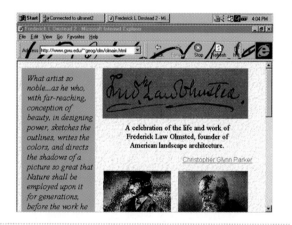

Figure 14.14 Notice how full this screen looks because there is so little breathing room surrounding the headline. Note also the flush-right link for the author's byline further fills the space.

Figure 14.15
The same content appears in a far more open environment when formerly centered and flush-right text elements are both aligned flush left. Now, the text is emphasized by a pool of white space which makes the page look more open.

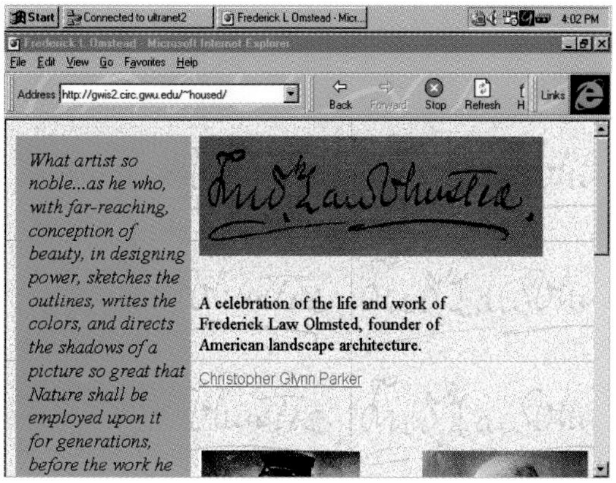

Here are some problems which limit the value of counters:

◆ *Embarrassingly low figures.* Counters with low totals project a bad image. If Web site visitors find that your site has only been visited 200 times during the past six months, they're likely to conclude that it doesn't have much to offer. Visitors, like sports fans, are more willing to invest their time with winners than losers.

◆ *Notoriously unreliable.* What, exactly, does the counter measure? Usually, it measures the number of times that a page has been accessed. If you place a counter on your home page, it will probably reflect an unrealistically high count because Web site visitors may have to return to the home page every time they want to access a different link! On the other hand, if you place the counter on the last page of your site, or your "How to contact us?" page, the counter's totals may be too low because not everybody may visit that page.

◆ *Quality versus quantity.* The biggest problem, however, is that counters don't measure the amount of time that visitors spend at your Web site. A visitor who accesses a page, only to immediately leave it, is counted the same as a visitor who spends fifteen minutes reading every word on the page, printing it out, and then sharing your content with their friends!

Ultimately, counters don't matter for the great majority of Web sites because there are other, more realistic, measures of the Web site's success. If your Web site contains forms, for example, the number of registration forms that you receive and the amount of information they contain are a far more important measures of success than numbers alone. Likewise, the number and profitability of the sales that can be traced to your Web site are far more important than the number of people who accessed a particular page—no matter how quickly they accessed it.

Simplifying and Improving Tables

Reviewing your Web site may reveal ways you can improve your use of tables as a design tool.

To start with, the default layouts for most tables are too complex. Rarely is it necessary to include gridlines separating every cell of the table. Try replacing borders with "None" or "0" so that the text appears against a plain background rather than being surrounded by a prison cell network of horizontal and vertical lines.

Cell padding is one of the command refinements you should consider adding to your tables. *Padding* refers to the amount of space separating text from the boundaries of each cell. Increasing cell padding adds air to the contents of your table, using fast-downloading space (rather than the slower to download buttons or icons) to separate the contents of each cell (see Figures 14.16 and 14.17).

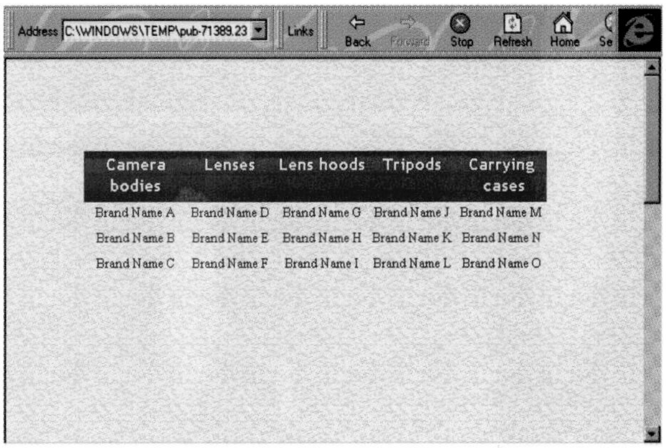

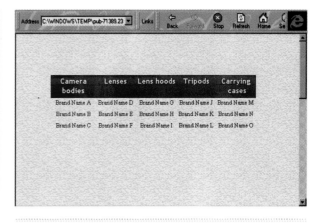

Figure 14.16 Default, or no, cell padding allows cell contents to closely approach the borders separating each cell.

Figure 14.17 Adding cell padding may slightly increase table size, but it allows the contents to be emphasized without adding distracting color or graphic elements.

Another way to simplify your Web site is to consider using style variations, such as bold and italics, to indicate visited links instead of adding second and third colors.

Replacing Graphics with Links

If your articles are long, consider replacing graphic elements—like horizontal rules or rows of repeating graphics—with subheads linked to the beginning of the article. The goal, as always, is to inform your Web site visitors, not entertain them with decorative eye candy.

◆ Eliminating horizontal dividers separating topics within articles simplifies the page by eliminating a visual distraction, making it easier for your Web site visitors to concentrate on your message (see Figure 14.18).

◆ Replacing horizontal graphic dividers with subheads, or bookmarks accessed by links at the beginning of the article, makes it easier for visitors to quickly access desired content (see Figures 14.19 and 14.20).

AWKWARD TYPOGRAPHY AND PHRASING

As discussed in earlier chapters, typography—the art of creating attractive, easy-to-read paragraphs—is more difficult on the Web than in print. Here are some things to watch out for as you review and improve your Web site.

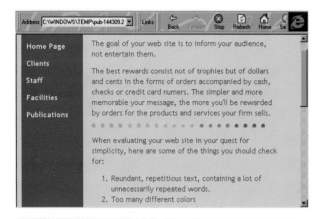

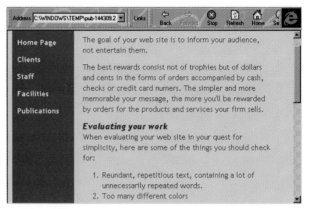

Figure 14.18 Graphic dividers may attract the eye, but they do little to introduce the text that follows.

Figure 14.19 By eliminating clutter, subheads project a more professional image and also help visitors quickly locate desired information.

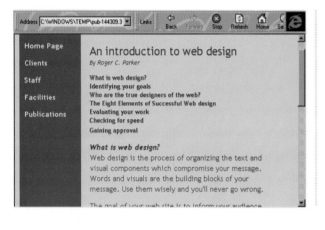

Figure 14.20
When you place links to subheads at the beginning of articles, visitors can easily judge the value of the content that follows as well as go directly to desired information, a far more valuable function than provided by decorative dividers.

Spell-check Problems

One problem that Web typography shares with print typography concerns words that are correctly spelled but incorrectly used. Most software programs used to create Web sites have built-in spell-checkers, but these remain unable to differentiate between what you typed and what you meant. As a result, we see many examples of the misuse of words like:

◆ To, too, and two

◆ Wend instead of wind

◆ Know, now

◆ Cant, can't

- Our, out, oar

- Now, not

The latter combination can be a source of a lot of trouble, as it completely changes the meaning of its sentence. "You can now cross the median divider" is entirely different than "You can not cross the media divider."

Since the words are correctly spelled, they are unlikely to be flagged. Although the grammar checkers in some word-processing programs may pick up misused words, this feature isn't yet implemented in most Web authoring tools. Always be sure you read your Web site out loud before you post it. Better yet, print out your Web site and have someone else proofread the hard copy version. (It's much easier to notice mistakes on paper than on screen.)

Broken Lines

Unusually short lines of text are often caused by use of the Paragraph Break HTML tag to break a line at a desired point, instead of placing the text in a table. What typically happens is that the visitor may have chosen a default text size on their Web browser that is different than what you had in mind. This causes line breaks to appear where they were not intended.

The problem is that, although the line break may appear very attractive on the screen of your computer, when previewed using the default typeface and type size you have chosen for your Web browser, the line may break completely differently for visitors using a different typeface and type size on their Web browser.

Oversize Pages

Have you ever noticed when surfing the Web how sometimes the horizontal scroll bar shows up along the bottom of the screen and the right-hand edge of each page is cut off, forcing you to scroll to the right to read the last words on each line?

REPAIRING TYPOGRAPHICAL ERRORS

When a Web site visitor takes the time to e-mail you, informing you of a typographical transgression, stifle the urge to be defensive and, instead, immediately thank them for taking the time to point out the mistake.

More important, immediately repair the mistake. The individual is likely to check back to see if you corrected "their" error, and your credibility and professionalism will suffer if the mistake remains.

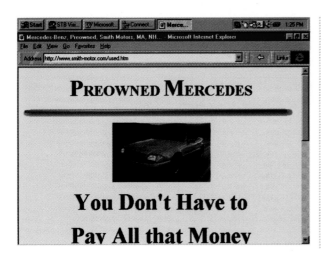

Figure 14.21
An alternative wording, such as "We can help you save money on your next Mercedes-Benz" might avoid giving the impression that you're apologizing for your high prices.

This often occurs when tables are used as the framework for a Web page, and the Width in pixels option is chosen instead of percentage. (Most Web authoring programs permit you to define table width in either the absolute [that is, pixels] or relative [percentage of] screen width.) If the table was created using a wider screen than available on the computer and Web browser used to view the page, the table will extend off the side of the visitor's screen.

Another cause may be long words set in columns created by tables. Since the Web does not permit hyphenation, when a long word appears on a line, the column of the table may expand to accommodate it, again creating a wider than desired table if the Relative option has been chosen.

The best way to avoid oversized Web pages is to design conservatively and allow extra room at the edges of your pages to accommodate Web browsers with narrower screens, often encountered on laptop computers.

That's Not What I Meant to Say!

Slip-ups are bound to sneak into your Web site, no matter how many times you and your co-workers proof your work. Between the time you post your Web site and return to review it, you'll gain the clarity to read every word from a fresh, that is, visitor's, perspective. This will help you avoid sending out signals that may give Web visitors a wrong impression…for example, that your products are impractically expensive (see Figure 14.21).

IMPROVING THE DESIGN OF YOUR OWN WEB SITE

There are several ways to improve the design of your own Web site.

◆ *Continue to analyze other Web sites.* Just because you've created and posted your Web site doesn't mean you stop spending an hour or two on the Web each week, analyzing a wide variety of Web sites. Check out Web sites within your field as well as Web sites from other fields. Choose a topic at random—for example, rodeos or railroading—and analyze a broad spectrum of Web sites in the field. Seek to visit those created professionally for Fortune 500 firms as well as those created in-house or by regional designers for smaller firms. As before, keep careful track of your observations and, whenever possible, make screen captures of various pages from each Web site and print out color samples.

◆ *Revisit Web sites you originally visited.* Note any changes in the Web site since the time you first visited it. What differences can you note? Are the differences major or minor? Do the changes strengthen or weaken the site?

◆ *Pay careful attention to the words your friends and co-workers use to describe your Web site.* Listen to their comments and attempt to determine honestly if their criticisms are valid and how their suggestions can be implemented.

◆ *Strive to constantly improve your Web design and production skills.* Although running your business should remain your first priority, allow yourself the luxury of mastering new software or, at least, reading about the capabilities of the latest software so you can do a better job of delegating production duties to others. *Knowledge is power!*

Most important, review your Web site using the Web Site Review Worksheet.

This Web Site Review Worksheet provides an opportunity to review many of the important points discussed in this book. More important, it provides you with an opportunity to objectively analyze your own Web site from an outsider's point of view. It will help you take a fresh look at your Web site and help you identify areas of possible improvement.

Again, feel free to photocopy this worksheet and distribute copies to your friends and co-workers and ask them to be as brutally honest as they can be in analyzing your Web site. No one likes criticism, (and you'll probably find your friends and co-workers will be as hesitant to criticize your work as you hate to criticize their efforts).

Yet, detailed and honest analyses are necessary tools in refining your Web site so that it performs as effectively as possible.

WEB SITE REVIEW WORKSHEET

1. Does the opening screen of your home page offer several navigation options?

    ❏ Yes ❏ No

2. Does the opening screen of your home page immediately involve visitors by describing (or beginning) an article or feature continued inside?

    ❏ Yes ❏ No

3. Does the opening screen of your home page project an appropriate image?

    ❏ Yes ❏ No

4. Are there text or graphic elements on the opening screen of your home page that could be reduced in size?

    ❏ No ❏ Yes (If yes, describe below)

5. Have you eliminated unnecessary space between text and visual elements as much as possible?

    ❏ Yes ❏ No

6. Does your Web site have something to offer visitors at various stages of the buying cycle?

    ❏ Yes ❏ No

    If yes, describe:

7. Is the content of your Web site significantly different than the content offered by your competitors?

    ❏ Yes ❏ No

    If yes, how?

8. Does your Web site look distinctly different than your competitors'?

    ❏ Yes ❏ No

9. Does your Web site offer compelling reasons to buy from you rather than anyone else?

    ❑ Yes ❑ No

    If yes, what?

10. How quickly does your Web site respond compared to your competitors'?

    ❑ Yes ❑ No

11. Have you included involvement devices to encourage visitors to quickly advance through the buying cycle?

    ❑ Yes ❑ No

12. What devices have you included to motivate visitors to act right now?

    (Describe):

13. Do your Web site's colors, typefaces, and layout project an appropriate image for your firm?

    ❑ Yes ❑ No

14. Do you use type, color, or some other technique to relate links to the pages they access?

    ❑ Yes ❑ No

15. Is your use of color, type, and layout consistent throughout your Web site?

    ❑ Yes ❑ No

16. Do you use color, type, or other graphic devices to visually tie links together with the pages they access?

    ❑ Yes ❑ No

17. Have you avoided long lines of text extending from the left to the right edges of the screen?

❑ Yes ❑ No

If Yes, how?

18. Does your Web use movement with restraint, that is, only when necessary to reinforce important messages?

❑ Yes ❑ No

19. Does your Web site include a registration form to make it easy to begin establishing a relationship with your visitors?

❑ Yes ❑ No

20. Have you delegated responsibility for tracking registrations and following up on requests for further information?

❑ Yes ❑ No

If "Yes," who?

How are you monitoring their performance?

21. Do you let visitors know when you have updated your Web site?

❑ Yes ❑ No

If "Yes," how?

22. Have you used cell padding to build air into your tables?

❑ Yes ❑ No

23. Have you used thumbnails so only those who want to view large photographs have to wait for their files to be downloaded?

❑ Yes ❑ No

24. Have you double-checked the spelling of your Web site and immediately corrected mistakes that Web site visitors have told you about?

    ❑ Yes ❑ No

25. Have you eliminated unnecessary graphic elements wherever possible?

    ❑ Yes ❑ No

26. Does your Web site contain a counter showing a disappointingly low total?

    ❑ Yes ❑ No

27. Do long articles contain links to subheads within the articles?

    ❑ Yes ❑ No

28. Have you checked your Web site on computers other than the one you used to create it?

    ❑ Yes ❑ No

29. Have you included full contact information so visitors can easily contact you by phone, fax, or e-mail?

    ❑ Yes ❑ No

30. When was your Web site last updated?

    Date:

Index

tables, 49-50, 51, 234
text, *See* text
theme, 25
tools for, 49-55
unifying look, development of, 126-127, 128
visual contrast, 59
visuals, *See* visuals
worksheets
    Design Analysis Worksheet, 124-125
    Design Goals Worksheet, 147, 148-151
desire stage of buying cycle, 7
dithering, 47, 133
domain name, registration of, 92
downloading Web graphics, 66

E

effectiveness of Web site, monitoring of, 155, 197-198, 218-219
e-mail, 27, 160, 194-195, 202
enhancement stage of buying cycle, 8
event calendars, 13, 14
Excite, 204
e-zines, advertising in, 207

F

feedback, 27
files
    graphics files, 54-55, 181-182
    naming and placement of, 118
    size of, 181-182
flyers, 17
follow-up and closure, 28-29, 193-200
    brochure requests, response to, 195
    delegation and monitoring of duties of, 195, 197, 198-199
    e-mail responses, 194-195
    information requests, response to, 195
    mailing lists, compilation of, 196
    planning considerations, 81
    sales fulfillment, 196-197
    staff awareness of Web site content, 194
    telephone follow-up, 195
    tracking responses to Web site, 155, 197-198, 218-219

worksheet, 200
font, 43
foreground/background contrast, 129, 131, 133
foreground colors, 46, 129
formatted text, 42-43
forms for registration, *See* registration forms for visitor involvement
frames, 52-54, 71, 140-142, 232, 233
frameworks for production of Web sites, 178
freelance Web designers, hiring of, 174
Frequently Asked Questions (FAQs), 154

G

glossary of relevant terms, 154
graphic design studios, hiring of, 174
graphics files, 54-55, 181-182
grunge typefaces, 136

H

handouts for promotion of Web site, 203
hardware requirements, 180-181
home pages
    analysis of, 65
    design of, 36-38
    hierarchy and color of, 228
    updating of, 218
HTML tags and styles, 51-52
HyperText Markup Language, *See* HTML tags and styles

I

icons, 39, 40
illustrations, 47
image maps, 39
image of site
    appropriateness of, 123
    color and, 129, 131
    Design Analysis Worksheet, 124-25
    symbols/metaphors, use of, 126, 128
    typeface choice and, 136-138
    unifying look, development of, 126-127, 128
improving existing Web sites, 225-243

buying cycle stages, 7-8, 217

obstacles, identification of, 111-14

primary markets, 8, 11

secondary markets, 9, 11

traditional media and Web marketing communications, 15-18

McCanna, Laurie, *Creating Great Web Graphics,* 133

meta-indexes, registration of Web site with, 205

meta tags, 205

Microsoft Explorer, 52

Microsoft FrontPage, 179, 180

Microsoft PowerPoint, 25-26

Microsoft Publisher, 179

movement, use of, 127, 144-146

N

navigation, 26, 34, 56, 154

links, *See* links

navigation bar, 39

Netscape Navigator, 52

newsgroups

as promotional tool, 210

visitor involvement through, 166-167

newsletters, 16-17

O

opening page/screen, 36, 70

P

padding, 234, 235

photographs, 5, 47, 56

planning of Web sites, 22-24, 77-86

content of site, 79-80

design considerations, 80

follow-up, 81

maintenance of site, 81-82

production considerations, 81

promotion of site, 81-82

purpose of site, 78-79

worksheet, 83-84

postcards, 17

press releases as promotional tool, 209

primary markets

composition of, 8

content geared to, 11

print design and Web page design compared, 55-57

procedures manuals, 18

production of Web sites, 28, 171-190

creating site yourself, 172-173

file size, 181-182

fine-tuning of details, 182-185

frameworks for, 178

freelance Web designers, hiring of, 174

graphic design studios, hiring of, 174

hardware requirements, 180-181

hiring outside vendor, 174-177

Internet Service Providers, by, 174

planning considerations, 81

software for, *See* software for production of Web sites

staff produced site, 173-174

templates for, 178

worksheets

hiring of outside vendors, 175-177

production worksheet, 186-190

promotion of Web sites, 29, 201-213

advertising, *See* advertising

co-marketing, 29, 208

e-mail signature, 202

handouts, 203

internal promotion, 202-203

keywords, 205

letters to the editor, 209-210

mailers, 203

meta-indexes, registration of site with, 205

meta tags, 205

newsgroup postings, 210

planning considerations, 81-82

press releases, 209

registration of Web site, 204-205

search engines, registration of site with, 204

self-promotion, 209-210

title tags, 205

worksheet for preparing promotional program, 211-213

purchase stage of buying cycle, 7

purpose of site, 78-79

R

receding colors, 131-132
registration
    of domain name, 92
    of URLs, 93, 96
    of Web site, 204-205
registration forms for visitor involvement, 26-27, 71, 154-161
    acknowledgment of receipt of form, 161
    advantages of, 155
    contact distinguished, 156
    designing registration forms, 156-157
    encouraging registration, 159
    incentives as means of encouraging registration, 159
    lead generation through, 155
    maintenance, visitor feedback leading to, 161
    sample registration form, 157-158
    tracking performance of Web site through, 155, 197-198, 218-219
replacement stage of buying cycle, 8

S

sales encounters, 18
sales fulfillment, 196-197
sans serif typefaces, 136
screen capture programs, 71-73
    Inner Media Collage, 71
    Inset Systems Hijack Pro, 71
    printing a screen capture, advantages of, 72
    XX Systems SnapJot, 71
script typefaces, 136
search engines, registration of Web site with, 204
secondary markets
    composition of, 9
    content geared to, 11
self-promotion, 209-210
serif typefaces, 136
shaded colors, 132, 133
site map, 42
software for production of Web sites, 179-180
    Adobe PageMill, 179
    Microsoft FrontPage, 179, 180
    Microsoft Publisher, 179
    text editors, use of, 179

    Web authoring programs, use of, 179-180
    word processing programs, use of, 179
Software Publishing ActiveOffice, 25-26, 48
spacing of elements, 231
spell-check, 236-237
strong colors, use of, 131-132
style of Web site, 117-118
    credibility, 118
    empathy, 118
symbols, use of, 126, 128

T

tables, 49-50, 51, 234
tagged text, 42
telephone calls, 17
telephone follow-up, 195
templates for production of Web sites, 178
text, 42-45
    broken lines, 237
    editing of, 230
    effective use of, tips for, 43-45
    font, 43
    formatted text, 42-43
    long lines of text, problems with, 45, 140-141
    spell-check, 236-237
    tagged text, 42
    typeface, *See* typeface
text links, 39, 232
theme, 25
thumbnails, 48
title tags, 205
tracking responses to Web site, 155, 197-198, 218-219
typeface, 42-43, 136-140
    color and, 139
    font distinguished, 43
    as formatted file, 42-43, 136
    grunge typefaces, 136
    image of site and, 136-138
    links and, 42
    sans serif typefaces, 136
    script typefaces, 136
    serif typefaces, 136
    types of, 136, 137-138

U

unifying look, development of, 126-127, 128
Universal Resource Locators, *See* URLs
URLs, 23-24, 29, 87-98
   descriptiveness of, 88, 89-90
   development of, 93, 94-96
   domain name, registration of, 92
   examples of creative URLs, 90-91
   geographical considerations, 97
   hyphens, use of, 92
   memorableness of, 88, 90
   product considerations, 97
   registration of, 93, 96
   researching, 92, 93-94
   shortness and simplicity of, 88-89
   supporting, 98
   testing of, 93, 96
   worksheet for selection of, 95-96

V

video, use of, 167
virtual reality, use of, 167, 168
Visio, 48
visitor involvement with Web site, *See* involvement
visuals
   business graphics, 48
   effective use of, tips for, 48
   graphics files, 54-55, 181-182
   illustrations, 47
   logo, size of, 226-227
   photographs, 5, 47, 56
   reducing size of visual elements, 226-227
   speed of download and, 48, 54, 55, 181-182

W

Web, 3-19
   color, *See* color, use of
   content, *See* content
   cost advantages of, 4-6, 15-18
   immediacy of information, 4
   marketing on, *See* marketing
   personalization of content, 5
   photography, 5

   quantity of information, 4-5
   sites, *See* Web sites
   strategy worksheet, 20
Web browsers
   Microsoft Explorer, 52
   Netscape Navigator, 52
Web Site Impression Sheet, 66-71
Web sites, 21-32
   address, *See* URLs
   analysis of, *See* analysis of Web sites
   balance, 21
   content, *See* content
   cyclical nature of, 30-31
   design of, *See* design of Web sites
   follow-up, *See* follow-up and closure
   improvement of, *See* improving existing Web sites
   involvement, *See* involvement
   maintenance of, *See* maintenance of Web sites
   planning, *See* planning of Web sites
   production of, *See* production of Web sites
   program, 21
   promotion of, *See* promotion of Web sites
why buy information, 12
World Wide Web, *See* Web

X

XX Systems SnapJot, 71

Y

Yahoo, 64, 204, 206